Intellectual Disabilit and Psychotherapy

M000312708

Intellectual Disability and Psychotherapy: The Theories, Practice and Influence of Valerie Sinason charts the transformative impact of the noted psychotherapist's work with children and adults with intellectual disabilities upon both a generation of clinicians and the treatment and services delivered by them.

Examining how contemporary Disability Therapists have discovered, used and adapted such pioneering concepts as the Handicapped Smile and Secondary Handicap as a Defence Against Trauma in their clinical work, the book includes contributions from renowned practitioners and clinicians from around the world. It shines a light on how Sinason's work opened doors for working with people who were previously thought of as unreachable.

Intellectual Disability and Psychotherapy will be an essential resource to anyone working with children or adults with disabilities, as well as psychotherapists interested in exploring Valerie Sinason's work.

Alan Corbett (1963–2016) was the author of a number of books, chapters, and papers on aspects of working psychoanalytically with trauma, abuse, and disability. Alan worked as a psychotherapist and supervisor in private practice and had been Clinical Director of Respond, ICAP, and the CARI Foundation in Dublin.

Intellectual Disability and Psychotherapy

The Theories, Practice and
Influence of Valerie Sinason

Edited by Alan Corbett
with assistance from
Tamsin Cottis

Routledge
Taylor & Francis Group

LONDON AND NEW YORK

First published 2019
by Routledge
2 Park Square, Milton Park, Abingdon, Oxon OX14 4RN

and by Routledge
711 Third Avenue, New York, NY 10017

Routledge is an imprint of the Taylor & Francis Group, an informa business

British Library Cataloguing in Publication Data
A catalogue record for this book is available from the British Library

Library of Congress Cataloging in Publication Data
Names: Corbett, Alan, editor.
Title: Intellectual disability and psychotherapy : the theories, practice, and influence of Valerie Sinason / edited by Alan Corbett.
Description: Abingdon, Oxon ; New York, NY : Routledge, 2018. | Includes bibliographical references.
Identifiers: LCCN 2018024841 | ISBN 9781138323612 (hardback) | ISBN 9781138323629 (pbk.) | ISBN 9780429451300 (master) | ISBN 9780429836305 (web) | ISBN 9780429836299 (ePub) | ISBN 9780429836282 (Mobipocket)
Subjects: | MESH: Sinason, Valerie, 1946– | Intellectual Disability–psychology | Intellectual Disability–therapy | Psychotherapy–methods | Festschrift
Classification: LCC RC570 | NLM WM 300 | DDC 362.3–dc23
LC record available at https://lccn.loc.gov/2018024841

ISBN: 9781138323612 (hbk)
ISBN: 9781138323629 (pbk)
ISBN: 9780429451300 (ebk)

Typeset in Times New Roman
by Out of House Publishing

Contents

Notes on contributors

Dr Alan Corbett (1963–2016) was the author of a number of books, chapters, and papers on aspects of working psychoanalytically with trauma, abuse, and disability including: *Disabling Perversions: Forensic Psychotherapy with People with Intellectual Disabilities* (2014) and *Psychotherapy with Male Survivors of Sexual Abuse: The Invisible Men* (2016). Alan worked as a psychotherapist and supervisor in private practice and had been Clinical Director of Respond, ICAP, and the CARI Foundation in Dublin.

Dr Noelle Blackman is the Chief Executive of Respond and a registered dramatherapist. In 1997 she founded a unique NHS bereavement therapy service for people with intellectual disabilities. She is the co-founder of the National Network for the Palliative Care of People with Learning Disabilities (PCPLD). Noelle moved to the charity, Respond, in 2003. Respond works with people (and their families) who have intellectual disabilities and/or autism, and who have experienced abuse or trauma and/ or are perpetrators of abuse. She is currently a visiting lecturer at Anglia Ruskin University, University College London, and the University of East London, and is an Honorary Research Fellow at the University of Hertfordshire. She has published work and presented papers nationally and internationally.

Tamsin Cottis is a UKCP registered child psychotherapist. She is a co-founder and former Assistant Director of Respond, the UK's leading provider of psychotherapy to children and adults with learning disabilities, including those with sexually harmful behaviours. More recently she has been Consultant Clinical Supervisor at Respond and a teacher at the Bowlby Centre. She also works as a child psychotherapist and clinical supervisor in primary schools and in private practice. Tamsin is a founder member of the Institute of Psychotherapy and Disability and a member of the International Association for Forensic Psychotherapy. She has written widely for books and professional journals, particularly regarding psychotherapy and intellectual disability, and has presented a range of academic papers. Publications include *Intellectual Disability, Trauma and*

Psychotherapy (2009), which she edited. Tamsin is also a prize-winning, published author of short stories.

Dr Pat Frankish is a clinical psychologist, past President of the British Psychological Society, and founder member and first Chair of the Institute of Psychotherapy and Disability. She shares, with Valerie, the experience of having parents who worked in the field of intellectual disability. Most of her career has been focused on developing and improving services for this client group. Pat recently published *Disability Psychotherapy: An Innovative Approach to Trauma-Informed Care* (2016) and often speaks at conferences. She has produced training courses for direct support staff and therapists in this area, pioneering a model called Trauma Informed Care (TIC). Pat has also been encouraged into the field of dissociative identity disorder by Valerie, and her company supports several people with holistic care packages. Recently, Pat has been working alongside statutory authorities with young people with disabilities, offering early intervention with the aim of preventing a later breakdown in mental health.

Graeme Galton was born in Australia and lives in London. He is an attachment-based psychoanalytic psychotherapist in private practice. He is also a consultant psychotherapist at the Clinic for Dissociative Studies, a small specialist outpatient mental health service for people suffering from severe trauma and dissociation. Graeme worked as a psychotherapist and clinical supervisor in the NHS for sixteen years. He is a registered member of the Bowlby Centre, where he is a training supervisor and teaches on the clinical training programme. Graeme is a member of the European Association for Psychotherapy and has been awarded the European Certificate of Psychotherapy. Graeme edited the book *Touch Papers: Dialogues on Touch in the Psychoanalytic Space* (2006), and co-edited *Forensic Aspects of Dissociative Identity Disorder* (2008).

Professor Sheila the Baroness Hollins is an independent, crossbench, life peer in the House of Lords, and Emeritus Professor of Psychiatry of Disability at St George's, University of London. She has been a clinical specialist, a researcher and policymaker in mental health, and has published many scientific and professional papers and books. In 1989 she founded the long-running *Books Beyond Words* series of picture books for young people and adults with intellectual disabilities, which includes stories about everyday life as well as about physical and mental health, trauma and abuse, and criminal justice. Baroness Hollins was President of the Royal College of Psychiatrists (2005–2008), President of the British Medical Association (2012–2013), and Chair of the Board of Science of the British Medical Association (2013–2016). She is currently a member of the Pontifical Commission for the Protection of Minors and Vulnerable Adults, and President of the Royal College of Occupational Therapists.

Professor Brett Kahr has worked in the mental health profession for over forty years. He is Senior Fellow at Tavistock Relationships at the Tavistock Institute of Medical Psychology in London, and Senior Clinical Research Fellow in Psychotherapy and Mental Health at the Centre for Child Mental Health. He was formerly Course Tutor in Mental Handicap in the Child and Family Department of the Tavistock Clinic and member of both the Mental Handicap Team and the Mental Handicap Workshop at the Tavistock Clinic. He became one of the founders of the Institute of Psychotherapy and Disability in 1999, and now serves as a fellow. A Consultant at both The Balint Consultancy and The Bowlby Centre, and a Trustee of the Freud Museum London, he is also the author or editor of ten books, including, most recently, *Coffee with Freud* (2017) and *New Horizons in Forensic Psychotherapy: Exploring the Work of Estela V. Welldon* (2018).

Liz Lloyd is a graduate in French from the University of Sussex. She went on to do her psychoanalytic training at The Guild of Psychotherapists in London. She joined Respond in the late 1990s as a psychotherapist working with individuals and groups, and also set up a twelve-week training course for health and social care staff working in this field. While working as a specialist at Respond, she developed her own mainstream private practice and also worked as a therapist for Valerie Sinason's Clinic for Dissociative Studies. Since returning to Wales some years ago, she became concerned at the lack of psychotherapy available for Welsh speakers in their mother tongue. She has organised conferences and, with other Welsh-speaking colleagues, set up a professionals' group (GIAT) to campaign on this issue. She currently works a few hours a week in her bilingual private practice.

Dr Eimir McGrath is a researcher, lecturer, and practitioner in several disciplines including psychotherapy, play therapy, critical disability studies, and dance. She works as a psychotherapist with both children and adults in a wide variety of educational and clinical settings, specialising in the areas of attachment, complex trauma, and disability. Her current research interests focus on the role of creative arts in psychotherapy, the critical analysis of societal perceptions of disability, and the application of interpersonal neurobiology to the psychotherapeutic process. Somatic practice informs her therapeutic work. Her recent publications include contributed chapters to the following edited books: *Disability and Social Theory: New Developments and Directions* (2012); *Play Therapy Today: Contemporary Practice with Individuals, Groups and Carers* (2014); *Creative Psychotherapy: Applying the Principles of Neurobiology to Play and Expressive Arts-based Practice* (2016); and *Dance, Disability and the Law: InVisible Difference* (2018).

David O'Driscoll has been a psychoanalytic psychotherapist for the Hertfordshire Partnership University NHS Foundation Trust, Intellectual Disability Service since 2000. He is a visiting research fellow and visiting lecturer at the Centre for Learning Disability Research, Hertfordshire University. He also teaches a short course on disability psychotherapy at the Bowlby Centre as part of the psychotherapy training. David is a council member and convenor for the Intellectual Disability section of the Association for Psychoanalytic Psychotherapy in the NHS, a founder member of the Institute of Disability and Psychotherapy (IPD), and is currently its Chair. He is a long-standing member of the Social History of Intellectual Disability Research Group based at The Open University. David has written widely in intellectual disability publications, including regular "opinion" pieces for the journal *Learning Disability Practice*, concerned with promoting psychoanalytic ideas to its nursing readership.

Susie Orbach is a psychoanalyst, writer, activist, and social commentator. She co-founded The Women's Therapy Centre in London in 1976 and The Women's Therapy Centre Institute, New York, in 1981. Her numerous books, which present new theory on women, the body, and the relationship between couples, include *Fat is a Feminist Issue* (1978; 1982), *Hunger Strike* (1986), *What Do Women Want?* (with Luise Eichenbaum) (1983), *The Impossibility of Sex* (1999), *Bodies* (2009), and *In Therapy* (2016). Susie has consulted to the World Bank, the NHS, and Unilever. She is a founder member of Psychotherapists and Counsellors for Social Responsibility, was convenor of Endangered Bodies (2017), an expert member of the steering group of the British government's Campaign for Body Confidence, a *Guardian* columnist for ten years, and a visiting professor at the LSE on psychoanalysis and social policy, also for ten years. In 2016, her BBC Radio 4 series *In Therapy* (2016) was listened to live by two million people, with an additional million listening on podcast. An annotated version is now in print: *In Therapy: The Continuing Story*. She has a practice seeing individuals and couples.

Georgina Parkes is a consultant psychiatrist in Intellectual Disability and has worked in the NHS for many years. She is also Secretary and out-going Chair of the Institute of Psychotherapy and Disability. Georgina is involved in training in psychiatry, as both a clinical and educational supervisor, and she supervises junior doctors to undertake weekly psychodynamic psychotherapy. She has specialist knowledge in gender dysphoria, trauma, and psychodynamic psychotherapy, and has written and published widely on these subjects, including contributing in 2016, to the *Diagnostic Manual in Intellectual Disability (DM ID)* (2017).

Professor Leslie Swartz is a clinical psychologist and distinguished professor of psychology at Stellenbosch University, South Africa. His work focuses on mental health and disability issues in resource-poor settings, with a focus on sub-Saharan Africa. He is founding editor-in-chief of the *African Journal of Disability*, and Associate Editor of *Transcultural Psychiatry*, and of the *International Journal of Disability, Development and Education*. Some of his current work focuses on cultural aspects of trauma, language and access to health care, and disability and development in sub-Saharan Africa.

Anders Svensson grew up in a small village in the south of Sweden and graduated from the gymnasium in Landskrona. He began his psychologist education at the University of Lund in 1972. On graduating, he worked for five years in the fields of addiction treatment, educational psychology, and adult and child psychiatry. In 1984 he began work with people with intellectual disabilities, their families, and their professional carers. Between 1991 and 1995 Anders was supervised by, and worked in professional collaboration with, Valerie Sinason. Now nearing retirement, Anders continues to work in Sweden with people with intellectual disabilities.

Jan Walmsley is an independent researcher and an advocate for the rights of people with intellectual disabilities. Her main interest is in the history of intellectual disabilities and how understanding the past might help shape a better future. She is the author of numerous books and articles, probably the best-known being on inclusive research, life stories of people with intellectual disabilities, and the history of community care. Her website is http://janwalmsleyassociates.com/

Shula Wilson is a practising psychotherapist. She is the founder of Skylark (1995–2012), an organisation that offered counselling and psychotherapy for people affected by disability, a founder member of the Institute for Psychotherapy and Disability and a consultant psychotherapist at St Thomas' Hospital and Great Ormond Street Hospitals, where she is also a lecturer and supervisor. Shula is the author of *Disability, Counselling and Psychotherapy* (2003).

Foreword

Susie Orbach

A living legend

Valerie Sinason is a byword for integrity, compassion, listening, hearing, thinking, bravery, and brilliance. We are blessed to have had her in our profession when she could so easily have continued life as a poet and writer. One only has to say her name to arouse the most extraordinary respect in the areas of disability, of abuse, of trauma, of dissociation, and therapeutic technique and practice.

Detectives and parliamentarians, social policy makers, budding psychotherapists, social workers, nurses, psychoanalysts, psychiatrists and trauma workers have learnt from her. Her writings, her talks, her open workshops in which she enabled other workers to hear and see what she has been able to see, hear, bear and communicate about are outstanding. No one leaves a talk by Valerie without growing, without experiencing a challenge that allows one to enter into a deeper sense of humanity on the one hand and of intellectual growth on the other.

As the late Alan Corbett writes, Valerie thinks and feels, and she is unafraid to combine the two. She uses her feelings to think and her thinking to understand her feelings. Perhaps more than anything, her concern for the people she worked with was paramount. She saw it as her duty to meet them where they were and to enable them to be who they could be. Strikingly, she made no superficial distinction between the "ordinary" psychoanalytic patient and the "disabled", seeing the fluidity in both their individual states of mind. She knew that difficult feelings and trauma affect how articulate, how self-censorious, how empathic one could be towards self and she worked hard to enable those who worked with the disabled to validate their own responses and difficulties in ways that gave them the courage and support to hang in there and dare to understand and feel the extreme challenges inherent in the work. With her patients, she made herself available to articulate what hadn't been able to be said and transformed the sense of uselessness and shame that impregnated the damaged sense of self that doubly harmed them.

Valerie's legacy will be enormous. In establishing the field of disability psychotherapy, she has shown the best of what psychoanalytically informed therapists are capable of. She has brought deep intelligence, learning, and flexibility to a population who are still considered "less than". Part of Valerie's genius is to enable us to find the "less than" in ourselves that can make a bridge to the other. I don't mean via un-thought-through identifications but by finding the parts of ourselves that feel unseen, stupid, rigid, and difficult – the parts of ourselves we often would rather not know. There is no easy "us and them" in the work Valerie has pioneered, there is only an "us"; and we have a duty to bring the troublesome "us" part of ourselves into sufficient consciousness to be able both to be connected to the people we see while being able to maintain without shame, without inhibiting guilt, the differences that allow us to be in the world in the ways we are.

Valerie is a campaigner. Never heavy with morality, never preachy, she tells us the world as she sees it and we cannot fail to be moved and persuaded. She is always in advance of the culture, absorbing what society would rather not know about and yet, in time, her persistent campaigning, sometimes crusading and sometimes just slowly inching her views forward, come to be understood and taken up. I often want to baulk at what Valerie tells me but I know better than to do so, for in every domain we have talked about together, she knows more than perhaps we wish her to know, not because we want to disparage her knowledge but because we don't know how she manages with what she knows and sees. She lives among stories of multiple traumas. She hears pain and suffering in the extreme. We are in awe at her capacity to hold the evidence of human cruelties and the pain of it. Her knowledge of such cruelties is matched by her capacious empathy and understanding. Often, we don't want to know what she has discovered because it is so disturbing and yet Valerie's ability to know about the very darkest of human practices, of the horrendous ways in which hurt becomes expressed in torturous expression, does not diminish her ability to relate to ordinary hurt. She can listen just as well to a dispute between a couple, to the burdens of community organisations and leadership, or to squabbling siblings. Those of us who have been touched by her, live with the imprint of her warmth, of her support, and of her deep intelligence. Her words and the way they are said, like the poet that she is, live inside of us, nourishing and accompanying us through our clinical and day-to-day lives. She is a true hero of our times.

Editorial notes

Tamsin Cottis

When Alan asked me to take on editorial duties for this book, he was seriously ill – it was just weeks before his untimely death. His determination and will to keep squeezing as much from life as possible throughout his illness was astonishing: he continued working and writing right to his final days. As we can read in his introduction, it was Alan's great wish that this book would be the first of a series and it is hoped that this will prove to be so. Alan was a gifted clinician, deeply committed to the field of disability psychotherapy. He was a consummate professional whilst being a highly compassionate and supportive friend and colleague. I miss him every day.

In completing the book on Alan's behalf, I have had the enormous privilege of being able to see the unifying threads that emerged from the different chapters, which are now contained in the pages ahead. From the accounts here, it is possible to see how, wherever she worked, Valerie was never afraid to say the difficult things and speak the truth as she found it. The accounts are often highly personal, the voices of the contributors unique and heartfelt. All the contributors write of how profoundly Valerie's ideas and writing affected them. Words such as "generous", "kind", "accepting", and "brave", recur many times. Valerie has been a prolific enabler and supporter of others, helping junior practitioners to develop confidence as well as skill and resilience. Valerie's key concepts of the "handicapped smile" (Sinason, 1986) and "secondary handicap", or handicap as a defence (Sinason, 1992), are also constant themes. Individual contributors show how these ideas have influenced their work with people with intellectual disabilities across many settings and in several countries and the book contains much vivid clinical material, all of which has been anonymised, illustrating direct practice. Many contributors highlight the way that Valerie's writing has helped them make sense of the underlying pain and hurt in the lives of their patients, but which the authors had not been able to conceptualise before encountering Valerie's ideas.

It is an honour to have a Foreword by **Susie Orbach**, a friend and colleague of Valerie's, who has done so much herself, through her clinical practice over many years and through her teaching, writing and broadcasting, to increase our knowledge and understanding of many complex psychological issues.

She has illuminated the process of psychotherapy itself, and has always made connections between psychotherapy and the political and social context in which it exists.

In 2002, **Graeme Galton** wrote a lengthy and important paper (Galton, 2002) about Valerie's work in the field of intellectual disability. It is a pleasure to include a revised and updated version of this paper in which Galton highlights: Valerie's work in regard to sexual abuse; a comprehensive account of her theory of secondary handicap; a description of her psychotherapeutic approach; and a summary of relevant clinical research.

As Alan says in his introduction, creativity is a core element of disability psychotherapy and **Eimir McGrath**, a founding member of the Institute for Psychotherapy and Disability in Ireland, describes, with detailed clinical and theoretical focus, her work with some of her most severely disabled patients, describing how her therapeutic practice is informed by more recent developments in our understanding of neuroscience.

Alan Corbett and **Tamsin Cottis** describe how Valerie played such a crucial part in their work in establishing Respond, a psychotherapy centre for people with intellectual disabilities who had experienced sexual abuse, some of whom were abusers themselves. Valerie was one of only a handful of people highlighting the issue of sexual abuse and intellectual disability at the time of Respond's inception, and she broke the ground in which the seeds of the organisation went on to take root and flourish.

Liz Lloyd also draws our attention to Valerie's invaluable yet, at the time, highly controversial work with people with intellectual disabilities who had been sexually abused. This was little believed, far less understood, in the late 1980s and early 1990s when Valerie was beginning to share her clinical findings. In her chapter, Liz Lloyd identifies the common themes in her work with people with intellectual disabilities and in her work with those who have little access to therapy in their mother tongue. She illustrates how Valerie's concept of the handicapped smile has fed into her understanding of this issue and has helped her in her work as a psychotherapist both at Respond and in her native Wales.

Noelle Blackman, herself another pioneer in the field of loss and intellectual disability, describes how Valerie influenced her in developing her innovative Loss and Bereavement Service in Hertfordshire, UK, and has helped her to develop a deeper understanding of the internal world of her clients, including those who have been both bereaved and abused.

The esteemed and influential Professor **Sheila Hollins**, who developed the psychiatry of intellectual disability as a discipline, has trained very many junior psychiatrists, including our contributor Georgina Parkes. Professor Hollins gives a personal account of her work with Valerie, in particular as her co-facilitator of a group for intellectually disabled men with sexually harmful behaviour. Professor Hollins was also Valerie's academic supervisor for her PhD. She now oversees *Books Beyond Words* (2017), volumes aimed at supporting discussions with people with intellectual disabilities on a range of difficult and pertinent subjects. Professor Hollins talks about Valerie's influence on, and contribution to, these important books.

In **Georgina Parkes'** chapter, we learn about Valerie's influence on the author's own medical career and also more about the clinical application of Valerie's ideas in a psychiatric setting.

Georgina Parkes' NHS colleague, **David O'Driscoll**, places Valerie's work in a historical context, and describes how her thinking and her personal interest and support influenced both his work with one of his patients in particular, and also his own development as a disability psychotherapist and teacher of allied professionals.

Psychologist **Pat Frankish**, who over many years has established a wide range of innovative intellectual disability services especially in the north of England, shows how Valerie's ideas are integral to the training she has developed and delivered to many hundreds of frontline staff as well as to therapeutic practitioners in the UK.

Another clinician, **Shula Wilson,** a long-term member of the Institute for Psychotherapy and Disability, and whose special interest is with people who have physical disabilities, gives an account of how Valerie's theory of secondary handicap has influenced her work as a supervisor in hospital settings.

Jan Walmsley, an academic from the Open University (OU), also highlights the longevity of Valerie's influence, describing how Valerie contributed to a highly influential and well-subscribed OU course for practitioners in intellectual disability in the early 1990s. Jan Walmsley reflects on how she has come to understand that Valerie's ideas connect to the work of Wolf Wolfensberger, who also spoke out about the ways in which the life of a disabled person is unwished for, and how there can be, in his view, systematic "deathmaking" (1980). The connections between Valerie's and Wolfensberger's ideas have great resonance in our contemporary world of specialist provision which seems, in some respects, to be regressing. This may be due to austerity but may also be due to lingering attitudes and policies, as evidenced by the ongoing scandal of thousands of people with intellectual disabilities being kept in inappropriate secure settings, or in assessment units far from home.

From his position as a psychologist and academic in South Africa, **Leslie Swartz** writes powerfully about how Valerie's sensibility and her capacity for looking at things which others may find unbearable, helped him and his colleagues to develop their ideas and practice in post-apartheid South Africa.

Swedish psychologist **Anders Svensson** gives a personal tribute, reflecting on what he has learned from Valerie, particularly through her supervision of his long-term work with an intellectually disabled patient with dissociative identity disorder.

Brett Kahr, Valerie's long-time friend and colleague, gives another very personal tribute, focusing on Valerie's bravery. He argues that she has shown great courage in pioneering and advocating tirelessly for psychoanalytic psychotherapy for people previously regarded as difficult, if not impossible, to treat. With close reference to the work of Sigmund Freud and Donald Winnicott, Kahr sets out his view that Valerie is deserving of a place in psychoanalytic history alongside these founding figures.

The book concludes with the transcript of an **interview with Valerie** herself, by **Alan Corbett**. This took place in November 2016, just a month before Alan died. Alan and Valerie discuss her influences, her early life, her thoughts about disability psychotherapy, how it can best be practised, and who can best practise it. The interview also touches on the controversy and difficulties which Valerie has faced during her career. Valerie's customary modesty and generosity towards others is evident in the interview. It was a privilege to listen in to this interview and it is a pleasure to be able to reproduce it here, bringing readers the chance to experience the thoughtful, compassionate voices of both Valerie and Alan, in conversation and creative connection.

This book is more than an account of Valerie's key theories and, as such, it is a volume which makes a valuable and important contribution to our developing understanding of the theory and practice of disability psychotherapy. It also provides much information and many insights into the past thirty-plus years of psychotherapeutic work with people with intellectual disabilities. Valerie, and her work as a clinician, writer, supervisor, and co-founder and President of the Institute of Psychotherapy and Disability, has been a constant throughout this time. As I believe was Alan's wish, this book stands as a multifaceted tribute to a remarkable woman.

The impetus for this book came from Alan: it was his idea and was well on the way to being realised at the time of his death. Completing his work has been a complex and emotional task for me. As with any book, especially one with multiple authors, the path to publication can only be partially predicted and planned. I have done my best to respond to any questions and issues that have arisen in the process which were unforeseen by Alan, by asking myself the question, "What would Alan do?" This is a question I asked of him many times when he was alive, too. His absence has been sharp indeed as, together with the contributors, I have worked to shape the individual chapters, and the volume as a whole, in the way which I understand Alan to have envisaged it. I have been especially assisted and supported in this process by Lorraine Hill; Peter McKeown, Alan's husband; Brett Kahr; Rod Tweedy at Karnac; and by Valerie herself. I hope I have succeeded in fulfilling Alan's wish that, in this book, Valerie's work would be honoured by those she has educated, supported, and inspired. Any mistakes or misjudgements made in this attempt are my own.

References

Beyond words. (2017). https://booksbeyondwords.co.uk/ [last accessed 30.12.2017].

Galton, G. (2002). New horizons in disability psychotherapy: the contributions of Valerie Sinason. *Free Associations*, 9(4): 582–610.

Sinason, V. (1986). Secondary mental handicap and its relationship to trauma. *Psychoanalytic Psychotherapy, 2*: 131–154.

Sinason, V. (1992). *Mental Handicap and the Human Condition: New Approaches from the Tavistock*. London: Free Association Books.

Wolfensberger, W. (1980). A call to wake up to the beginning of a new wave of 'euthanasia' of severely impaired people. *Education and Training of the Mentally Retarded, 15*: Guest Editorial, 171–173. [reprinted in: D. G. Race (Ed.) (2003). *Leadership and Change in Human Services: Selected Readings from Wolf Wolfensberger* (pp. 189–190). London: Routledge.]

Introduction

Alan Corbett

It is entirely apt that this, the first book in a planned Institute of Psychotherapy and Disability Monograph series, should centre on the work of Dr Valerie Sinason. Disability psychotherapy would not exist in its current form without Valerie's unique combination of clinical bravery and intense theoretical knowledge. It is one thing to feel instinctively, as so many of us do, that psychotherapy for people with intellectual disabilities is, in large part, an equality issue, and to withhold it is a violation of human rights. It is quite another thing to do what Valerie has done. She has created a school of thought which provides evidence for those instinctive feelings about equality and social justice that stands not only on its own, but also in the context of psychoanalytic history. Valerie feels and thinks, and is unafraid to combine the two.

Threaded throughout this book are concepts that we, in the disability world, take entirely for granted, most notably the "handicapped smile" (Sinason, 1986) and "secondary handicap" (Sinason, 1992). Over the years, I have worked alongside Valerie in a variety of settings. Initially, this was as her supervisee. In later years, I had the honour of introducing Valerie at various conferences and events, experiences that taught me that no matter how often one hears her speak, she always has something new, unexpected, and inspiring to say.

I suspect that, as the years go by, we will find more examples of Valerie's unique ideas and concepts seeping out into the world, just as words such as the "conscious", the "unconscious", and "projection", which were initially specialist psychoanalytic terms, now populate mainstream discourse. Before we reach that point, however, there is work to be done in alerting the world of psychotherapy to the ideas and concepts that we, in the disability psychotherapy field, are developing. Hence this series being aimed not only at those already working in the field but also at those working with patients without (apparent) disabilities. While disability psychotherapy shares the DNA of psychotherapy, it also has some genetic variants that necessitate differences in some aspects of clinical approach. I believe that the more the principles of disability psychotherapy are adopted in work with patients without disabilities, then the better the quality of their therapy.

It is important that the mother of disability psychotherapy is honoured in this first volume. Set against the history of psychoanalysis and its various offspring, disability psychotherapy is a baby, still finding its feet and its voice. Its identity is not set and nor, I argue, should it be, although there are certain principles of disability psychotherapy that I believe are important which are outlined in the core ethos below. It is important that we begin with a picture of what disability psychotherapy looks like now, in the knowledge that it may look very different in decades to come.

Disability psychotherapy describes the use of psychological therapies in work with people with disabilities. It is used by people with intellectual disabilities, physical disabilities, and autism. Its founders were clinicians who had worked with patients with disabilities in a variety of settings for many years, and who formed the Institute of Psychotherapy and Disability (IPD) (2017). At its inception in 2000, the IPD was described as, "...the inauguration of a new variety of psychotherapy: ... which will sit alongside child psychotherapy, family therapy, forensic psychotherapy, group psychotherapy, marital psychotherapy, and other such identities..." (Kahr, 2000, p. 194). More recently, the work and values of the IPD have been echoed in the formation of Disability Psychotherapy Ireland (2017).

The founding conference of the IPD was titled "Treating with Respect", and these words still inform the overall therapeutic approach adopted by the Institute. It is an organisation with a wide membership including psychotherapists, counsellors, psychiatrists, and psychologists from a range of settings who work according to differing theoretical orientations. These orientations include psychoanalytic, psychodynamic, play, person-centred, art, existential, gestalt, and group therapy. As is reflected in the accounts of disability psychotherapy practice in this book, what unites all these modalities is a core ethos. This ethos is informed by:

Respect

People with disabilities tend to occupy the lowest rungs of society's ladder. Cultural, socio-economic, and psychosocial factors increase the tendency for people with disabilities to experience disproportionately high levels of deprivation, abuse, and trauma. The power imbalance inherent in the lives of many people with disabilities is vulnerable to being magnified within the consulting room. It is incumbent on disability therapists to be particularly mindful of this power dynamic and to conduct themselves in ways that do not increase their client's sense of powerlessness.

Trauma

Most disability psychotherapists subscribe to a trauma model, which accommodates two key aspects of clients' traumatogenic history: first, disability is an intrapsychic and interpsychic trauma; and second, societal responses to disability tend to exacerbate the primary trauma. For these reasons, in the context of deep trauma, disability psychotherapy tends to consider the presenting symptoms the clients bring, be they behavioural and/or psychological.

Awareness of cultural issues

A key component of disability psychotherapy is understanding the social context in which many people with disabilities live. For example, many clients rely on a social care network to facilitate their attendance at therapy, and psychotherapy is often paid for by a third party. Also, the confidentiality required of a therapy session may be at odds with how those supporting the client view privacy. It is rare for disability psychotherapy to work without the willingness of the psychotherapist to engage with the client's support network in some way, whilst also protecting the boundaries of the clinical work.

Boundary

The more profound the client's disability, the more consideration disability psychotherapists need to give to the boundary surrounding the work. While the normal ethical boundaries of therapeutic work govern disability psychotherapy, consideration is also given to, for example, the need for the client to have sessions that are shorter or longer than the optimum fifty minutes, or for transitional objects to be brought into the session to help the client manage his or her anxiety.

Unconscious

There is a historical tendency for people with disabilities to be treated in overly behavioural ways that tend to ignore the fact that, like all human beings, people with disabilities have an unconscious. Disability psychotherapists are interested in finding ways to access the unconscious, no matter how severe the disability. The work is informed by such psychoanalytic theories as the "handicapped smile" (Sinason, 1986), "secondary handicap" as a defence (Sinason, 1992), and "the three secrets" (Hollins & Sinason, 2000). As it is a relatively new specialism, its theoretical underpinning is growing and evolving.

Using creativity

As with boundary, the more profound the disability, the more consideration needs to be given to creative ways of working. Disability psychotherapy rejects the notion that psychotherapy is primarily a talking cure. It is a relational process in which many forms of non-verbal communication can be used. Given that some patients with intellectual disabilities may struggle to form narratives or have the vocabulary with which to describe their feelings, disability psychotherapists take care to find alternative ways of facilitating communication. This can include the use of communication aids, the assistance of advocates, and the therapist him- or herself being more active than usual in voicing suggestions as to what the patient may be trying to communicate.

The practical

Disability psychotherapists have a responsibility to take practical steps to prevent the disabling obstacles to psychotherapy that often prevent patients with physical disabilities from being seen. Consulting rooms should be accessible to all.

Pluralism and beyond

Disability psychotherapy is a pluralistic discipline that seeks to encompass a wide range of modalities. The breadth of these modalities reflects the broad range of levels of disability and trauma that present in the consulting room. The ethos of disability psychotherapy is also applicable to other minority groups and capable of being practised by clinicians who do not work predominantly with disability.

These guiding principles all originate from Valerie's approach, most vividly described in her 1992 seminal work, *Mental Handicap and the Human Condition*. As mentioned above, however, these principles should not be set in stone. What we know from our work with patients at the margins of society is that too rigid an approach tends not to work, and that we, as psychotherapists, have to adapt both to the specific cognitive and relational needs of our patients, but also to the organisational needs of the setting in which therapy is being practised. A hallmark of this work is to expect the unexpected. I never dreamt when I started this work that one day I would be happily supervising the work of a therapist whose sessions with a client with intellectual disabilities were conducted while jogging in a circle in the middle of a muddy field! Perhaps this is why it has historically been extremely difficult to get a specialist disability psychotherapy training off the ground. What training manual could possibly encompass the challenges thrown at us every day we practise, and how could we presume to provide answers to questions that have yet to be formulated?

The Monograph series will thus seek to question as well as to answer and I envisage the series becoming a library in which to store our developing theories. This stance is a good fit with Valerie's, as reflected in the contents of this book. Her approach, both individually with patients and before audiences in their thousands, has always been to avoid the easy, pat answer. The inspiration for this series has been Professor Brett Kahr's ground-breaking Forensic Psychotherapy Monograph series, published by Karnac Books (2017). Because of this series, there is now a library of texts specific to forensic work where none existed before. There is, of course, a risk inherent in this kind of specialising: the danger that we create yet another ghetto into which the messiness, shame, and trauma of disability itself can be deposited, relieving the wider therapeutic world of its responsibility to look at disability through an equal lens.

Ultimately, I hope that there will cease to be a need for this specialist series. I hope that "mainstream" psychotherapy will come to see people with disabilities as patients, first and foremost; that training institutes will, in all cases, accept patients with disabilities as valid training patients; and that the teaching and writing about the needs of this heterogeneous and varied group will be within the context of mainstream, non-specialist theory. In reality, this goal is many years away, so while there remains a powerful, unconscious aversion to the integration of children and adults with disabilities into mainstream therapeutic provision, there also remains a need for the IPD and for this series. However, we should not give up on the hope that such specialist distinctions will one day fall away under the glare of human rights and equality considerations, and that the gulf between us and them will fade.

I think I am arguing for the term "disability psychotherapy" to be thought of as a transitional phrase describing a transitional phase. It is already the case that some, such as child psychotherapist Tamsin Cottis who works with children both with and without disabilities, argue that in their disability psychotherapy work the similarities with "mainstream" psychotherapy far outweigh the differences, to the point that, for Cottis, calling herself a disability psychotherapist sits uneasily with her (Cottis, 2016). This is particularly interesting given the preponderance of child analysts and therapists who have laid the foundation stones of disability psychotherapy, among them Anne Alvarez and, of course, Valerie, herself. Their approach has made me consider what I do with my identity as a disability psychotherapist when I am working with a patient without disabilities. I hope that much of it remains, just as I hope that my identity as a psychoanalytic psychotherapist remains in my work with patients with disabilities.

I wonder if our need for a specific label has been fed partly by our fear of danger. It would be surprising and rather grandiose to think that, by dint of our training, analysis, and supervision, we are immune to the prevailing notion that psychotherapy with patients with disabilities is not "real" therapy, and that there may be something flawed and rather dangerous about the whole enterprise. Our patients are vulnerable to psychosocial and individual perceptions of themselves as not being the "right kind of person" and, indeed, of being the kind of person who should have been aborted and whose own potential for procreation should be curtailed.

Small wonder that we, as therapists immersed in the world of disability, should experience a fractal part of these projections of hatred and disavowal. We need to be careful that our need for a specific label does not become overly defensive in nature.

Disability psychoanalysis and its variants have been engaged with disability for over a century now, even though disability, as a description and a construct, is in in a constant state of flux and meaning. I have been considering the disabling illness endured by Sigmund Freud, the founder of psychoanalysis, in the latter years of his life. In reading *The Death of Sigmund Freud* (Edmundson, 2007), I was struck by the presence of disability in Freud's Viennese and London consulting rooms. The overwhelming smell of the prosthetic device lodged in his jaw eventually forced him to end his work with patients. The device, the partial result of many operations to arrest the development of his cancer, was a primitive one. It affected, among many things, the sound and clarity of Freud's voice. For a discipline forged not just on listening, but also on communicating interpretations, this must have been a painful disability for both analyst and patient to negotiate. This led me to reflect on the way in which the clinicians and practitioners who have written for this book seek to notice and accommodate the disability in their patients and, at the same time, want to see beyond it, in order to encounter the patient's real self. In introducing this series, it is important for me to thank those who have helped this first volume come to life. Professor Brett Kahr provided the encouragement and support to put the initial ideas together; without him the series would not exist. Oliver Rathbone, owner of Karnac Books, has recognised the value in publishing books like this one, with a highly specialist focus, and has been supportive of the plans for a series. Dr Georgina Parkes and David O'Driscoll, and their colleagues from the board of the Institute of Psychotherapy and Disability, have been staunch supporters of the series since I first suggested it. Ann Scott, editor of the *British Journal of Psychotherapy* (BJP), helped bring to life a "pilot" for the series whereby I guest-edited a special issue of the BJP focusing on disability psychotherapy (Scott, 2017). I would like to say a special thank you to Tamsin Cottis who took on editing duties for this book when ill health held me back. Enormous thanks, too, to all the contributors to this book. They have brought a rich tapestry of thoughts, theories, and creativity to the project. My final heartfelt thank you goes to Valerie herself, for her generosity in helping me identify potential chapter authors and, of course, for providing the inspiration for this book, and those that will follow. This book stands as a tribute to Valerie, with the love and respect owed to her by generations of clinicians.

References

Cottis, T. (2016). Personal communication.

Disability Psychotherapy Ireland. (2017). www.disabilitypsychotherapyireland.com/ [last accessed 27.11.2017].

Edmundson, M. (2007). *The Death of Sigmund Freud: Fascism, Psychoanalysis and the Rise of Fundamentalism*. London: Bloomsbury. [reprinted London: Bloomsbury, 2008].

Hollins, S., & Sinason, V. (2000). Psychotherapy, learning disabilities and trauma: new perspectives. *The British Journal of Psychiatry*, *176*(1): 32–36.

Institute of Psychotherapy and Disability. (2017). https://instpd.org.uk/ [last accessed 27.11.2017].

Kahr, B. (2000). The adventures of a psychotherapist: a new breed of clinicians – disability psychotherapists. *Psychotherapy Review*, *2*: 193–194.

Karnac. (2017). www.karnacbooks.com/SeriesDetail.asp?SID=90 [last accessed 27.11.2017].

Scott, A. (Ed.) (2017). Special issue on Disability Psychoanalysis, introduced by Dr Alan Corbett. *British Journal of Psychotherapy*, *33*(1): 1–141.

Sinason, V. (1986). Secondary mental handicap and its relationship to trauma. *Psychoanalytic Psychotherapy*, *2*: 131–154.

Sinason, V. (1992). *Mental Handicap and the Human Condition: New Approaches from the Tavistock*. London: Free Association Books.

Townsend, S. (2002). *Number Ten*. London: Michael Joseph.

Chapter 1

Including the excluded

Valerie Sinason, psychoanalytic pioneer

Graeme Galton

Introduction

I first met Valerie in 2001, after she had written much of her pioneering work about intellectual disability and achieved an international reputation in the field. By the time I met her, the focus of her clinical and theoretical work had moved away from intellectual disability. She was, by then, focusing her attention on a further group of clients who had been excluded and marginalised: those who had suffered organised criminal abuse and had developed dissociative identity disorder as a result.

I had the privilege of working closely with Valerie as a friend and colleague in this latter field, at the Clinic for Dissociative Studies, from 2004 until her retirement in 2016. I worked alongside her almost daily during those years and I was in constant awe of her huge creative intellect, as well as her generosity, her warmth, and her humanity.

I was struck by the power of the extraordinary journey Valerie had taken through the field of intellectual disability and I set about reading and assimilating her prolific writing on the subject. The result was that in 2002 I wrote a lengthy paper about her work for the journal, *Free Associations* (Galton, 2002). This present chapter is an updated and revised version of that earlier paper.

Valerie's early work showed that a client does not need cognitive intelligence in order to benefit from psychotherapy and that an intellectually disabled client is likely to make considerable improvements in linguistic and emotional functioning following treatment with psychoanalytic psychotherapy. In addition, she was one of the first clinicians to recognise the particular vulnerability of intellectually disabled clients to sexual abuse, the prevalence of such abuse, and the ways in which psychotherapy can be used to treat its debilitating effects. These ideas are now widely accepted but were viewed with disbelief and hostility when she first presented them in the 1980s. Much of this change in attitude is the result of her work.

All of Valerie's work is in fields which attract enormous amounts of painful and unwanted associations; consequently, the terminology used to describe these frequently changes. As she points out (Sinason, 1992a), when a term becomes contaminated by association with impulses society wishes to disown, it is replaced by a new, as yet uncontaminated, term. In the United Kingdom, the phrase "intellectual disability" is replacing the term "learning disability" which, in turn, replaced the term "mental handicap" and, before that, "mental retardation". One of Valerie's clients told her, "I've got four handicaps. I've got Down's Syndrome, special needs, learning disability and a mental handicap." (Sinason, 1992a, p. 39).

When Valerie joined the Subnormality Workshop at the Tavistock Clinic (Stokes & Sinason, 1992) and began to treat severely disabled patients there, she received a lot of referrals and found it difficult to turn people away. As a result, she was soon seeing a large number of patients, most of them without charge. By 1984, she was treating children and adolescents in three clinical settings and had become increasingly aware that a significant number of her clients, including some who were intellectually disabled, were unable to play with the standard set of toys in her consulting room. She provided new toys, which included large and ordinary-sized dolls and teddy bears. She writes, "The effect was devastating. Within the first session of their use, nine children in three settings disclosed physical and sexual abuse." (Sinason, 1988a, p. 349) Only after she had worked through her feelings of nausea and disbelief, was Valerie able to realise that she had, up until then, been avoiding knowledge of the abuse because she was unable to tolerate the possibility of its occurring, a process which had been identified by Bowlby (1988).

Valerie was working with a client group who were not usually treated with psychotherapy and this enabled her to feel free from an internal orthodoxy. She felt able to use whatever psychoanalytic technique worked, without knowing why it worked, and then conceptualise afterwards. Gradually, the theoretical underpinning of her clinical work took shape. Between 1986 and 1988 Valerie published four key papers about her work with intellectually disabled clients (Sinason, 1986; 1987; 1988a; 1988b). In addition to introducing a number of important new concepts, the papers are full of compassion and understanding for her clients and contain a large amount of clinical detail. Valerie followed them with a large and continuous output of published work on the understanding and treatment of intellectually disabled clients. In 1992 she published *Mental Handicap and the Human Condition: New Approaches from the Tavistock* (Sinason, 1992a), which I consider a landmark publication in the history of psychotherapy publishing.

Secondary handicap

Symington (1981) had found that his patient's level of disability would vary, even from one moment to the next, suggesting that not all of the disability was organic. Sinason (1986) expands and develops this concept and describes a number of defence mechanisms frequently employed by intellectually disabled individuals to protect themselves from the awfulness of realising they are different. These defence mechanisms are defences against meaning and constitute secondary handicaps. These are additions to the original, organic disability, and they attack and deny otherwise intact skills and intelligence. They can also represent a revengeful attack on what is healthy in the client and others, to assuage some of the pain of the original disability (Sinason, 1999a).

By exaggerating a speech defect or lack of language knowledge, or a disabled walk, the intellectually disabled person is able to feel they have some control over their disability. Also, they achieve a narcissistic victory over non-disabled people by fooling them into believing the exaggerated speech or walk is their real voice or real walk. Frequently, the defence mechanism takes the form of an appeasing, disabled smile to create a false, happy self and to keep the outer world happy with them. These concepts do not use any new theoretical ideas; they are a version of Freud's secondary gain (Freud, 1901) and Winnicott's false self (Winnicott, 1960 [1965]). These are familiar ideas showing themselves in a different way with this client group.

Secondary handicap can also take the form of severe personality maldevelopment which is linked to, and added to, the original disability. Intellectual disability depletes a person's inner resources, and excites and attracts emotional difficulty and disturbance (Sinason, 1988b; Stokes & Sinason, 1992). The resulting secondary handicap may be an exaggeration of the organic disability as defence against dangerous impulses such as sexual or violent feelings (Stokes & Sinason, 1992) and may include a hatred of the parents who made them, a hatred of the sexuality involved, a hatred of normality, and an inability to mourn their own lost, healthy self (Sinason, 1986). This personality maldevelopment exacerbates the original loss of normality, as with one lonely, adolescent client who desperately wanted a sexual relationship (Sinason, 1988b). He had such a deep fear of needing help or being humiliated that he aggressively avoided any possibility of meeting or learning to care about someone.

Secondary handicap can also serve as a psychotic defence against trauma (Sinason 1986; 1987). Behaviour which is often explained as part of the original organic disability can be reframed as a version of unrecognised post-traumatic stress disorder. This form of secondary handicap protects against the unbearable memory of trauma, either the trauma of the original organic disability, or the trauma of subsequent sexual or physical abuse. Violent and aggressive behaviour such as kicking, biting, and headbutting can be understood as a psychotic attempt to manage the helplessness inherent in trauma and to omnipotently compensate for the disability. For example, headbanging can be understood as an attempt to rid the mind of bad thoughts. If there has been sexual abuse, violent and sexualised behaviour can be understood as a way of repeating the trauma in an attempt to assimilate it and as a defence against further attack. Eye-poking, cutting, and other forms of self-injury can be understood as attacks on the client's despised body for being unable to prevent the abuse.

Secondary handicap as a psychotic defence against trauma is also evident in the aggressive cuddling by Down's Syndrome children through which they enjoy the violence of abusive physical contact whilst showing ostensible affection (Sinason, 1986; Stokes & Sinason, 1992). In another client, compulsive and aggressive masturbation is a way for him to avenge himself on his parents for the attack he fantasises they made on him at birth (Sinason, 1995b).

Sinason (1986; 1990b; 1995a) identifies the therapist's initial task as elimination of the aspects of secondary handicap which include an exaggerated, disabled, physical appearance, such as a disabled smile, posture or speech. The therapist must acknowledge to the client that there is a better functioning self underneath his or her twisted movements and guttural sounds. The therapist needs to acknowledge the angry, hurt, and painful feelings that lie behind the "handicapped smile" (Sinason, 1986). There follows an opportunity to treat the more pathological kind of secondary handicap represented by the disturbed, envious, and destructive aspects of the personality. The therapist becomes an auxiliary brain, helping the thinking process, and filling in missing words or sentences, whilst being careful not to continue when the client is capable of managing without it (Hollins, Sinason, & Thompson, 1994). This is likely to be a period of crying, rage, grief, and depression as the client mourns his or her lost, healthy self, and his or her limitations, dependency, and terrible feeling of aloneness (Sinason, 1995a). The trauma can be remembered, acknowledged, and healed, in a safe setting with the therapist as protector (see Chapter 7 in this book, by Georgina Parkes; Sinason, 1986).

If treatment can be maintained, there is usually an improvement in internal and external functioning by this point. If there is an accompanying psychosis, the likelihood of which increases with the severity of the disability (Sinason, 1990b), this may now be treated. Valerie has found that a relatively small input of psychotherapeutic resources can make a big difference to an intellectually disabled client's functioning, which can improve dramatically although not to normal. The improvement in functioning may not be constant and is likely to fluctuate (Hollins, Sinason, & Thompson, 1994; Sinason, 1989; Stokes & Sinason, 1992). Improvement is especially likely to fluctuate if a client has been sexually abused.

Sexual abuse

Valerie was particularly concerned at the high proportion of her intellectually disabled clients who had been sexually abused. In these cases the traumatic experience of the original disability is compounded by the further trauma of abuse. Over a two-year period, out of 200 referrals of emotionally disturbed children and adults with an intellectual disability, Valerie found that 140 had been sexually abused (Sinason, 1994). Intellectually disabled children and adults are particularly vulnerable to sexual abuse for a number of reasons (Sinason, 1988b; 1989; 1992a; 1993a; 1994; 1995b). Their lack of sexual knowledge and assertiveness may make it very difficult for them to say "No" to the perpetrator. They also may be physically dependent on those abusing them. Their guilt and shame at being disabled, and the fear that comes from knowing some people wish they were dead, makes them feel they do not have the right to say "No".

When abuse has occurred, the intellectually disabled victim is likely to find it harder to communicate about the abuse so it is more likely to continue. Diagnosis is particularly difficult if the victim is nonverbal. He or she is more likely to be disbelieved because of the widespread belief that sexual attractiveness plays a part in abuse. The psychological symptoms and the disclosure of the abuse are often wrongly diagnosed as psychotic fantasies arising from the original organic disability, and convictions are extremely difficult to achieve (Cooke & Sinason, 1998). Likely symptoms will include self-injury, excessive masturbation, and in children, highly sexualised play (Sinason, 1987; 1992a; 1994).

Sexual abuse is more likely to lead to psychological disturbance in an intellectually disabled victim than a cognitively more able victim (Cooke & Sinason, 1998; Sinason, 1989; 1993b; 1996b). An intellectually disabled victim is more likely to have pre-existing psychological and social problems and, possibly, past psychiatric illness. Past victimisation experiences, low self-esteem, and the lack of a supportive social network combine to exacerbate the impact of the trauma. The disbelief of others increases the likelihood of psychosis in this group (Sinason, 1990a; 1993b; 1994).

These victims often lack a cognitive process to aid healing and enable the painful aspects of the abuse to be processed and symbolised (Cooke & Sinason, 1998; Sinason, 1997d). Self-injury such as cutting and poking – the most common reason for referral of the sexually abused intellectually disabled client (Sinason, 1993b) – is an attack on the client's own, despised body as the hated, helpless victim who was not strong enough (Sinason, 1996a). The client may even have experienced an involuntary orgasm or sexual awakening as the body's survival mechanism to accommodate the intrusion (Sinason, 1996a), in which case the body is even more despised. Valerie has found that the effects of sexual abuse on an intellectually disabled victim can be so severe that in some cases it can even become the primary cause of intellectual disability (Sinason, 1989). Disability becomes a defence against the memory of sexual abuse because, as Sinason writes, "To throw out the knowledge of an abusing trusted adult means throwing out other learning..." (1987, p. 104). Valerie has found that when intellectually disabled clients are able to disclose abuse, they often reveal their intelligence. She notes some clients show a dramatically improved level of language and other functioning after they have remembered and disclosed the abuse in the safe presence of a psychotherapist able to bear the knowledge of the abuse (Sinason, 1986; 1987; 1989; 1992a). However, she notes that, over the long term, a client's improvement will fluctuate and that none of her clients have regained their potential for more than part of each day (Sinason, 1989).

Some victims of abuse go on to become abusers themselves, whether intellectually disabled or not. Evidence indicates that approximately one victim out of every fourteen is likely to do so (Sinason, 1996a) in response to a need to transmit the same complex sequence of pain followed by pleasure as they experienced themselves in the original trauma. Male clients are more likely than female clients to repeat the abuse cycle (Sinason, 1994). Such a cycle of repetition was noted by Klein (1932) and others as victims find that, "the only way to deal with an intolerable experience, the memory of which cannot be borne, is to expel it by making someone else experience it instead" (Sinason, 1990a, pp. 550–551). Valerie notes that intellectually disabled offenders, whether committing sexual or other crimes, are less likely to be taken seriously as offenders by professionals (Sinason, 1997a). Such lack of acknowledgement of their crimes can actually increase the offender's sense of guilt and level of disturbance and cause further sexually disturbed behaviour (Sinason, 1997a; 1997d).

Whether a client's cognitive deficit is the result of chromosomal abnormality, organic illness, birth injury, violence, sexual abuse, lack of attachment, poor schooling, malnutrition, or a combination of factors (Sinason, 1997d), the level of emotional disturbance increases with the severity of the disability (Sinason, 1992b; 1999b). Moreover, the emotional distress is often not recognised and the symptoms are ascribed to the disability rather than to the emotional state of the individual (Hollins, Sinason, & Thompson, 1994). At a World Congress for the Scientific Study of Mental Deficiency in 1989, out of 500 papers, only ten were concerned with emotional disturbance (Sinason, 1990b). In 1987 in the United Kingdom, a study of 596 self-injuring intellectually disabled adults and children showed that only twelve were receiving any psychological treatment, only one of which was psychoanalytical, and this was with Valerie herself (Sinason, 1990b). This was despite Valerie's evidence that even severely and profoundly intellectually disabled clients can show a reduction in symptoms when treated with psychoanalytic psychotherapy.

Challenges for the psychotherapist

There are significant challenges for the psychotherapist treating an intellectually disabled client because of the particular demands of this group, as is seen in many of the chapters that follow in this book. The therapist has first to come to terms with his or her own guilt about not being disabled (Sinason, 1988b), and his or her fears of not understanding the client's speech (McCormack & Sinason, 1996; Sinason, 2000). The therapist must also accept the limitations of what can be achieved because the emotional disturbance might be treatable but the actual organic disability is not. Differences of technique are required as visual contact is needed by the client; it is not possible, for example, for the client to lie on the couch (Hollins, Sinason, & Thompson, 1994). More affective colouring is required in the therapist's speech (Sinason, 1999b), and negative transference interpretations require a facilitating tone of voice or they will be understood as direct complaints from the therapist (Hollins, Sinason, & Thompson, 1994). At times there is a need for a straightforwardly educational comment (Sinason, 1997b). The therapist must also be prepared to be part of a larger care and treatment team (Sinason, 1999b). Crucially, the therapist must be able to accept the possibility that sexual abuse has occurred (Sinason, 1989).

The most challenging aspect of working with clients with intellectual disabilities is the therapist's need to withstand and interpret the client's extremely powerful projections (Sinason, 1997c). Valerie shows an enormous capacity to do this as evidenced in her remarkable ability to sustain and expand her work in the intellectual disability field. She uses her countertransference as a key diagnostic and therapeutic tool and maintains that this is particularly essential when working with this client group because of the combined effect of their impaired cognitive ability and their communication difficulties (Sinason, 2002).

In her case studies, Valerie describes the powerful feelings projected into her by her clients as they, on occasion, make her feel completely helpless, stupid, disgusted or nauseous. In the consulting room she has had incontinent clients urinate or defecate, then smear their faeces or throw their used sanitary pads onto the floor, and then sometimes roll their wheelchairs over them so the smell and mess is spread (Sinason, 1992a; 1997c). On other occasions clients have poked their fingers or other objects into their anus or vagina and then sometimes licked the object (Sinason, 1987). Sinason (1992a; 1997c) describes how her primitive response of disgust when made witness to these actions has made her unable to think properly. She describes the effort she has had to make to understand these actions and interpret them back to the client as expressions of powerful feelings of stupidity, self-disgust, and self-loathing, and as attempts to project into the therapist the same stupefaction, disgust and loathing.

Valerie also recognises the powerful feelings that intellectually disabled people evoke in those who live or work with them. As with projections into the therapist, "feelings in learning-disabled clients of being, for example, stupid, useless, uncomprehending, powerless, unattractive, socially denigrated and unwanted are projected into the workers" (Sinason, 1997c, p. 105). Valerie raises concerns that workers with the intellectually disabled are often not adequately trained or supported (Sinason, 1988b), allowing these negative projections to be internalised and to grow into hatred for those in their care (Sinason, 1993a). There is denial of these negative feelings out of guilt for not being disabled themselves (Sinason, 1988b; 1993a).

For the intellectually disabled client, this hostility forms part of a general death wish which is felt about them by society in general, unconsciously or otherwise (see Jan Walmsley's chapter in this book, Chapter 11). The ubiquitous handicapped smile and outward friendliness of intellectually disabled clients is a defence against this accurately perceived societal death wish (Sinason, 1986). Valerie's understanding of the handicapped smile as a defence against pain is, perhaps, of all her work, the aspect which has become most recognised, and which has also lost its direct connection with her (Sinason, 2002). Society's guilt about not being disabled leads to collusion, and the creation of defensive myths about intellectually disabled children being friendly, even when there is clear evidence that they are not (Sinason, 1986; 1993a; 1999b).

Formal research

It was many years before Valerie realised the importance of testing and measuring the improvement in her clients' functioning in a formal way. Only as she began work on her doctoral thesis, did she fully appreciate the need for evaluative outcome research, if her findings were to achieve credibility in the wider professional fields of medicine and psychology.

The first published study which tested Valerie's clinical findings was undertaken at the Tavistock Clinic from 1989 to 1993 (Bichard, Sinason & Usiskin, 1996). Valerie collaborated with Sheila Bichard, a psychologist, who used the Draw-a-Person (DAP) test to assess changes in clients' functioning following psychoanalytic psychotherapy. The study looks at clients with IQs ranging from 30 to 69, some of whom received psychotherapy and some of whom received no treatment and served as the contrast group. Clients were also assessed with other projective tests, including House–Tree–Person, Kinetic Family Drawing, TAT and Rorschach, as well as cognitive testing.

The study confirms what Valerie already knew, and shows that over a two-year period the great majority of the treatment group, regardless of IQ, had improved cognitive and emotional functioning as measured by increased DAP scores. In the contrast group, all except one client showed a deterioration in functioning over the period of the study. Bichard, Sinason and Usiskin (1996) conclude that an increase in emotional functioning leads to an increase in cognitive functioning, but not necessarily to an increase in IQ. The study also shows that it is difficult to predict, at the outset, an individual's potential for improvement or likely rate of improvement.

Valerie was keen to make up for the lack of outcome research studies and hoped to accumulate a body of formal evidence to back her pioneering clinical findings. She conducted a significant research study with Sheila Hollins at St George's Hospital Medical School (Carlsson, Hollins, Nilsson, & Sinason, 2002). The study used two psychoanalytic tests, the Defence Mechanism Test and Perceptual Object Relations Test, which were originally developed at the

Tavistock Clinic but had fallen out of use in the United Kingdom. These tests were widely used in Sweden and the study linked St George's Hospital with five other treatment centres abroad, including one in Lund, Sweden. The tests were used to assess the effect of psychotherapy on patients in two of Valerie's psychoanalytic groups at St George's Hospital. In one group the patients were all female victims of abuse, while the other group consisted of male sex offenders. The effectiveness of group analytic treatment with intellectually disabled clients was also assessed in an interview study published by Macdonald, Sinason, and Hollins (2003).

A further study, which was not published, measures changes in clients' language structure following psychoanalytic psychotherapy (Sinason, 2002). The study examines mean length of utterance in matched pairs of clients, one of whom is in treatment and the other of whom is not, and is in a contrast group; the pairs were matched for gender, age, symptom, and IQ. The study shows that language structure improves for those in treatment but remains the same for those in the contrast group, proving what Valerie had known for a long time. Valerie concludes that before treatment there is a defensive gap between clients' expressive vocabulary (words such as, "nice", "good", and "clean") and their large receptive vocabulary of insults (words such as "disgusting", "revolting", and "devastating"). After a year in therapy, the negative vocabulary to which they have been exposed is able to emerge.

Institutional responses

From the beginning of Valerie's work with intellectually disabled patients at the Tavistock Clinic, she had received a very warm and enthusiastic response from outside agencies. In 1985, psychologist Vicky Turk suggested to Valerie that she run a short course for outside workers in order to share her understanding of working with intellectually disabled adults and children. Even without advertising, that first ten-week course was immediately very popular, so it was repeated. Soon there were up to three such courses running at any one time. The ten-week course in psychotherapeutic approaches to working with people with intellectual disability became part of the Tavistock Clinic's official training programme. The course presented a psychoanalytic perspective on intellectual disability, something no other course had ever done in the United Kingdom, and led to the eventual establishment of the Post-Graduate Certificate in Psychotherapeutic Approaches to Working with People with Learning Disabilities in partnership with the University of East London.

Valerie returned to South Africa every year for many years following her first visit in 1994 and in 1997 she was appointed Honorary Consultant Psychotherapist at the Cape Town Child Guidance Clinic in the Psychology Department of the University of Cape Town (see Lesley Swartz' Chapter 12 in this book). She became a key person in training psychologists in South Africa to use psychotherapy with disabled people who had also been abused. She spent three or four weeks every year lecturing and working without payment in the South African townships, giving supervision to clinicians and treating disturbed children, many of whom had seen members of their family tortured and killed. In Sweden, too, psychotherapists listened to Valerie and began applying what she had to say; this happened notably more quickly than in the United Kingdom. Her work is highly regarded in Sweden and she has been awarded life membership of Sveriges Handikappsykologers Förening, the Swedish organisation for psychologists working in the field of intellectual disability.

As others have noted in this volume, Valerie achieved a long-held ambition in January 2000 with the establishment of the Institute of Psychotherapy and Disability (Kahr, 2000a; 2000b; Sinason, 2002). Valerie made a singular contribution to this landmark step and, through the Institute, she hopes to bring about further improvements in the treatment of intellectually disabled clients. The establishment of the Institute marked another milestone in twenty years of progress in disability psychotherapy.

Conclusion

Valerie's work with intellectually disabled clients served as good training for her later work with clients suffering with dissociative identity disorder. Indeed, she first became involved in the field of dissociation through supervising the psychotherapy of an intellectually disabled woman being treated by a colleague in Sweden (see Anders Svensson's Chapter 13 in this book). This intellectually disabled woman had developed dissociative identity disorder as a result of organised, criminal abuse. Valerie has never lost her close connection with intellectual disability and, in her subsequent years at the Clinic for Dissociative Studies, about a quarter of her dissociative clients had an intellectual disability.

Intellectual disability and dissociative identity disorder have some key features in common. In contrast to mainstream psychoanalytic psychotherapy, there is nothing symbolic about the chronic and painful reality of both conditions. Many of the countertransference feelings of helplessness and hopelessness are present in work with both client groups. In both, the psychotherapist also has to bear the client's depression at the lack of change that can be achieved. The projections from both these client groups can be particularly powerful and many therapists find them intolerable. Society has a wish to deny the existence of both groups and would frequently prefer these clients were not seen and not heard. Furthermore, there is a societal wish to deny the truth of associated trauma and abuse so people in both groups can face denial, fear of difference, stigma, re-abuse, and scapegoating. Thanks to Valerie's theoretical contributions, all of us working in these fields are better equipped to understand this and to offer more effective help to our clients.

References

Bichard, S. H., Sinason, V., & Usiskin, J. (1996). Measuring change in mentally retarded clients in long-term psychoanalytic psychotherapy: 1. the Draw-A-Person Test. *National Association for Dual Diagnosis (NADD) Newsletter, 13*(5): 6–11.

Bowlby, J. (1988). On knowing what you are not supposed to know and feeling what you are not supposed to feel. In: *A Secure Base: Clinical Applications of Attachment Theory* (pp. 99–118). London: Routledge.

Carlsson, B., Hollins, S., Nilsson, A., & Sinason, V. (2002). Preliminary findings: an Anglo-Swedish psychoanalytic psychotherapy outcome study using PORT and DMT. *Tizard Learning Disability Review, 7*(4): 39–48.

Cooke, L. B., & Sinason, V. (1998). Abuse of people with learning disabilities and other vulnerable adults. *Advances in Psychiatric Treatment, 4*(2): 119–125.

Freud, S. (1901). The psychopathology of everyday life. [reprinted in: *The Standard Edition of the Complete Psychological Works of Sigmund Freud, Volume VI (1901): The Psychopathology of Everyday Life.* (trans. J. Strachey). London: Vintage, 2001.

Galton, G. (2002). New horizons in disability psychotherapy: the contributions of Valerie Sinason. *Free Associations, 9*(4): 582–610.

Hollins, S., Sinason, V., & Thompson, S. (1994). Individual, group and family psychotherapy. In: N. Bouras (Ed.), *Mental Health in Mental Retardation: Recent Advances and Practices* (pp. 233–243). Cambridge: Cambridge University Press.

Kahr, B. (2000a). The adventures of a psychotherapist: a new breed of clinicians – disability psychotherapists. *Psychotherapy Review, 2*: 193–194.

Kahr, B. (2000b). Towards the creation of disability psychotherapists. Paper presented at the launch of the Institute of Psychotherapy and Disability, held at St George's Hospital Medical School, London, 20 May [unpublished].

Klein, M. (1932). *The Psycho-Analysis of Children.* (trans. A. Strachey). London: Hogarth Press and The Institute of Psycho-Analysis. [reprinted London: Vintage, 1997, 3rd edn].

MacDonald, J., Sinason, V., & Hollins, S. (2003). An interview study of people with learning disabilities' experience of, and satisfaction with, group analytic therapy. *Psychology and Psychotherapy: Theory, Research and Practice, 76*: 433–453.

McCormack, B., & Sinason, V. (1996). Mentally handicapped children and adolescents. In: P. Kymissis & D. A. Halperin (Eds.), *Group Therapy with Children and Adolescents* (pp. 225–241). Washington DC: American Psychiatric Press.

Sinason, V. (1986). Secondary mental handicap and its relationship to trauma. *Psychoanalytic Psychotherapy, 2*(2): 131–154.

Sinason, V. (1987). Smiling, swallowing, sickening and stupefying: the effect of sexual abuse on the child. *Psychoanalytic Psychotherapy, 3*: 97–111.

Sinason, V. (1988a). Dolls and bears: from symbolic equation to symbol. The significance of different play material for sexually abused children and others. *British Journal of Psychotherapy, 4*: 349–363.

Sinason, V. (1988b). Richard III, Hephaestus and Echo: sexuality and mental/multiple handicap. *Journal of Child Psychotherapy, 14*(2): 93–105.

Sinason, V. (1989). Uncovering and responding to sexual abuse in psychotherapeutic settings. In: H. Brown & A. Craft (Eds.), *Thinking the Unthinkable: Papers on Sexual Abuse and People with Learning Difficulties* (pp. 39–40). London: Family Planning Association Education Unit.

Sinason, V. (1990a). Child sexual abuse. In: H. Wolff, A. Bateman, & D. Sturgeon (Eds.), *University College Hospital Textbook of Psychiatry: An Integrated Approach* (pp. 541–553). London: Duckworth.

Sinason, V. (1990b). Individual psychoanalytic psychotherapy with severely and profoundly handicapped patients. In: A. Došen, A. van Gennep, & G. J. Zwanikken (Eds.), *Treatment of Mental Illness and Behavioural Disorder in the Mentally Retarded: Proceedings of the International Congress, Amsterdam, 3–4 May 1990* (pp. 71–80). Leiden, The Netherlands: Logon Publications.

Sinason, V. (1992a). *Mental Handicap and the Human Condition: New Approaches from the Tavistock*. London: Free Association Books.

Sinason, V. (1992b). Psychotherapy with profoundly handicapped children. In: S. Ramsden (Ed.), *Psychotherapy – Pure and Applied: Papers and Workshops Presented at the ACPP Study Day, London, 9 October 1991* (pp. 38–42). London: Association for Child Psychology and Psychiatry.

Sinason, V. (1993a). Hate and mental handicap: issues in psychoanalytical psychotherapy with children with mental handicap. In: V. Varma (Ed.), *How and Why Children Hate: A Study of Conscious and Unconscious Sources* (pp. 186–198). London: Jessica Kingsley.

Sinason, V. (1993b). The vulnerability of the handicapped child and adult: with special reference to mental handicap (learning disability). In: C. J. Hobbs & J. M. Wynne (Eds.), *Baillière's Clinical Paediatric: International Practice & Research. Volume 1: Child Abuse* (pp. 69–86). London: Baillière Tindall.

Sinason, V. (1994). The treatment of people with learning disabilities who have been abused. In: J. Harris & A. Craft (Eds.), *People With Learning Disabilities at Risk of Physical or Sexual Abuse* (pp. 123–132). Kidderminster: British Institute of Learning Disabilities.

Sinason, V. (1995a). Individual psychoanalytical psychotherapy with severely and profoundly handicapped patients. In: J. Ellwood (Ed.), *Psychosis: Understanding and Treatment* (pp. 153–161). London: Jessica Kingsley.

Sinason, V. (1995b). Revenge and learning disability. *Self & Society*, *23*(1): 16–18.

Sinason, V. (1996a). From abused to abuser. In: C. Cordess & M. Cox (Eds.), *Forensic Psychotherapy: Crime, Psychodynamics and the Offender Patient. Vol. 2: Mainly Practice* (pp. 371–382). London: Jessica Kingsley.

Sinason, V. (1996b). Introduction. In: A. Corbett, T. Cottis, & S. Morris (Eds.), *Witnessing, Nurturing, Protesting: Therapeutic Responses to Sexual Abuse of People with Learning Disabilities* (pp. vii–x). London: David Fulton.

Sinason, V. (1997a). A relationship with the law. *Bulletin of the Association of Child Psychotherapists*, *73*: 22–28.

Sinason, V. (1997b). Gender-linked issues in psychotherapy with abused and learning disabled female patients. In: J. Raphael-Leff & R. J. Perelberg (Eds.), *Female Experience: Three Generations of British Women Psychoanalysts on Work with Women* (pp. 266–280). London: Routledge.

Sinason, V. (1997c). Stress in the therapist and the Bagshaw Syndrome. In: V. P. Varma (Ed.), *Stress in Psychotherapists* (pp. 83–93). London: Routledge.

Sinason, V. (1997d). The learning disabled (mentally handicapped) offender. In: E. V. Welldon & C. Van Velsen (Eds.), *A Practical Guide to Forensic Psychotherapy* (pp. 56–61). London: Jessica Kingsley.

Sinason, V. (1999a). Challenged bodies, wounded body images: Richard III and Hephaestus. In: J. M. Goodwin & R. Attias (Eds.), *Splintered Reflections: Images of the Body in Trauma* (pp. 183–194). New York: Basic Books.

Sinason, V. (1999b). The psychotherapeutic needs of the learning disabled and multiply disabled child. In: M. Lanyado & A. Horne (Eds.), *The Handbook of Child & Adolescent Psychotherapy: Psychoanalytic Approaches* (pp. 445–456). London: Routledge.

Sinason, V. (2000). *Traumatic Attachment, Cognitive Impairment and Psychoanalysis.* Audio tape of workshop conducted on 14 October 2000. Los Angeles: Los Angeles Institute and Society for Psychoanalytic Studies Audio & Video Library.

Sinason, V. (2002). Personal interviews with Valerie Sinason conducted between 21 May 2001 and 14 March 2002.

Stokes, J., & Sinason, V. (1992). Secondary mental handicap as a defence. In: A. Waitman & S. Conboy-Hill (Eds.), *Psychotherapy and Mental Handicap* (pp. 46–58). London: Sage.

Symington, N. (1981). The psychotherapy of a subnormal patient. *British Journal of Medical Psychology, 54*: 187–199.

Winnicott, D. W. (1965). Ego distortion in terms of true and false self (1960). In: *The Maturational Processes and the Facilitating Environment: Studies in the Theory of Emotional Development* (pp. 140–152). London: Hogarth Press. [reprinted London: Karnac, 2007].

Chapter 2

Creativity and the analytic condition

Creative arts approaches within a psychoanalytic frame

Eimir McGrath

Introduction

Talking therapies that focus on the spoken word as a primary means of creating connection can be inadequate for those whose lived experience compromises their effective use of language, whether that is due to trauma or environmental factors, or as a consequence of disability. The use of creativity in psychotherapy provides a conduit for finding a voice that is not reliant on the spoken word. The fundamental basis of any psychotherapeutic intervention is the interpersonal relationship that grows between therapist and client, and the building of relationship depends on pathways of communication that are infinitely greater than just words. Creative arts approaches within psychotherapy can provide the tools for finding many of those pathways, leading to a prelinguistic level of intersubjectivity that is the foundation of human interaction (Stern, 2004; Trevarthen, 2006).

Contemporary research into the neurobiological aspects of relationship (Cozolino, 2006; Schore, 2012; Wilkinson, 2010) has enhanced our understanding of the psychodynamic concepts of attachment, and of transference and countertransference, both of which are essential to the therapeutic process especially where language is compromised (Sinason, 2010, p. 67). This research also provides a rationale for the inclusion of creative elements within the therapeutic relationship as a means of building connection that is emotionally based rather than being dependent on higher cortical processes where language is situated. The combination of these elements will be explored in this chapter through the lens of writer, child psychotherapist, and adult psychoanalyst, Valerie Sinason (1992; 2010), with her pioneering approach to working psychotherapeutically with people who have an intellectual disability. The focus will be on clients with severe to profound intellectual disabilities who experience emotional pain and who seek to find their voice through a connection not primarily dependent on language, but rather, through the intersubjective space where meaning making occurs, facilitated by shared creativity.

I first heard Sinason's voice through the medium of the printed word. As a psychotherapist specialising in play therapy who had recently begun working in residential settings for children and adults with multiple disabilities, I felt the lack of an appropriate theoretical framework with which to underpin my developing disability psychotherapy practice, in environments that were unused to thinking psychotherapeutically. Despite many years' experience of working with vulnerable children and adults in the community, my understanding of intellectual disability at that time did not adequately encompass the complexities of the lives of those with whom I came into daily contact in these residential disability settings. My discovery of Sinason's seminal work, *Mental Handicap and the Human Condition* (1992), was the beginning of a journey that transformed that understanding, providing me with the concepts of primary and secondary handicap, the handicapped smile, and disability as a defence against trauma. These were essential elements that I needed in order to make sense of the pain and distress which confronted me in the therapy room, and for which, at the beginning of my work, I had no coherent understanding, but rather a collection of loose threads that would be woven into a cohesive theoretical fabric over the next few years. This theoretical fabric developed through the application to intellectual disability of a neurodevelopmental understanding of brain growth and relationship building, an exploration of the neurobiology of attachment and the consequences of failed relationship, and by investigating the impact of trauma, whether relational or through physical, emotional, or sexual abuse. This was all held together on the bedrock of Sinason's psychoanalytic approach.

Sinason recognises the absolute humanity of each client regardless of the level of disability, and also the painful "not knowing" (Sinason, 2010, p. 1) of the human condition where intellectual disability is present. Both of these principles were fundamental to my understanding of the very complex dynamics contained in disability services, where the humanity of patients was defended against because of the pain it contained, and unknowingly became a negative force that buried thinking underneath a busy regime of "doing" that could be measured, monitored and objectified. This reflected the tendency of non-disabled professionals involved in the care of disabled clients to be drawn into accepting a societally imposed regulatory role, containing their clients either within a regime of attempted normalisation and acquiescence (Sinason, 2010), or upholding an exclusionary, ableist understanding of disability as "not really human" (Campbell, 2012, p. 215).

My practice evolved with each new challenge that required me to be adaptable, and flexible, and to find solutions through making use of my training in play therapy and my background in the creative arts. The very structure of the therapeutic session often had to be thought about in a more creative way to enable clients to engage with me in a relationship that was beyond the realm of their prevailing experience. Disability psychotherapy requires the recognition and consideration of a multiplicity of complex concepts. Fundamental to these is the hegemony of the sociocultural notion of disability itself, and how disability is seen.

Disability: the power of the gaze

Apart from individual disabled clients' specific experience of trauma, emotional pain for these clients can arise from the commonalities of an existence where disability is marginalised and ejected from the communal psyche. Sociologist Bill Hughes states, "Disability, in modernity, has been produced in the ontological household of the abject, as the antithesis of communication and community" (2012, p. 23). He speaks of the ableist reaction of disgust when faced with disability, reflecting the inability to face the vulnerabilities and imperfections that are part of every person's life. The need to project this disquiet into those who are perceived as different establishes a dichotomy, a separation of the bearable from the unbearable, so creating the barriers that make communication and community a struggle rather than a given of social life (Hughes, 2012). Sinason refers to the consequent pain of being different as the result of becoming "the dustbin for the primitive fears for others" (2010, p. 41).

Cozolino (2002) speaks of these primitive fears arising from societal perceptions of disability, where being seen (or not) can become a negation of the intellectually disabled person's aliveness. The power of the gaze is a fundamental aspect of the development of social behaviour, and the mutual gaze at the beginning of life between an infant and the primary caregiver is vital for the early experience of positive emotional attunement. This, in turn, releases the cascade of neurochemicals that are needed for the creation of new neural pathways, the basis of brain growth and development (Hughes, 2007; Schore, 1997; Trevarthen, 2009). For an infant with an intellectual disability, the sharing of the gaze can be seriously disrupted where the primary caregiver is unable to successfully meet a rhythm of interaction that may be unexpectedly slow or appear disjointed, thereby leading to multiple misattunements. Sometimes the primary caregiver cannot bear and contain the communications of an infant that represents Hughes' notion of "the abject" (Hughes, 2012, p. 23). When this happens, this is the beginning of what Sinason calls "the handicapping process" (2010, p. 67), inhibiting brain development and social communication, and compounding the organic deficit that is already in place. Cozolino states, "The eyes and the information they communicate are windows to our interpersonal histories as well as our souls" (2002, p. 176).

Being seen in a wider social context can bring further pain. Shared social communications that perceive disability negatively, are instilled into children from a very young age by the adults in their environment. If, upon seeing a disabled person, an adult displays a negative emotional response in front of a child, this will communicate complex emotional information to the child who is looking at difference. The adult's response does not have to be based in verbal communications of dismay, disapproval, or perhaps revulsion; the eye gaze and facial expression alone will communicate this. Looks of disgust and disapproval trigger feelings of shame in both the disabled person and in the child and adult who look, and so the adult's internal world and belief system are transferred within the triad, creating a potentially toxic state from a neurobiological perspective due to the neurochemicals produced (Schore, 2012, p. 98). The toxicity of such rejection is not purely chemical, it is also a symptom of Hughes' "ontological household of the abject" (2012, p. 23), where the marginalisation of disability is embedded in cultural belief systems, passed from adult to child. Neuroscientist Antonio Damasio speaks of the primitive sense of contamination caused by disgust and the feeling of contempt. He says: "... many of the actions in the human disgust program, including its typical facial expressions, have been co-opted by a social emotion: *contempt*. Contempt is often a metaphor for moral disgust" (2010, p. 117, author's italics). The inability to cope with difference leads to denial and Sinason's notion of stupidity as, "a defence against the trauma of knowing too much of a painful kind" (2010, p. 18). This is a stupidity that may be shared by those who look, as well as those who are the object of that destructive gaze. Disability scholar Rosemarie Garland-Thomson speaks of the blank stare of those who are the victims of societal inequity, including those with significant physical and intellectual disabilities whose appearance is non-typical. She asserts:

> The supposed dumb look, blind eye, and idiotic expression are highly stigmatized ways of appearing that draw interrogative stares from those who are properly focused. This type of purportedly empty stare demands no response, initiates no interchange, and produces no knowledge. Blank stares function, then, as visual impotence.
>
> (2009, p. 23)

It creates a striking impression to think of the juxtaposition of Garland-Thomson's "blank stare" with Sinason's notion of the "handicapped smile" (2010, p. 119), where the perceived deadness of gaze is accompanied by the abject smile of compliance, the smile that perverts and denies any recognition of the awful emotional, physical, and mental pain that hides behind. Sinason speaks of the guilt this pain generates in others, leading to the insistence on an appearance of happiness rather than any expression of the depth of pain. She very eloquently says, "I now see the shadow of the smile forms the shape of loss in exact proportion to the excess of the upward curve" (2010, p. 124).

Transforming the gaze

In order to provide a therapeutic space where such pain can be recognised and witnessed, and to create a reparative experience for those with a severe or profound intellectual disability, it is necessary to take a neurodevelopmental approach. By doing this, it makes it possible to meet each person at the point of earliest rupture. Neuropsychologist and psychotherapist Allan Schore

(2009) has extensively researched affect regulation in infants and the role of attachment, in order to create a neuropsychoanalytically informed mode of practice that benefits from strong foundations in affective neuroscience. This is particularly relevant to therapeutic work in the field of intellectual disability where implicit, right-brain communications between therapist and client are the basis of transference and countertransference, providing the means of building a therapeutic alliance that can be reparative. Schore states, "Within the therapeutic dyad, not left brain verbal explicit patient–therapist discourse but right brain implicit nonverbal affect-laden communication directly represents the attachment dynamic" (2012, p. 127). As social beings whose brains are hardwired to connect with others, our earliest experience of attachment provides the foundation for relationship, the heart of psychotherapeutic practice. In his research, Schore has shown that through the use of an attachment-based relationship, the change mechanism contained in the therapy is not necessarily mediated by insight, but is the product of an experience of therapeutic synchrony. He states that, "psychotherapy is not the 'talking cure' but the affect communicating and regulating cure" (2009, p. 128). Where symbolic thought is absent and communication is non-verbal, "relatedness becomes more important than cognition" (Corbett, 2009, p. 62), and interpretation can be communicated in a way that is receivable; it can be "held" in the therapist's mind rather than verbalised. The therapist becomes a thinking presence on behalf of the client and gives meaning to interactions through his or her embodied self and use of voice. The pitch, timbre, and rhythm of vocalisations can "provide an aural sense of holding and containment" (Corbett, 2009 p. 62).

These early patterns of engagement can be awoken not only through the transference and countertransference, but also through the use of pre-linguistic, creative approaches in psychotherapy, regardless of intellectual ability. The initial gaze of the primary caregiver holds the seed of attunement that allows an infant to be seen. With disability, being seen holds a much wider, more painful significance.

The rhythm and musicality of relationship

Many of my clients would have been the receptacle of others' looks of disgust and horror as their multiple disabilities gave them a physical appearance that created a hypervisibility due to their physical difference (Kuppers, 2003, p. 49). Consequently, the very act of being seen carried an unbearable amount of emotional pain for some clients, dominating the beginning of their therapeutic engagement. Each clinical case that follows is a composite of more than one client's story in order to respect the privacy and confidentiality of the shared relationships contained within the therapy room.

"Maura" was a nonverbal young woman with a severe intellectual disability and physical limitations that limited her mobility due to extreme childhood neglect. Her entry into the therapy room was painfully tentative. With averted gaze and lowered head, she would shuffle her way around the door, retreating hastily in the fearful anticipation of being seen. This was repeated time and again for several sessions until she became accustomed to my neutral presence as I sat quietly on the floor in the middle of the room. Her fascination with shiny objects that she hoarded within her clothing became the entry point for our relationship. Alvarez discusses the reclamation of those whose intersubjective relationships have gone drastically wrong. She speaks of the "chronic apathy about relating, which goes beyond despair" (2012, p. 21), where there may never have been the creation of a healthy attachment. The process of reclamation with Maura centred on recreating within her a sense of curiosity about another living, responsive object. There was an apparent reversal of the normal sequence of intersubjectivity (Trevarthen & Aitken, 2001). It can be presumed from her history of extreme rejection during infancy and early childhood that the maternal gaze of primary intersubjectivity (ibid.) had been experienced in such a perverse way that any future look of interest, or engagement with her very being, became unbearably threatening. She could not tolerate being seen by me so we had to begin our relationship in the less threatening arena of her defensive, relational fascination with objects.

The starting point was through shared attention on small shiny objects, the secondary intersubjectivity that is formed by the triad of intentional communication with another through the use of objects (Trevarthen, 2006). With my attention firmly fixed on my own collection of shiny things, Maura very cautiously began to approach me. My visual focus remained on my collection, but my therapeutic focus was on being an external regulator for Maura's emotional hyperarousal and I used my voice as a means of regulation and attunement (Schore, 1994). Starting with a low humming tune, I sang to Maura as one would to a newborn, creating a rhythmic, melodic accompaniment to her slow entry into the room. Over several sessions, I continued singing, ritualising her entry into and exit from the room with the exact same, very simple, repetitive song that contained both our names. This concrete expression of containment not only represented the psychic containment of the therapeutic space, provided by repetition and predictability, but also marked the boundaries of our coming and going. I began to create songs that reflected her exploration of the room, directing my gaze towards the object of interest, with fleeting glances at Maura which were becoming more bearable for her as she began to realise that I was a benign presence. Maura's desire for my shiny objects became more urgent than her need to maintain distance and she finally approached me, sitting beside me and reaching out cautiously for the objects in my collection. The first experience of reciprocity followed soon after as we exchanged objects, accompanied by her fleeting glances at me, and all the time accompanied by my singing and humming.

My voice gradually moved to the protoconversational patterns of early infancy (Malloch, 1999). Sinason speaks of the need for the therapist to become the provider of the voice for clients who cannot think or speak easily; this is informed by the therapist's countertransference in the immediacy of the moment as events unfold (2010, p. 107). As I continued to provide a voice, Maura began to make small, guttural noises in reciprocation. Malloch (1999) demonstrated that in protoconversations, mothers and infants mutually adjust the pulse of their vocalisations and vary the quality of their expression systematically in order to produce a narrative lasting tens of seconds. During these protoconversations they can respond synchronously or alternately and gradually develop a coordinated timing. Interactions become progressively more complex and lively and, as the infant matures, the protoconversations become faster, with a wider range of rhythms and qualities of expression (Trevarthen, 2005; 2009). Maura and I created such narrative patterns through our rhythmic, playful interactions and our increasingly complex use of song. The emotional content of her inner experience and the external, reciprocal expression of emotion contained in each rhythmic interaction became more and more predictable. Through this embodied form of empathic attunement, she ultimately became fully present in our interactions and a healthy therapeutic attachment was formed. As Trevarthen says, the use of speech and song can "turn the rhythms and accents of the mind into events that can bridge space between distant human bodies" (2005, p. 66).

Making a move

The neurobiologically primitive power of rhythm can be applied in diverse, creative ways within the therapeutic environment (McGrath, 2014; 2016). Sharing rhythms through the use of musical instruments, creating songs, listening to music, and embodying rhythm within movement all provide the means to recreating these early infant patterns of communication and attachment building. Trevarthen states that, "matching rhythm or pulse of movement offers a powerful correspondence by which mind states may be coupled and 'march in step'" (2005, p. 64). Movement and dance likewise offer a way of developing relationship through an embodied experience of empathic attunement, and with this discovery of social connection, a client with severe intellectual disability is able to explore his or her inner emotional life. The therapist must be finely tuned to all the embodied communications that pass between him or herself and the client for this exploration to be adequately supported. Sensorimotor psychotherapist Pat Ogden describes this process: "The therapist meticulously watches for incipient spontaneous actions and affects – the beginning of a smile, meaningful eye contact, a more expansive and playful movement – calling attention to them and expressing curiosity, enabling the moment to linger" (2009, p. 221). In order to know about the client's unconscious process, we need to become not only keen observers of our clients' physiology and the associated bodily changes, such as body position, facial expression, shifts in eye gaze, changes in muscle tension and breathing, but also to be fully aware of our own physiological responses and what they are communicating, along with the emotional content of our presence. In the dance of communication, both literally and figuratively, therapist and client can achieve synchrony through a pattern of engagement, arousal, withdrawal, and re-engagement (Schore, 2012). This replicates the early pattern of rupture and repair where infants learn to differentiate and separate from their primary caregivers, develop self-regulation, tolerate waiting and frustration, and experience synchrony with another (Trevarthen, 2003). Neuroscientists Marco Iacoboni and John Mazziotta (2007) have created an understanding of the mirror neuron system in humans, stating that their role in intersubjectivity is to create an interdependence that is based on shared existential meanings, leading to a deep interpersonal connection. Psychotherapist Suzanne Maiello, talks of the "rhythmicity of maternal embodiment providing the music of the life dance ... where mirror neurons are creating the groundwork for the development of empathy through rhythmic sound and movement" (2001, p. 81). For someone with a profound intellectual disability, rhythmic sound and movement provides a link that makes the outside world accessible, shifting from a position of isolation towards an emerging sense of self (Maiello, 2001, p. 182), which in turn leads to intentional communication with another.

I experienced this emerging sense of self through the use of movement when working with "Julia", a tiny, delicate, three-year-old who had suffered extensive brain damage due to a non-accidental injury as an infant, resulting in profound intellectual disability. She lived in her own isolated world, cocooned from any interaction with others by her compulsive rocking to and fro. Her body became stiff and resistant whenever there was any attempt to physically soothe her when she was distressed. She was unresponsive to touch and unable to mould her body or allow her weight to be supported when held, as would be expected of a child her age. We began with my mirroring of her rocking movements, matching the rhythmic speed and intensity that was governed by her internal metronome. This gave me the vital clues as to when her level of arousal was becoming too intense. By withdrawing and re-engaging, my presence and absence gave her the experience of the basic patterns of rupture and repair that are necessary for the awareness of another than can lead to a developing sense of self (Schore, 2012). Over several months we engaged in floor play that incorporated movement games based on rocking and weight giving. She slowly began to intentionally interact, initiating hand-holding while rocking in unison with me and seeking proximity through being cradled, thereby progressing from isolation to an awakening of self within a relationship at the very infantile level of primary intersubjectivity.

Making a mark

Through his very extensive research in this field, (Trevarthen, 2005) asserts that infants have an innate capacity to share understanding and collaborate in intentions long before there is intellect. For infants with intellectual disabilities who are not fortunate enough to cultivate this innate capacity through a healthy relationship with a primary caregiver, the very creation of intersubjective meaning is contaminated. Sinason (2010) considers the absent mother, the mother who is unable to think about or feel with her infant and so becomes a persecuting, frightening absence that haunts the baby. She speaks of the infant's mind that is, "permanently emptied to avoid being annihilated from within" (2010, p. 159), where nothing can be experienced as good; rather everything is "instantly transformed into something dangerous and annihilating" (ibid.). A significant number of the patients in my caseload had experienced not just this frightening emotional absence, but also the physical annihilation of the parent–child relationship when placed into residential care, with either very limited or no further contact with their birth families.

The pain of abandonment was overwhelming for "Jamie", an eight-year-old boy with severe intellectual disability. His mother had found life with Jamie so traumatic that she had intentionally harmed him in order to have him taken into residential care. His rage was palpable whenever he entered the therapy room and one day, having attacked the toys with huge, destructive energy, randomly scattering anything within his reach, he focused on the paints and sensory materials used for messy play. This became the primary expression of his inner turmoil and over the next few weeks, he repeatedly mixed everything into a large, muddy puddle on a sheet of plastic which he would then push towards me violently, leaving me with the product of his pain. Fonagy, Gergely, Jurist, and Target discuss the role of play in such a scenario, stating that the child's "affective investment in his play may directly reflect the extent to which his phantasy incorporates a disguised piece of 'serious' reality" (2004, p. 262). The use of metaphor provided by the muddy mess allowed Jamie the space to reflect on his thoughts and feelings regarding his life experience, and through my presence as containing therapist, he was provided with "a necessary frame [to] insulate him from the compelling character of external reality" (2004, p. 263).

A breakthrough came when Jamie gradually discovered the possibility of making intentional patterns with his fingers in the chaos of paint, flour, sand, and glitter. This culminated in him very suddenly running to the door one day as I gave him warning that our session was about to end. He created two hand prints as he placed his hands on the door. He then stood back and looked at me with intensity, saying, "Jamie". Jamie had arrived at a sense of self that started to blossom as we moved on to mark making on paper, so creating his artwork. I kept his artwork carefully from week to week, always having it readily available for us to ponder over together. Sinason states that writing (in Jamie's case, intentional mark making) "acts in the absence of speaking subjects. It uses space to indicate itself by defying time. It is also symbolic as it replaces or represents something that is absent" (2010, p. 168). Jamie had found a way of making sense of presence and absence, where his sense of self could survive by being held in mind within the therapeutic containment of his precious artwork.

Being creative: the arts in psychotherapy

Psychotherapy that includes creative arts therapies focusing on dance, music, art, drama, and play allows for the exploration, expression, and communication of inner emotional life. It also allows for an embodied sense of "being in the world". In discussing the evolutionary sociocultural development of the arts, neuroscientist Antonio Damasio describes the arts as being "a means to induce nourishing emotions and feelings ... a way to explore one's own mind and the minds of others" (2010, p. 296). He also views the arts as being "a compensation for emotional imbalances caused by fear, anger, desire, and grief" (ibid.). Engaging in arts activities within the therapeutic space offers an invaluable means of accessing emotional life and building interpersonal connection with another in a way that is not reliant on any cognitive threshold or linguistic ability. Damasio's more recent research (2010) has highlighted that emotional-affective processes arise from the subcortical regions of the brain, not from higher cortical sources, and it is in these subcortical regions that psychotherapeutic change can come about. When considering a client with profound intellectual disability, this is of primary importance, as it confirms the possibility of building relationship through emotional connection, even with such extreme cognitive deficit. Neuroscientist Jaak Panksepp and psychotherapist Lucy Biven state: "... affective neuroscience highlights how primary-process, pre-propositional emotional energetic states have minds of their own as ancient forms of affective mentation that preceded language and thought by vast spans of evolutionary time" (2012, p. 453). Through building a relationship based on these "ancient forms of affective mentation" (ibid.), it is possible to gain a window into the world of someone whose distress may be expressed by behaviours rather than by voicing words.

Conclusion

In a milieu where behavioural management may often be prioritised over exploration of emotional life, there has historically been a lack of expectation with regard to engaging people with severe and profound intellectual disability in therapeutic interventions. There was the perception that the more a person's cognitive ability fell below an accepted norm, the less able that person was to engage in psychotherapy. The previously held 'top down' understanding of brain development meant that cognition was believed to lead emotional growth; now the 'bottom up' concept of brain development has begun to take precedence, where more primitive, emotion-led structures must be positively engaged in order for cognitive development to occur. Neuroscientists such as Damasio (2010) and Trevarthen (2006) have led research from which our current knowledge of human development has emerged, demonstrating that healthy attachment, emotional regulation, and social connection are vital for growth of mind. This research dovetails well with Schore's extensive writings on the integration of psychoanalytic concepts of the unconscious mind into a neurobiological understanding of human development. He speaks of the historical "paradigm shift from behavior, to cognition, to bodily based emotion" (2012, p. 4) in which scientific research has transitioned from studies of language-based cognitive processes and voluntary motor functions, to emotional processing and embodied systems independent of cognitive processes.

This is of huge significance when looking at the relevance of a neurobiologically informed approach to the practice of disability psychotherapy as it makes it possible to move from the realm of the cognitive ability to the realm of embodied, experience-based emotional growth, where relationship is paramount. When a neurodevelopmental approach is taken in therapy, it allows for appropriate interactions that reflect the developmental level that is present in the client at any given moment. As Sinason points out, despite some aspects of organic impairment being fixed, the level of disability can be fluid from one moment to the next and provision should be made to meet the person at both their highest and lowest level of functioning (2010, p. 5). Child psychotherapists are very aware of the constantly fluctuating developmental needs of the child during any therapy session, reflecting the different states of being where repair is needed. This is usually expressed in playful engagement at the appropriate developmental level and is most often experienced as a creative alignment with the therapist, embodied through the medium of the arts. The use of rhythm and music, dance, movement, dress up, role play, messy play with paint, and creating images with clay are all examples of embodied play where child and therapist join together in bringing the child's inner world and lived experience into the safety and containment of the therapeutic space. Here, conflicts and confusions can be explored and processed, and pain can be witnessed and absorbed.

Transferring this embodied approach into the practice of disability psychotherapy opens up the possibility of utilising a developmentally informed way of working that can be tailored to fit the fluidity of disability. From neurobiologically very primitive interactions to highly complex symbolic play, the use of creative arts and playful engagement within the therapeutic space can support the development of intersubjectivity where connection and repair can take place. Trevarthen describes how meaning is discovered in playful collaborative relationships long before the emergence of language, and "its discovery is motivated by pleasure in dynamically responsive company" (2005, p. 58). The offer of "dynamically responsive company" (ibid.) in disability psychotherapy, replicating these basic building blocks of relationship that are present from birth, can create a sound basis upon which to bring about growth and change, even where intellectual disability is at its most extreme.

The final thought must centre on Valerie Sinason. Without the benefit of her enormous insight, clinical wisdom, and deep humanity, my work would have faltered at the start. The constant message that sustained me throughout these years of professional growth and all the difficulties associated with working in the field of intellectual disability was this: "… however crippled someone's external functional intelligence might be, there still can be intact a complex emotional structure and capacity" (2010, p. 63). This was my mantra that contained the certainty that psychotherapeutic engagement is possible for those even with the most profound intellectual disability.

References

Alvarez, A. (2012). *The Thinking Heart: Three Levels of Psychoanalytic Therapy with Disturbed Children*. New York: Routledge.

Campbell, F. K. (2012). Stalking ableism: using disability to expose 'abled' narcissism. In: D. Goodley, B. Hughes, & L. Davis (Eds.), *Disability and Social Theory: New Developments and Directions* (pp. 212–230). Basingstoke: Palgrave Macmillan.

Corbett, A. (2009). Words as a second language: the psychotherapeutic challenge of severe intellectual disability. In T. Cottis (Ed.), *Intellectual Disability, Trauma and Psychotherapy* (pp. 45–62). New York: Routledge.

Cozolino, L. (2002). *The Neuroscience of Psychotherapy: Healing the Social Brain*. New York: Norton.

Cozolino, L. (2006). *The Neuroscience of Human Relationships: Attachment and the Developing Social Brain*. New York: Norton.

Damasio, A. (2010). *Self Comes to Mind: Constructing the Conscious Brain*. New York: Pantheon Books.

Fonagy, P., Gergely, G., Jurist, E., & Target, M. (2004). *Affect Regulation, Mentalization, and the Development of the Self*. London: Karnac.

Garland-Thomson, R. (2009). *Staring: How We Look*. Oxford: Oxford University Press.

Hughes, B. (2012). Civilising modernity and the ontological invalidation of disabled people. In: D. Goodley, B. Hughes, & L. Davis (Eds.), *Disability and Social Theory: New Developments and Directions* (pp. 17–32). London: Palgrave Macmillan.

Hughes, D. (2007). *Attachment Focused Family Therapy*. New York: Norton.

Iacoboni, M., & Mazziotta, J. C. (2007). Mirror neuron system: basic findings and clinical applications. *Annals of Neurology, 62*: 213–18.

Kuppers, P. (2003). *Disability and Contemporary Performance: Bodies on Edge*. New York: Routledge.

Maiello, S. (2001). On temporal shapes: the relation between primary rhythmical experience and the quality of mental links. In J. Edwards (Ed.), *Being Alive* (pp. 179–193). Hove: Brunner-Routledge.

Malloch, S. (1999). Mother and infants and communicative musicality. *Musicae Scientae, 3*(1 suppl): 29–57.

McGrath, E. (2014). Group play therapy for children with multiple disabilities. In: E. Prendiville & J. Howard (Eds.), *Play Therapy Today: Contemporary Practice with Individuals, Groups and Carers* (pp. 130–146). Abingdon: Routledge.

McGrath, E. (2016). The role of music and rhythm in the development, integration and repair of the self. In: E. Prendiville & J. Howard (Eds.), *Creative Psychotherapy: Applying the Principles of Neurobiology to Play and Expressive Arts-Based Practice* (pp. 83–100). Abingdon: Routledge.

Ogden, P. (2009). Emotion, mindfulness and movement: expanding the regulatory boundaries of the window of affect tolerance. In D. Fosha, D. Siegel, & M. Solomon (Eds.), *The Healing Power of Emotion: Affective Neuroscience, Development and Clinical Practice* (pp. 204–231). New York: Norton.

Panksepp, J., & Biven, L. (2012). *The Archaeology of Mind: Neuroevolutionary Origins of Human Emotions*. New York: Norton.

Schore, A. N. (1994). *Affect Regulation and the Origin of the Self: The Neurobiology of Emotional Development*. Hillsdale, NJ: Lawrence Erlbaum Associates.

Schore, A. N. (1997). Interdisciplinary developmental research as a source of clinical model. In: M. Moskowitz, C. Monk, C. Kaye, & S. Ellman (Eds.), *The Neurobiological and Developmental Basis for Psychotherapeutic Intervention* (pp. 1–71). Northvale, NJ: Jason Aronson.

Schore, A. N. (2009). Right brain affect regulation: an essential mechanism of development, trauma, dissociation and psychotherapy. In: D. Fosha, D. Siegel, & M. Solomon (Eds.), *The Healing Power of Emotion: Affective Neuroscience, Development and Clinical Practice* (pp. 112–144). New York: Norton.

Schore, A. N. (2012). *The Science of the Art of Psychotherapy*. New York: Norton.

Sinason, V. (1992). *Mental Handicap and the Human Condition: New Approaches from the Tavistock*. London: Free Association Books.

Sinason, V. (2010). *Mental Handicap and the Human Condition: An Analytical Approach to Intellectual Disability* (2nd edn). London: Free Association Books.

Stern, D. (2004). *The Present Moment in Psychotherapy and Everyday Life*. New York: Norton.

Trevarthen, C. (2003). Neuroscience and intrinsic dynamics: current knowledge and potential for therapy. In: J. Corrigall & H. Wilkinson (Eds.), *Revolutionary Connections: Psychotherapy and Neuroscience* (pp. 53–78). London: Karnac.

Trevarthen, C. (2005). "Stepping away from the mirror: pride and shame in adventures of companionship" – reflections on the nature and emotional needs of infant intersubjectivity. In C. S. Carter, L. Ahnert, K. E. Grossmann, S. B. Hardy, M. E. Lamb, S. W. Porges, & N. Sachser (Eds.), *Attachment and Bonding: A New Synthesis* (pp. 55–84). Dahlem Workshop Report (92nd: 2003: Berlin, Germany). Cambridge, MA: The MIT Press.

Trevarthen, C. (2006). The concepts and foundations of infant intersubjectivity. In S. Bråten (Ed.), *Intersubjective Communication and Emotion in Early Ontogeny* (pp. 15–46). Cambridge: Cambridge University Press.

Trevarthen, C. (2009). The functions of emotion in infancy: the regulation and communication of rhythm, sympathy and meaning in human development. In: D. Fosha, J. Siegel, & F. Solomon (Eds.), *The Healing Power of Emotion: Affective Neuroscience, Development and Clinical Practice* (pp. 55–85). New York: Norton.

Trevarthen, C., & Aitken, K. J. (2001). Infant intersubjectivity: research, theory and clinical applications. *Journal of Child Psychology and Psychiatry*, *42*(1): 3–48.

Wilkinson, M. (2010). *Changing Minds in Therapy: Emotion, Attachment, Trauma and Neurobiology*. New York: Norton.

We are who we see looking back at us

Valerie as a supporter of a developing organisation

Alan Corbett and Tamsin Cottis

The words in the title of this chapter were spoken by Valerie at a conference (Sinason, 2015). They capture the way that a child's sense of self is significantly shaped by the way they are experienced by their parents. A child needs to see in their parents' eyes that they are beautiful, delightful, and loveable in order to feel that way about themselves. This is the thinking that has informed Valerie's understanding of how relationships between intellectually disabled children and their families may be thrown out of kilter if the infant experience is one of stress, anxiety, disappointment, and loss. She says:

> When a child is born who is clearly "not all right" or who is noticeably handicapped, parents receive a terrible blow. Most parents hope for a child at least as healthy and fortunate as themselves. When that wished-for baby does not appear, it is hard for even the most loving, resourceful parent to feel deeply attached.
>
> (Sinason, 1992, p. 123)

In the 1980s, Valerie talked and wrote about the experience of having an intellectually disabled child in the family and it resonated very powerfully then, and still does now. She highlighted the potential for parental anxiety, fear, dread, disappointment, and unhappiness at such a birth. It is gratifying that the work of psychotherapists such as Alvarez (2012) and Sunderland (2006), neuroscientific practitioners such as Schore (1994; 2003), Tronick (2007) and Tronick et al. (1998), and babywatchers such as Trevarthen and Aitken (1997) have also identified a place for the role of joy, pleasure, love, and delight in the developing of secure attachments which underpin good mental health. Sian Davey (2015), whose daughter, Alice, has Down's Syndrome, describes her own anxieties and fears when she brought Alice home:

> ...she didn't feel like my other babies had. I was fraught with an anxiety that rippled through every aspect of my relationship with her and that penetrated my dreams ... I could sense that Alice was feeling my rejection

of her and knew that the responsibility lay with me to work this out and find a way through the fear that was getting in the way of loving her. As my fears dissolved I fell in love with my daughter.

(2015, p. 1)

From the beginning of her work with people with intellectual disabilities, with her concept of the "handicapped smile" (1992), and what it may be covering up, Valerie spoke of the need to name difficult feelings in order to move forwards with emotional authenticity. This thinking of Valerie's is considered in this chapter in relation to organisations, and the authors' experience at one organisation in particular. We experienced how Valerie was able, with her unflinching yet tirelessly humane eye, to bring this same capacity to a newborn organisation.

Twenty-five years ago, the authors of this chapter were both part of a very small group of people who set up Respond. This voluntary sector organisation is now Britain's leading independent provider of psychotherapy to people with intellectual disabilities. It has grown from two people sketching out an idea on a kitchen table, to an organisation employing over twenty people, with a central London clinic base. Over this time it has supported many hundreds of people with intellectual disabilities, as well as their families and carers. Respond currently works in schools, in the community, with sex offenders, and as a training and consultancy agency for a wide variety of organisations. It is a campaigning voice for greater justice, equality, and safety in the care of vulnerable people who have experienced trauma and disability, and whose place in society puts them at risk of poor care and sometimes death, through neglect and lack of concern (Hampshire Adult Safeguarding Board, 2009; Mencap, 2012a; 2012b; Mortimer, 2015; Sheikh, Pralat, Reed, & Hoong Sin, 2010).

When Respond was at the kitchen table stage in 1991, we contacted Valerie. She was one of a handful of people who we knew were concerned about both the sexual abuse of, and therapy for, people with intellectual disabilities. Though experienced in working with people with intellectual disabilities in a variety of settings, we were not psychotherapists at that time, and we felt our inexpertise as a weight and potential barrier to progress. We could not have been more startled when, after one phone conversation, Valerie suggested a meeting. We went into the Tavistock Centre for the first time and, in a small and inauspicious-looking room, we told her we were thinking about setting up a service that might, in time, be able to provide both counselling for people with intellectual disabilities and training for their carers. We thought she might, perhaps, suggest some courses we could do or some books we could read, or she would share some of her experiences for us to reflect on, or suggest some names of people she knew who were qualified to develop our ideas "properly". What, in fact, happened was that she encouraged us to get on and do it ourselves and she offered us her ongoing support. How risky that was! But also, how fantastic, and how empowering. When we looked at her face as we talked, we saw pleasure, encouragement, and a belief in us and in the worth and potential of our idea as well as in our capacity to take it further. It set us on a path which we are still walking. And although Valerie has less direct involvement in Respond today, she continues to be a companion on that path.

We were motivated to act on our idea for Respond due to the fact that many of the adults with intellectual disabilities with whom we had worked in our previous roles as counsellors, teachers, support workers and advocates, had been sexually abused. We saw how vulnerable they were, how ill-served they were by law and employment practices, and how scarce was the availability of therapeutic support for them in the wake of abuse. Too often they were not believed or were blamed, while their abusers (whether family members, other service users, or people paid to support them), went unchallenged and untreated. At that time, we were also meeting many other carers and professionals who wanted to do more to support victims and who wanted to be part of a process of changing the landscape. At that time, Valerie was publicly highlighting the issue of sexual abuse as a feature in the lives of her learning disabled patients at the Tavistock Centre. Her concerns were clinical but, as with so much of her work, her thinking had a sharp interface with social justice campaigns and an understanding that some of the worst care came from an unspoken belief that some lives were seen as less valuable, or just too difficult, to be accorded the same worth as others. Her thinking was heady, strong stuff; it was unflinching and painful to encounter and we sometimes struggled to take it all in. However, there was a warmth, humanity, and respect, as well as truth, to her ideas which we found irresistible.

By 1993, Respond had a name, a base, and some trustees. We were now three people (the authors and Stephen Morris) working directly with survivors of sexual abuse, and delivering training as a way of both reaching care providers and of generating income for the organisation to augment our small government grant. In particular, Valerie helped us to work in ways which brought the experiences of the people with intellectual disabilities with whom we worked into the light. This was so that others could be made aware of their experiences, and things could change for the better. By this time, we had undertaken a number of training courses ourselves and knew a lot more about the experience of sexual abuse, and also about the terrible vulnerability to it of people with intellectual disabilities. In this regard, we had also been supported in person and by the work of the late Ann Craft (Craft & Brown, 1989). However, we were not, and nowhere near being, psychotherapists. Although, in time, both the authors of this chapter went on to become fully qualified psychotherapists, there is no doubt that to have had Valerie as a supervisor in those early days, was to receive a significant initial training.

Supervision as training

Szecsödy (1997) highlights the Swedish term for supervision, "handledning", which means "to lead by the hand", and it is this term that most clearly describes the role that Valerie played in her supervision of the initial Respond clinical team. It was Valerie we turned to, ostensibly for supervision, but in practice for training, in this disturbing new world of disability, trauma, and abuse. A form of supervision was required that could be a container for the horrifying levels of trauma and the severity of the abuses that were being presented by our patients. We met weekly, initially in St George's Hospital Medical School, where Valerie was conducting her forensic group work with Professor Sheila Hollins, and then in our first base in a converted GP surgery in Wandsworth, and latterly in Respond's own and current base in central London.

Most models of supervision are essentially Oedipal: the supervisory triangle comprising the therapist, the supervisor, and the patient. The third person is always absent from the supervision, and therein lies the risk of their humanity, their essence, being missed. While this is true of all psychotherapeutic supervision, it is particularly the case in disability psychotherapy. No matter how well intentioned we think we are, disability is an attack upon the self and this increases the potential for "losing sight" of the patient who has intellectual disabilities. Close encounters with disability provoke multilayered unconscious responses. To be a psychotherapist working intensively with disability involves the processing of hatred. This is necessary in order to love those parts of our patients that induce hope in us, and bring pockets of insight and attunement that oil the wheels of the therapy. Winnicott (1949) taught us that hate is an essential component of the analytic process and, through her writing and her work, Valerie has taught us that it is particularly alive in our encounters with disability. In the field of disability psychotherapy, the matrix could, in fact, be experienced more as a quadrangle as it involves the other unseen player: the carer or supporter of the patient. Valerie helped us understand this, too, and the way that she helped to develop this sensibility is reflected in other chapters of this book, for example, those by David O'Driscoll (see Chapter 8) and Georgina Parkes (see Chapter 7).

The initial Respond clinical team had come from work settings such as day and residential centres and adult education, in which kindness and empathy abounded and negative feelings were supposedly disavowed. In reality, all of these settings were brimming with hatred and aggression, only there was nowhere to process these responses. Part of the huge and continuing question of how to provide services for people with disabilities, which are not prone to objectifying, infantilising and, in the worst cases, abusing, rests on the capacity of services to think honestly about what disability evokes in themselves. Unless ambivalence, and its close relation, hatred, can be thought and talked about, they become enacted, as we have seen in the seemingly endless litany of services that abuse those they are paid to care for, whether by acts of omission or commission. These have included Atlas care homes (McNicoll, 2017), Winterbourne View care home (Hill, 2012) and Southern Health NHS foundation trust (Campbell, 2015). Evidently, there is still much to be done and recent government austerity has given the enacting of hate a new face. Film director Ken Loach put his finger on this when, in speaking about his film, *I, Daniel Blake*, he spoke of the "conscious cruelty" (Taylor, 2015) of this austerity programme as it has affected the most vulnerable in society, including those with disabilities.

The Respond Model (Blackman & Cottis, 2013) has placed therapeutic-ally informed work with carers and families at its heart, and initial research (Blackman & Cottis, 2013) indicates that affective change in carers leads to positive shifts in empathy for clients which is then reflected in their care. However, it is rare for us to acknowledge the feelings of shame and disgust evoked in us by disability and, as such, we tend to displace them into more acceptable forms of anxiety. This anxiety embeds itself deeply into both indi-viduals and organisational systems and, unless processed through personal analysis, supervision and/or organisational consultancy, it can produce enactments that are forensic in nature. Hatred must be voiced. The poet William Blake wrote in 1794:

> I was angry with my friend:
> I told my wrath, my wrath did end.
> I was angry with my foe:
> I told it not, my wrath did grow.

Supervision must be a place to which feelings of shame, guilt, disgust, and rage can be brought without fear of retribution.

Valerie's book, *Mental Handicap and the Human Condition* (Sinason, 1992), was our textbook throughout the period of Respond's development in the 1990s. It is an extraordinary book: a hybrid of case studies, sociology, and psychoanalytic theorising that is immensely readable. It refuses to presume that the readers of a deeply psychoanalytic book know much about psy-choanalysis – hence the glossary of psychoanalytic terms at the end of the book. Valerie's definition of countertransference demonstrates her clarity of thought and her desire to ensure her reader can apply this thinking to real life situations. It reads:

> The conscious and unconscious reactions and feelings of the ther-apist who is responsive to the transferred feelings of a patient and uses her understanding of those feelings to further the work. When faced with a patient with no words, countertransference is a crucial tool to understanding. When Ronald, aged six, banged his head, I would learn from my countertransference response what the meaning of his action

was. One time when he banged his head I felt immensely sad for him and could speak of his longing to bang out the bad thoughts that hurt him. Another time, I felt angry and knew he was attacking me by hurting himself in front of me.

(Sinason, 1992, pp. 323–324)

Similarly, Valerie's explanation of projective identification is illuminated by a powerful direct example:

As with projection, part of the self is split off and projected into the external object. However it then becomes 'possessed by, controlled and identified with the projected parts' (Segal, 1973, p. 27). For example, one deprived woman battered her baby when it cried. She could not bear the cry because she felt it was her own. Everything dependent and fragile in her that she could not bear had been projected into the baby. The baby's cries were then intolerable.

(Sinason, 1992, pp. 324–325)

What Valerie provided at Respond was far more than the normal space in which cases are discussed, transference and countertransference responses analysed, and plans for the future of the therapy examined. Her particular form of supervision was a training. She used the cases we presented as a launching pad for a weekly lesson in the practice of a discipline that, at that point, did not even have a name but would come to be known as disability psychotherapy (Kahr, 2000).

Supervision is traditionally a form of thinking about thinking. As practised by Valerie, it was a form of thinking about non-thinking, a space in which we struggled to withstand the attacks on thinking that trauma, abuse, and disability had caused within our patients. From early on in our work together, Valerie found ways of ensuring that the core of the patient was present, encouraging us to imbue our reading of transcripts with as much of our patient's accent, intonation, and affect as possible. This extended to sessions where no words were spoken. Working with patients with no verbal communication, of course, presents a profound challenge to the concept of psychotherapy as a "talking cure", and it was in this area of the work that we found ourselves being encouraged to find creative ways of bringing our silent patients into the supervision space.

In his writing about his almost silent patient, "Barry", Alan Corbett (AC) (Corbett, 2009), one of the authors of this chapter, describes a man who lacked words to describe the sexual attacks that had been inflicted on him. Valerie supervised the five years of this work with an astonishing attention to detail, to the point where it became a kind of life support system for the therapy. The work was often deeply confusing and AC writes of his struggle to bear the dead weight of Barry's silences and the exhaustion of trying to spark into life a brain that was slow and unwieldy. Over time it became clear that Valerie had two main interests: the meaning of Barry's non-verbal communications, which included rocking, pulling his fingers back, dancing, dribbling, farting, and staring longingly at the therapist; and the capacity of the therapist's countertransference to decode all of these communications. AC was encouraged to talk about how sick he sometimes felt when faced with Barry's drooling, how much he sometimes wanted to shake his patient into mental life, and how much hatred he could feel towards the agonisingly slow pace of the therapy. In relation to Barry, and to many other patients who challenged and demanded much from us as therapists, Valerie taught us to be brave about our countertransference – not just to be aware of it, but to dare to talk about it with our peers.

Our supervision faced various other challenges too. Valerie supervised us as a group and as Bion writes, a "work group is constantly perturbed by influences which come from other group mental phenomena" (1961, p. 129). We were a young and inexperienced group, relying heavily on the authority and experience that Valerie brought, to dilute our shared anxieties. In addition, the context of any supervision group determines the field in which the group operates and the context of this group was a vulnerable one. Respond was, and is, a voluntary sector organisation, dependent on charitable fund giving, and shrinking government grants. Disability psychotherapy was not just a discipline without a name; it also lacked a history. O'Driscoll (2009) has written of the curious gaps and lacunae in the history of disability psychotherapy: how there have been sporadic pockets of activity across the twentieth century but that it did not begin to cohere as a body of thought and work until Valerie's work in the 1980s.

It was not just the fact that we were working psychoanalytically with patients with intellectual disabilities that placed our group outside the frame of traditional therapeutic work. We were also working with people who had experienced sexual abuse. Denial surrounding the incidence of sexual abuse in the population in general began to shift in the 1980s. This shift in awareness, however, did not extend to the recognition that people with disabilities were also affected. The fact that possessing a disability rendered a person four times more likely to experience sexual abuse (Sobsey, 1994) was too painful for most people to accept. In a deeply depressing example of a double bind, this denial served to perpetuate the high levels of abuse; the more society denied the fact that people with disabilities were particularly vulnerable to abuse, the longer abusers would be able to abuse. A few years into the life of Respond, we added another complicating factor into the mix: we began to treat perpetrators of abuse. We did so in response to the fact that many of the abused people referred to us were now presenting a sexual risk to others.

The supervision group became the auxiliary brain of Respond, or in Oedipal terms, the id: the place where creativity and play helped reinforce the Self of the organisation. It also modified the pressures of the superego: the harsh world of limited funding, scepticism about the value of psychotherapy for patients with disabilities, and our own internal ambivalence about the work we were doing. The creation of the forensic work in Respond originated within the group, as did most of the innovations that followed, such as: a national helpline for people with disabilities and their carers; a group for young people who were at risk of become adult abusers; and a project that sought to reach potential patients from non-white populations.

The authors have to be careful not to idealise this group. Kalsched describes supervision groups as "breeding grounds for unconscious processes, including projection, splitting, acting out, to say nothing of dysfunctional family dynamics such as sibling rivalry, envy, scapegoating, triangulated collusive alliances, co-dependency, etc." (1995, p. 111). He also cites Bion, who says that, "every group is really two groups. The first is a work group, and the second, a basic assumption group (the B-a group), characterised by primitive unconscious fantasy dynamics, high levels of anxiety, and paranoid/schizoid splitting defences" (1995, p. 111). This was true of our supervision group at Respond, and over time it became clear that a separate space was needed in which, in Jungian terms, the "shadow" (Jung, 1938, p. 131) of Respond's success could be held. This development was precipitated by an organisational trauma in which one of the founders was found to have engaged in fraudulent behaviour and was sacked from the organisation, the narrative of which has been recorded elsewhere (Corbett, Cottis & Lloyd, 2012). Initially, this trauma was responded to in purely clinical ways. Valerie encouraged us to consider the fraudulent behaviour of the sacked founder much as we had learnt to consider the abusive behaviour of our forensic patients: it was an enactment of trauma, the playing out of some unconscious process.

An important component of Valerie's supervision of Respond as it developed was her insistence that disability psychotherapy should not be ghettoised as an adaptation of psychotherapy, nor as a form of "applied" treatment. It was, she continually reminded us, psychotherapy – a relational, intersubjective process that involves a careful interweaving of the psychodynamic and the creative. In positioning disability psychotherapy on the spectrum of therapeutic approaches, there was a temptation to focus on the differences (slower pace, often non-verbal) rather than the similarities (relational, attuned to the unconscious, transference-based) between our work and that which we tended to view as the mainstream. This is as important a political statement as it is a clinical statement, as it demands that a truly democratic and egalitarian stance is adopted by the disability psychotherapist and, by implication, all psychotherapists. Patients should not be discriminated against on any grounds. It is as unethical to refuse to work with a patient with a low IQ as it is to refuse to work with someone because of their ethnicity, gender, or sexual orientation.

Hopper (2012) describes the paradox of disability psychotherapists consciously both dis-identifying and identifying with their patients, often simultaneously. The danger of overidentification with disability and damage is high, with supervision functioning as a form of psychic barometer with which to guard against the attendant danger of overcompensation and burnout. Psychotherapists new to disability psychotherapy often express horror at the high levels of neglect and deprivation in the lives of their patients. We are familiar with both of these factors being part of the early lives of many of our non-disabled patients. Part of the shock of working with adults with disabilities, however, is the reality that deprivation and neglect can still exist in their lives, meaning that their present, as well as their past, needs to be processed. The reality of working with patients vulnerable to the modern-day atrocities that have been uncovered in recent years, such as that at Winterbourne View care home (Hill, 2012), adds a heavy weight of responsibility and anxiety upon the therapeutic endeavour.

Supervision must be alive to the dangers of disability psychotherapists taking on too much in an attempt to defend against the trauma of disability. They may seek relief from the agony of disability by becoming "super-able": taking on too many cases; promising astonishing change to patients and to referrers; and generally avoiding the reality of life with a disability. The work can contain joy, transcendence, and love, but it can also contain rage, shame, and hatred. If this central fact is not considered in supervision, there is the risk of therapist and supervisor colluding in a disavowal of reality, a risk that exists for the supervisor as much as for the therapist.

Sedlak (1997) identifies the importance of personal analysis or therapy to help supervisees recognise the damage in their patients. She writes this in the context of the supervision of untrained psychotherapists, and raises important questions about how possible it is to provide supervision to those who are not trained in therapeutic theory and, perhaps more importantly, who have not undergone their own therapeutic process. Supervisors of disability psychotherapy have an ethical responsibility to recognise the limits of supervision in those situations where the trauma of disability has unravelled something in the supervisee that necessitates a return to personal therapy.

The importance of teaching

The majority of psychotherapy trainings continue to contravene legislation enshrined in the Equality Act (2010) by failing to equip their trainees to work with people with intellectual disabilities. The adult psychotherapy training provided by The Bowlby Centre (2017) is a notable exception. Few trainings include any theoretical input in this field and some discriminate by not allowing trainees to take on a disability case as a training patient. This deficit has had to be compensated for in supervision through the incorporation of a strong teaching component. This applies on two levels: the supervision of psychotherapists who have received no teaching on disability throughout their years of training; and the supervision of those from other clinical disciplines, such as psychology or psychiatry, who come to supervision with dual needs – to learn about the intrapsychic world of patients with intellectual disabilities, and to learn more about psychotherapeutic techniques. Changes are beginning to be made through the development of courses, such as that pioneered by Dr Pat Frankish and described in this book (see Chapter 9) and those of institutes such as Respond and the Tavistock Clinic, but progress is inevitably slow.

When words are not enough

Supervision of disability psychotherapy needs to acknowledge that words are not the only language used by our patients, particularly those with profound or severe levels of disability. Just as disability psychotherapists have had to learn to be creative in how they work with patients whose receptive and/or expressive language skills are severely limited, supervisors likewise need to formulate supervisory techniques for analysing sessions in which patients may communicate non-verbally, such as with grunts or groans or by using media such as sand trays. Where the patient's words are limited, careful analysis of the psychotherapist's countertransference is required in order to help decode the hidden language that lies beneath. In analysing countertransference responses, the new concept of the disability transference (Corbett, 2009) has emerged, as a useful way of conceptualising the complex projective processes most often at play in this field of work. Being in the presence of disability in its raw, unprocessed state, such as that reached through intensive, long-term psychotherapy (or even at the very beginnings of such work), is an affective, intersubjective process in which the therapist's capacity to think, to form words, and to hold memory can be attacked or broken down in the service of understanding the enormity of living with a cognitive deficit.

Valerie's role as a supervisor and trainer, albeit not formally identified as such, is invaluable. To us and to Respond, as to many others, she has brought her gaze of encouragement, her warmth, and her capacity to see potential and help it flourish. These are the very qualities she brings to her own clinical work and which she describes in *Mental Handicap and the Human Condition* (Sinason, 1992). They are also at the heart of early human relationships, where we increasingly recognise them as being central to the development of a healthy brain wired to make the most of the human capacity for attuned relationship.

References

Alvarez, A. (2012). *The Thinking Heart: Three Levels of Psychoanalytic Therapy with Disturbed Children*. Hove: Routledge.

Bion, W. R. (1961). *Experiences in Groups And Other Papers*. London: Tavistock Publications.

Blackman, N., & Cottis, T. (2013). *Psychotherapy at Respond: The Relational and Attachment-Based Systems Model* [unpublished].

Blake, W. (2000). A Poison Tree (1794). *The Selected Poems of William Blake* (p. 82). London: Wordsworth Poetry Library.

The Bowlby Centre. (2017). www.thebowlbycentre.org.uk/ [last accessed 11.9.2017].

Campbell, D. (2015). NHS trust 'failed to properly investigate deaths of more than 1,000 patients'. *The Guardian*, 9 December. Available at: www.theguardian.com/society/2015/dec/09/southern-health-nhs-trust-failed-investigate-patient-deaths-inquiry [last accessed 16.9.2016].

Corbett, A. (2009). Words as a second language: the psychotherapeutic challenge of severe disability. In: T. Cottis (Ed.), *Intellectual Disability, Trauma and Psychotherapy* (pp. 45–62). Hove: Routledge.

Corbett, A., Cottis, T., & Lloyd, L. (2012). The survival and development of a traumatized clinic for psychotherapy for people with intellectual disabilities. In: E. Hopper (Ed.), *Trauma and Organizations* (pp. 111–126). London: Karnac.

Craft, A., & Brown, H. (1989). *Thinking the Unthinkable: Papers on Sexual Abuse and People with Learning Difficulties*. Family Planning Association (Great Britain) Education Unit.

Davey, S. (2015). *Looking For Alice*. London: Trolley Books.

The Equality Act. (2010). Available at: www.legislation.gov.uk/ukpga/2010/15/contents [last accessed 11.9.2017].

Hampshire Safeguarding Adults Board. (2009). Available at: www.hampshiresab.org.uk/learning-from-experience-database/serious-case-reviews/fiona-pilkington-leicestershire/ [last accessed 29.12.2016].

Hill, A. (2012). Winterbourne View care home staff jailed for abusing residents. *The Guardian*, 26 October. Available at: www.theguardian.com/society/2012/oct/26/winterbourne-view-care-staff-jailed [last accessed 21.7.2017].

Hopper, E. (2012). Some challenges to the capacity to think, link and hope in the provision of psychotherapy for the learning disabled. In: J. Adlam, A. Aiyegbusi, P. Kleinot, A. Motz, & C. Scanlon (Eds.), *The Therapeutic Milieu Under Fire: Security and Insecurity in Forensic Mental Health* (pp. 229–239). London: Jessica Kingsley.

Jung, C. G. (1938). Psychology and religion. [reprinted in: *The Collected Works of C. G. Jung, Volume 11, Psychology and Religion: West and East*. (trans. R. F. C. Hull). Abingdon: Routledge, 2014, 2nd edn]. p. 131

Kahr, B. (2000). The adventures of a psychotherapist: a new breed of clinicians – disability psychotherapists. *Psychotherapy Review*, 2: 193–194.

Kalsched, D. (1995). Ecstasies and agonies of case seminar supervision. In: P. Kugler (Ed.), *Jungian Perspectives on Clinical Supervision* (pp 107–119). Einsiedeln, Switzerland: Daimon.

McNicoll, A. (2017). Thirteen convicted over 'systemic' abuse at care homes. *Community Care*, 7 June. Available at: www.communitycare.co.uk/2017/06/07/thirteen-convicted-systemic-abuse-care-homes/ [last accessed 21.7.2017].

Mencap. (2012a). *Stuck at Home: The Impact of Day Service Cuts on People with a Learning Disability*. Available at: www.mencap.org.uk/sites/default/files/2016-08/Stuck_at_home.pdf [last accessed 16.9.2016].

Mencap. (2012b). *Death by Indifference: 74 Deaths and Counting*. Available at: www.mencap.org.uk/sites/default/files/2016-08/Death%20by%20Indifference%20-%2074%20deaths%20and%20counting.pdf [last accessed 16.9.2016].

Mortimer, C. (2015). Hate crime against disabled people rises 41 per cent in one year. *The Independent*, 8 November. Available at: www.independent.co.uk/news/uk/hate-crime-against-disabled-people-rises-41-per-cent-in-one-year-a6713546.html [last accessed 29.12.2016].

O'Driscoll, D. (2009). Psychotherapy and intellectual disability: a historical view. In: T. Cottis (Ed.), *Intellectual Disability, Trauma and Psychotherapy* (pp. 9–28). Hove: Routledge.

Schore, A. N. (1994). *Affect Regulation and the Origin of the Self: The Neurobiology of Emotional Development*. Hillsdale, NJ: Lawrence Erlbaum Associates.

Schore, A. N. (2003). The human unconscious: the development of the right brain and its role in early emotional life. In: V. Green (Ed.), *Emotional Development in Psychoanalysis, Attachment Theory, and Neuroscience: Creating Connections* (pp. 23–52). Hove: Brunner-Routledge.

Sedlak, C. A. (1997). Critical thinking of beginning Baccalaureate nursing students during the first clinical nursing course. *Journal of Nursing Education*, *36*(1): 11–18.

Segal, H. (1973). *Introduction to the Work of Melanie Klein*. London: The Hogarth Press.

Sheikh, S., Pralat, R., Reed, C., & Hoong Sin, C. (2010). *Don't Stand By: Hate Crime Research Report*. Available at: www.mencap.org.uk/sites/default/files/2016-08/Don't%20stand%20by-research-report%20(1).pdf [last accessed 16.9.2016].

Sinason, V. (1992). *Mental Handicap and the Human Condition: New Approaches from the Tavistock*. London: Free Association Books.

Sinason, V. (2015). *Trauma in Infancy and Building A Secure Base*. Talk at School of Infant Mental Health Conference, London. [unpublished paper]

Sobsey, D. (1994). *Violence and Abuse in the Lives of People with Disabilities: The End of Silent Acceptance?* Baltimore, MD: Paul H. Brookes Publishing.

Sunderland, M. (2006). *The Science of Parenting*. London: Dorling Kindersley.

Szecsödy, I. (1997). (How) Is learning possible in supervision? In: B. Martindale, M. Mörner, M. E. Cid Rodríguez, & J.-P. Vidit (Eds.), *Supervision and its Vicissitudes* (pp. 101–116). London: Karnac.

Taylor, D. (2015). 'Conscious cruelty': Ken Loach's shock at benefit sanctions and food banks. *The Guardian*, 23 November. Available at: www.theguardian.com/film/2015/nov/23/ken-loach-benefit-sanctions-jeremy-corbyn-food-banks [last accessed 12.6.2017].

Trevarthen, C., & Aitken, K. J. (1997). Infant intersubjectivity: research, theory and clinical applications. *Journal of Child Psychology and Psychiatry*, *42*(1): 3–48.

Tronick, E. (2007). *The Neurobehavioral and Social-Emotional Development of Infants and Children*. New York: Norton.

Tronick, E. Z., Bruschweiler-Stern, N., Harrison, A. M., Lyons-Ruth, K., Morgan, A. C., Nahum, J. P., Sander, L., & Stern, D. N. (1998). Dyadically expanded states of consciousness and the process of therapeutic change. *Infant Mental Health Journal*, *19*: 290–299.

Winnicott, D. W. (1949). Hate in the Counter-Transference. *International Journal of Psychoanalysis*, *30*: 69–74.

Chapter 4

The handicapped smile

Language and identity

Liz Lloyd

Note: All patients referred to are fictitious composites but are based on clinical material encountered during my work as a psychotherapist at Respond, London, and in my private psychotherapy practice in Wales.

A group of psychotherapists is silently reading the transcript of a therapy session together. It is of an intellectually disabled patient who has a history of sexually aggressive behaviour, both abused and abusing:

> Lovely uncle, lovely uncle [sweetly ingratiating smile] me upstairs, upstairs, people downstairs praying, praying, singing, singing, second uncle [the smile vanishes] turns me over, inside, inside, hurting, hurting, downstairs praying, third uncle comes in with cousin, hurting, hurting, can't see, downstairs singing, singing, so loud, loud, can't hear me, me, can't breathe, stupid, stupid, dead, dead, singing, singing.

This account of his abuse at the hands of the elders of his religious community whilst a service is taking place, continues for about twenty minutes. At the end, the ingratiatingly desperate smile returns as he says, "Lovely, lovely, hurt, hurt, prayers, prayers." A stunned and appalled silence follows. However, the group's clinical supervisor, Valerie Sinason, takes the discussion immediately into the unconscious gaps and spaces between the patient's words, through her free associations to the material. This method frees up the group's own unconscious associations and begins to reach the material defended against by the exaggeratedly "handicapped" speech of the patient. His own unconscious demonstration of his "stupidity' – in the original sense that Valerie has noted as "stupefied" or "numbed with grief" (1992, p. 2) – is here an instance of the "handicapped smile" (1992) being enacted in words, and inviting the listener to stay with the defensive surface of the exchange.

This was my introduction to the experience of Valerie's meticulously creative style of supervision. I was the therapist whose work was under discussion and who was fortunate to have joined Respond, a London-based voluntary organisation founded by Alan Corbett and Tamsin Cottis in 1991 to provide psychoanalytic psychotherapy for people with intellectual disabilities, specifically but not exclusively, around issues of sexual violence (see also the chapters by Alan Corbett, Tamsin Cottis, and Noelle Blackman in this book). Valerie was at a point when she was crystallising her psychoanalytic understanding of working with intellectually disabled patients in the field of disability and sexual abuse.

Valerie's theory of the handicapped smile and its role as a defence against the knowledge of trauma – significantly, not only in the patient, but also in the therapist – has proven to be immensely important, not only for work in the field of intellectual disability, but also in mainstream psychotherapy, especially where there could be a complicit refusal in both patient and therapist to recognise a reality too painful to bear. Perhaps a smiling, cultural handicapping is enacted collusively and operates most effectively in those areas of society where there is a complicit refusal to remember. The progress of the therapy – the growth of a disavowed self-knowledge – would then be expected to go hand in hand with a growth in the capacity to think the unthinkable: that the defence of "handicap" would become no longer necessary.

It is these areas I want to consider in this chapter: my work with the people with intellectually disabled smiles whom I encountered at Respond; and then, later, the verbal, metaphorical, handicapped smiles of those who are similarly unrecognised in their own separateness of experience, which I found in my work in Wales as a Welsh-language psychotherapist. These patients of mine were offered, usually for the first time, an opportunity to understand their experiences using their own language. They could, at last, think about their own histories: not only their personal histories but also, inextricably interwoven with these, their own cultural narratives.

The concept of the handicapped smile was developed by Valerie through her work as a psychotherapist at the Tavistock Clinic Workshop on Mental Handicap (Stokes & Sinason, 1992) and is elaborated clinically and theoretically in her groundbreaking work, *Mental Handicap and the Human Condition* (1992). Valerie describes in precise clinical detail her therapeutic work with patients at the clinic and, particularly relevant for this chapter, with Ali's "learning disabled" behaviour, body language, and smile (1992, pp. 137–177), which exacerbated his original disability. This not only served as a defence for him against the awful self-knowledge of his history of abuse, but also protected everyone else, whether carers, family, or therapist, from that knowledge. Confronted with this smile, everyone was invited to share the clown-mask of vacant jollity. Valerie's careful and painstaking therapy with Ali took place over some years, and her account charts both his and her own painful lurches into knowledge, following each challenge from the therapy to the "happy" reality he tried to inhabit.

My work with the young man mentioned at the beginning of this chapter, whom I shall call "Harry", was immensely influenced by Valerie's work with Ali, and by the need for the therapist not to be seduced by the smiling surface of stupefied handicap. When Harry was first referred, he arrived with a winsome and pleading expression which immediately endeared him to others, and which, no doubt, played a part in getting him the referral to therapy. This was a therapy which he desperately needed, ironically, in order not to be seen as endearing and for him to be able to recount his very un-endearing history of abuse and extremely frightening fantasies (both for him as much as for the listener) of sexual violence. He had been referred to Respond because of concerns about his sexually intrusive behaviour towards young boys, and for his repeated dialling of 999 for emergency services – a reflection of his desperate, but unacknowledged, awareness of his own dangerousness.

The winsomeness remained as a smooth and untroubled (as well as untroubling) surface for the first months of therapy. Then it mutated into something far less endearing, and even menacing. At the same time, Harry began to speak. Initially he used very limited language, but over the course of several months, he began to construct basic sentences. It is from around this time that the extract above was taken. He told me of being groomed and abused by a circle of adults who were senior members of a local community religious group, some of whom were his own family members. Each time he disclosed a name, or an experience of abuse or betrayal, he would stare fixedly at me and the sickly-sweet, endearing gaze would return. In terms of transference, he was inviting me to collude with the seduction and betrayal he had experienced, by seducing me into not hearing the menace.

Valerie's concept of the handicapped smile was vital in being able to hear the menace. Her supervisory input underlined this: the free associations in the group supervisions would catch the unconscious menace through allusions to fairy stories and folk myths, such as the smiling wolf in "Little Red Riding Hood" or the beguiling fox, which could also catch its own capacity to menace, in Beatrix Potter's *Jemima Puddleduck* (Potter, 1908). This is what emerged through the therapy: the unconscious mask of winsomeness cracking, over time, to reveal the sadistic fantasies Harry had internalised through his own experiences. The handicapped smile was no longer needed to placate and appease either the external world, or, crucially, Harry's own internal hatred and destructiveness. He could recognise his need to be protected, not only from the abuse of others, but from his own capacity to abuse. Eventually he began disclosing the very concrete steps he was taking to enact his sadistic fantasies, and in speaking about them, he was able to see his need to be protected from acting them out. He was able, himself, to alert the Probation Service, and with support from myself in the therapy, was given much firmer boundaries, which protected him and others.

The relationship of the handicapped smile, not only to the internal but also to the external world, is important. It is needed to placate and reassure those who might be troubled by encountering "otherness"; in this case, not only the intellectual disability itself, but crucially, its menacing, non-smiling aspect which does not fit society's expectations of mindlessness and which needs to be confronted. Refusing to smile becomes a refusal to, in Goffman's term, "minstrelise" disability (Burns, 1992, pp. 28–31). Any disability, and perhaps intellectual disability particularly, is an uncomfortable reminder of our own vulnerability. Society's unconscious expectation of someone with an intellectual disability is that he or she should at least be smiling and jolly, lest we be discomfited by their presence.

Another version of the handicapped smile could be found in a young woman, "Holly", who came to therapy at Respond. She shrieked with laughter on greeting each person she met on her way to see me – carers, taxi drivers, staff members, and escorts of other patients. But, as soon as the swing door between the waiting area and the therapy rooms swung closed, the manic grin disappeared from her face in an uncannily parallel movement. Even while this door was still swinging shut and before the door to my therapy room had been opened, there remained no trace of Holly's smile and no sound of her laughter. This area had become a truly transitional space, bridging the gap between the external world and the internal; between two separately held notions of herself. Once inside the therapy room, she sat and stared fixedly at me and announced clearly, with no trace of intellectual disability in her voice, that she wanted to kill herself.

Holly's care staff were sensitively aware of her despair and her urgent need to talk about it, hence her referral for psychotherapy. However, they were also aware that she, and they, needed the protection of her unconscious defence against that despair, lest it become overwhelming for her and for them. The defence had an essential protective role in enabling her to survive. Although there could be a safely demarcated hour in therapy for her to experience and speak about that despair, there were also all the other hours when she needed her defence in order to function. Holly had found a way to use the ritual swinging shut of the door as a marker of a literal transition from smiling defence to bleak self-knowledge. The same process operated in reverse at the end of our session. On leaving, Holly literally "put her face on".

It was known that Holly was someone who had silently and smilingly endured years of sexual abuse by her stepfather, fearing that as soon as she could no longer bear to go on smiling, then her family would have to know what they were choosing not to know, and the family would fall apart. Her intuition proved right: when she finally spoke out about the abuse, the knowledge was unbearable to them. Although there was conclusive forensic evidence of her stepfather's abuse, her mother chose to blame Holly. She never forgave her and chose to side with Holly's stepfather. Holly was forced to leave home and lost all contact with her family. Little wonder that she had felt it safer to keep silent and to keep smiling. With the help of the dedicated team of carers at the group home where she subsequently lived, she began to let go of her grip on the defensive smiling, and very slowly through her therapy she came to terms with the part of herself who did not want to smile, but that had not initially been able to envisage a different way of being alive.

The handicapped smile can be seen to operate as a defence in a far wider context than that of disability, however. It is a concept I found myself returning to after I had left Respond and my work as a psychotherapist for people with an intellectual disability.

As a psychotherapist living and working in a Welsh speaking part of Wales, I was shocked to discover that there is a large geographical area of the UK, albeit with a low population density, where people are largely unable to gain access to psychotherapy in their native tongue. Moreover, pointing this out could be seen as pathological and trouble-making; it was far simpler, to wear the handicapped smile of the appeasing and compliant victim. This could apply as much to professionals as to patients, in light of the defensively dismissive words of one leading health professional: "But they all speak English, don't they?" We subsequently used this phrase as inspiration for the title of a conference, "Siarad yr Anweledig / Speaking the Invisible" (2000), held at the Theater Felinfach in West Wales, in which we began to examine the issue of language in psychological care in Wales. For the aforementioned health professional, the otherness of language and culture was so discomfiting that it had to be disavowed.

This phenomenon is developed very movingly in the Welsh novel, *Wrth fy Nagrau i*, by a leading contemporary cultural figure, Angharad Tomos (2007). This work has not, so far, been translated into English but the title is roughly translatable as *Faced with My Tears*. The novel is loosely based on Tomos' experiences as a Welsh speaker being treated for post-natal depression in a North Wales psychiatric unit. The psychiatric staff in the hospital, which served an almost totally Welsh-speaking area, was entirely English-speaking. The only staff who were also Welsh-speaking were the cleaners, and it was with them that Tomos found herself able to talk about her experience, and in particular about the Welsh poetry, especially that of T. H. Parry-Williams, which spoke to her experience.

Tomos' novel explores the impact this cultural isolation has on a severely depressed woman, trapped in the impossibility of conveying the depth of her experience to an English-speaking psychiatrist, other than with a banality that only a handicapped smile could mediate. Her experience of mothering, and of being mothered, had naturally been through the medium of Welsh, and so its meanings and allusions were for her steeped in Welsh culture. She finds herself despairing of finding meaning through her conversations with the psychiatric staff, and dully acquiesces to a bland Anglo version of her experience, resigning herself with a linguistic "disabled smile". The novel's protagonist finds solace and understanding, instead, from her mind's evocation of similarly culturally silenced women poets and writers from the past.

Thus, in my work as a Welsh-speaking psychotherapist, I have found myself repeatedly thinking about Tomos' experience, especially as I have encountered patients who have never been able to reflect on, and fully understand, the impact of their earliest experiences which had been saturated with the language and values of their own, Welsh-speaking culture. An expectation of not being understood in English at on this cultural level, played a significant part in what they experienced as an annihilation of their narrative. This came to life only when it was possible to follow their unconscious associations and to analyse their dreams and phantasies through their mother tongue of Welsh. An English patient in analysis with an English-speaking therapist can assume a cultural common ground. He or she can allude to Shakespeare or to Keats in trying to convey their understanding of the world. This was not possible for a Welsh-speaking patient, as Tomos' central character finds to her cost when trying to articulate her response to a well-known Welsh poet as a way of describing her feelings to her psychiatrist. This is my English translation:

> In my clumsy English I tried to convey how much hope I got from the coming of spring each year, but I couldn't feel any of that this year. Had he been Welsh I could have used one of R. Williams Parry's sonnets but this chap wouldn't have had a clue. The sentence that appeared in the letter summarising our exchange was: "She has been unable to enjoy the daffodils this spring which are normally a great joy for her."
>
> Well yes, that was true. But it was a far bigger problem. I didn't need treatment because I couldn't appreciate daffodils. The problem went deeper than that.
>
> (Tomos, 2007, p. 47)

The platitudes and compliance of the linguistic version of the handicapped smile become a defence against the pain of such dismissive non-understanding.

This bland non-understanding by the English-speaking professional, although no longer sanctioned in law as it was in the nineteenth century, has extended for several generations through all aspects of professional administration in Wales, both statutory and voluntary, and it has bred, in its wake, its own self-parodying and self-handicapping response. One of my patients, "Gareth", was a man in his early sixties who worked for a local charity. It was one that was run along the neo-colonial lines of a white organisation from Britain's colonial past: a management and trustee structure that was wholly English-speaking, with an unofficial no-Welsh-speaking policy in the office. This was despite being sited in an area where the vast majority of its clients were themselves Welsh-speaking. Gareth had found a niche as the ever-smiling, compliant Welshman, a cultural figure redolent of literature and English parody. He came to me with severe alopecia: a bodily enactment of the impossibility of feeling comfortable in his own skin; of things falling apart from the intense pressure of his divided selves. This was a pressure he had known since childhood. As a child he had passed his entrance examination for the local grammar school but had found in it no place for his Welsh identity. He became the "token Taffy", as he put it, and learned early on to defend himself against any painful self-knowledge through his own variant of the handicapped smile, a jocular self-parody: "Uncle Dai", a Welsh equivalent of a black Uncle Tom. At the time of his therapy, he had, likewise, unconsciously found for himself in his workplace an almost exact parallel with this role. Perhaps this was a defence not unlike that employed by children in other parts of Britain, who are uprooted from a working class culture and are striving to "pass" in the dominant culture.

The added twist Valerie gave to this familiar story is that the defence also protects the dominant culture from the discomfort of recognising this difference or acknowledging its own role in this alienation. In Gareth's case, it absolved his academically excellent, and in many ways enlightened, school from recognising the colonial roles it perpetuated, which thus would have subverted its perception of its own ethos. This defence had continued throughout Gareth's working life but now that he was about to retire, the split would no longer serve, and the dispossessed and repressed rage kept breaking through the smiling surface of Gareth's scalp in a rash of livid weals, and cracking his compliant voice in outbursts of fury and tears.

Gareth was surprised to be offered a choice of Welsh or English for his therapy, and he frequently slipped between the two in a reflection of his slippage between identities. Through this, however, he was able to trace the various threads which he had woven together into his current workplace persona. In untangling these threads, it helped to bear in mind Valerie's concept of the handicapped smile, particularly the way it serves to emphasise the original handicap to the point of caricature. Perhaps this could be a useful way of understanding the tenacity of cultural stereotypes and how eagerly they come to be embraced by both sides of a cultural divide. A film such as *The Full Monty* (1997) could, thus, be seen in terms of a handicapped cinematic smile from a ravaged, post-industrial North of England which defends against, and so avoids having to confront and own, the rage at its own destruction. The trivialising and "minstrelising" of the defeated, through their own complicity in their defeat, is a relief not only for themselves, but for everyone else, uncomfortable with the catastrophe wrought in their names.

The relief at not having to perform a handicapping version of themselves was palpable for those patients I have seen who were able to choose their analysis in their mother tongue of Welsh. This was particularly the case for those who had suffered early physical, emotional, and sexual abuse while immersed in this damaging mother tongue. Reaching the roots of the earliest patterns of experience needs an immersion in a shared cultural and linguistic context. Perhaps also, paradoxically, it needs the opportunity to simultaneously step outside of this context, to find a different perspective through a shared, different, non-abusive language in therapy, before returning again and again to a non-abusing version of the mother tongue. In my work I have found that this slippage between Welsh and English has allowed for an altering of perspective in which the fixity of the cultural handicapped smile could be allowed to shift in and out of focus.

Another example of this cultural dislocation is that of a young woman called "Siân", whom I saw for some years. She had a history of severe self-harming behaviours but presented herself as a rural innocent who smiled determinedly through the most harrowing accounts of childhood sexual abuse. Adam Phillips' paper, "On Translating a Person" (Phillips, 2000), which was first presented at the Gwyn Jones Memorial Lecture in Cardiff in 2000, comments on this experience of cultural dislocation. He explains that the structure of the Welsh language has a strict linguistic hierarchy between the everyday "demotic" colloquial language of day-to-day life and the academic "higher" literary speech of the chapel and the bardic tradition. Alongside this was the neo-colonial insistence on English as the language of education and administration, a situation which is only now being painfully redressed through cultural change and political legislation. Siân's role in the family was constrained by her class and gender: while her father and brothers could take the English route of education or the Welsh route of the chapel, she was left with no place to speak. The abuse she suffered came from within the family's Welsh-speaking nonconformist aspirational members (much as Harry's had come from within his revered religious hierarchy). This left Siân no option but to try to engage with an uncomprehending English education system where she was dismissed as a failure because of her poor English language skills. She dealt with this, as Harry had done, by creating an intellectually disabled and smilingly compliant persona for herself, although the intolerable splits would break through in the self-harming of her cutting.

This is an area which has, perhaps, been investigated in poetry and fiction more than in psychotherapeutic writing. The poet Gillian Clarke writes in *At the Source* (2008) of her mother's embargo on their shared Welsh mother tongue which was perceived, realistically, not to be the language of the upwardly mobile. She writes of her rediscovery of her Welsh identity through her father, and says:

> I grew up in a Tower of Babel. English was the proper tongue. The world spoke it, according to my mother. She spoke it to me, so it was my mother tongue. Yet the family language was Welsh. It was literally the familiar language.
>
> (2008, p. 56)

As for Gareth, Siân's "handicapped" persona had protected her from the self-knowledge not only of the abuse she had suffered from within the community, but from an awareness that she had colluded with her own silencing. Like Harry, and Valerie's Ali, Siân had silenced herself behind a veneer of smiling simplicity. The various hospital admissions and interventions she had received remained on the outside of her experience; there had been no way she could speak about the impact of being trapped in a close-knit but abusive community. Moreover, because of the marginalisation of her mother tongue during those early years, she herself had wanted to identify with the dominant language. She had wanted, like her brothers, to find a way out of a language that she had experienced as inferior as well as oppressively abusive. She could only do that, however, when she could begin to understand the oppression. Hence, as with Gareth, the slippage between Welsh and English in the therapy was an attempt to reposition herself so that she was able to choose Welsh as a non-abusive and non-oppressive mother tongue, as a choice freely made between Welsh and English. In the transference, I had to hold these constantly shifting positions. It took some years for her to be able to give up the ingratiating smile and the self-deprecating laugh in which she had shrouded herself; and it was, quite literally, a shroud because inside, as she often said, she "felt dead".

The situation Siân described when she was growing up has changed radically, thanks to legislation sparked by Welsh language activists. Cymdeithas yr Iaith / The Welsh Language Society (2017) became active in the late 1960s and forced legislation through direct action, giving Welsh equal status with English in all fields of public life. However, as this chapter illustrates, there is still some way to go on the ground. There remain strong neo-colonial residues whereby language is a signifier of an imbalance of power. Seemingly liberal English speakers living in Wales can bristle in outrage at the existence of Welsh areas of life. They retaliate with hostility against what they perceive to be the self-same feelings of being marginalised and excluded that my Welsh-speaking patients have experienced. An example is the psychiatrist in an almost wholly Welsh-speaking area who responded to my question as to whether he planned to learn Welsh with a furious, "Not if I can help it". Language is not only a powerful means of communication but, because it is so inextricably bound up with an existential sense of being, any challenge to the security of its borders challenges a fundamental sense of existence. This bond between language and being has been well understood by colonisers, as Harold Pinter shows so powerfully in his short play, *Mountain Language*, where the violence of the annihilation of the people's language is the means of subjugating the population:

> Now hear this. You are mountain people. You hear me? Your language is dead. It is forbidden. It is not permitted to speak your mountain language in this place. You cannot speak your language to your men. It is not permitted. Do you understand? You may not speak it. It is outlawed. You may only speak the language of the capital. That is the only language permitted in this place. You will be badly punished if you attempt to speak your mountain language in this place. This is a military decree. It is the law. Your language is forbidden. It is dead. No one is allowed to speak your language. Your language no longer exists. Any questions?
>
> (Pinter, 1998, p. 255)

At a conference, organised by myself and Gudrun Jones, entitled "Language, Culture and Identity" held in Machynlleth in August 2008, therapists from across Wales came together to try to and understand and tackle this issue. Angharad Tomos gave the keynote paper at this event, presenting through the medium of Welsh with simultaneous translation facilities available. She spoke movingly and passionately of her experience as a patient. Therapists from many different fields then addressed the issue of language in their own clinical practices. Despite this effort, however, this issue still remains a huge and neglected problem.

Valerie's later work has taken her into the field of dissociation and the founding in 1998 of the Clinic for Dissociative Studies (2017). For my patients, their feelings of despair and disintegration did not lead to a total shattering of their sense of themselves as in dissociative identity disorder, but it did lead to impossibly creative and fragile constructions of themselves as a way of dealing with impossibly conflicting demands. They felt their Welsh identity to be invisible and so created not just a smiling stupidity, but a whole performance of exaggerated otherness so that everyone could thereby feel reassured, and so that no troubling history, be it personal, cultural or linguistic, need disturb the surface.

I have therefore come to understand Valerie's concept of the handicapped smile as one more element in the armoury of defences which we all use. In *The Four-Gated City* (1969), Doris Lessing's final novel in her series, *The Children of Violence*, the character of Martha Quest struggles to prevent herself falling back at moments of stress into her self-creation of the self-deprecating, good-humoured and humouring "Matty". As the title, *The Children of Violence* implies, Martha had had to create "Matty" in order to deal with the violence which had saturated her growing up as a white child in colonial Southern Rhodesia. As an adult, she had found a political voice to oppose the violence and injustice, but as a child, it had permeated her whole being, whilst not being spoken about. She had learnt to defend against it with a self-mocking parody of herself. "Matty" was her version of the smiling, inwardly screaming, abuse survivors at Respond or the compliant, inwardly seething, Welsh self-caricatures of today's neo-colonial Wales whom I have met in my consulting room.

Valerie Sinason's work has had an impact, not only on all subsequent psychoanalytic work in the field of intellectual disability, but also on a deeper understanding of the defences thrown up in response to certain aspects of the prejudices and inequalities of contemporary Britain and elsewhere.

References

Burns, T. (1992). *Erving Goffman*. London: Routledge.
Clarke, G. (2008). *At the Source: A Writer's Year*. Manchester: Carcanet Press.
Clinic for Dissociative Studies. (2017). www.clinicds.co.uk/ [last accessed 19.10.17].

Conference on Culture, Identity and Psychiatry. (2000). *Siarad yr Anweledig / Speaking the Invisible*. Felinfach Theatre, Ceredigion, West Wales, 4 November 2000.

Cymdeithas yr Iaith / The Welsh Language Society. (2017). http://cymdeithas.cymru/hafan [last accessed 19.10.17].

The Full Monty. (1997). Directed by P. Cattaneo [Film]. UK: 20th Century Fox.

Lessing, D. (1969). *The Four-Gated City*. London: Random House.

Phillips, A. (2000). On translating a person. In: *Promises, Promises: Essays on Literature and Psychoanalysis* (pp. 125–147). London: Faber and Faber. Presented at Gwyn Jones Memorial Lecture, Cardiff, 2000.

Pinter, H. (1998). *Harold Pinter: Plays 4: Betrayal; Monologue; One for the Road; Mountain Language; Family Voices; A Kind of Alaska; Victoria Station; Precisely; The New World Order; Party Time; Moonlight; Ashes to Ashes; Celebration; Umbrellas; God's District; Apart from That*. London: Faber and Faber.

Potter, B. (1908). *The Tale of Jemima Puddle-Duck*. London: Frederick Warne. [reprinted 2002].

Sinason, V. (1992). *Mental Handicap and the Human Condition: New Approaches from the Tavistock*. London: Free Association Books.

Stokes, J., & Sinason, V. (1992). Secondary mental handicap as a defence. In: A. Waitman & S. Conboy-Hill (Eds.), *Psychotherapy and Mental Handicap* (pp. 46–58). London: Sage.

Tomos, A. (2007). *Wrth fy Nagrau i*. Llanrwst: Gwasg Carreg Gwalch.

Chapter 5

Death, loss, and the struggle for non-disabled grief

Noelle Blackman

Introduction

This chapter describes the impact that Valerie has had on my professional and personal development over the last couple of decades. Meeting Valerie and discovering her writing was a turning point in my life: it was as though she were shining a torch on the path ahead; up until this point I had been working in the dark. My training as a drama therapist had not prepared me at all for working as a therapist with bereaved people with intellectual disabilities. As with many therapy trainings, it was broad, and there was a gaping hole in the curriculum where the literature and lectures on working with people with intellectual disabilities should have been. Valerie's book, *Mental Handicap and the Human Condition* (1992), showed me a rich and deep understanding of the inner world of people with intellectual disabilities. Valerie helped me to see communication that I had overlooked before, and to recognise emotional pain in my clients that, up until then, I had only glimpsed. Discovering Valerie's way of thinking, and having her as my clinical supervisor, enabled me to make sense of what I was experiencing, and to build meaningful relationships with my clients who had intellectual disabilities. Valerie's book introduced me to concepts such as the "handicapped smile" and "secondary handicap". It helped me to feel less disabled within my work, and I began to be able to conceptualise that which I had experienced. Discovering the book emboldened me. In this chapter I will describe how I came to set up a unique loss and bereavement service for people with intellectual disabilities and I will illustrate some of Valerie's theories with vignettes of my own work.

It was while working as a trainee dramatherapist that I first came across Maureen Oswin's seminal book, *Am I Allowed to Cry?* (1991). It built on the unrecognised grief that she had observed during a previous study (1971) in newly bereaved children and young people with intellectual disabilities who had been placed into an institution after the death of a parent. The book sparked my interest in this subject and within two years of completing my training, I had set up the loss and bereavement service (Blackman, 2011).

I was then lucky enough to recruit to the service the psychotherapist, David O'Driscoll, and it was at his invitation that I went to Valerie's workshop at the Tavistock Clinic.

Sitting amongst a small group of health professionals from a variety of disciplines while Valerie conducted an open clinical supervision session, was revelatory. We were each encouraged to present something from our clinical work and to consider the previously hidden, unconscious communications and relational transactions that might be going on, even when, at first, it appeared that there was very little occurring. At the end of the session, David suggested that I might ask Valerie if she would consider becoming my clinical supervisor, which I did; to my utter surprise, she accepted. It was through the many wonderful years of supervision with Valerie that I began to really develop my own practice, experience, knowledge, and confidence, and it is also at this point that I began to be able to understand and theorise my work. Valerie gave me the courage to challenge the status quo and to go beyond the labels that people had been saddled with, to fully meet the human being beyond the label. I began to see more clearly the resourcefulness and resilience within each person and not just the disability and vulnerability.

Bereavement, mourning and the state of grief

There are several reasons why it is important to pay particular attention to the grief of people with intellectual disabilities. Over the last century, due to the benefits of improved medical treatment and better living conditions, there has been a rise in the longevity of the entire UK population (Office for National Statistics, 2015). This means that there has also been a rise in the population of adults, particularly older people, with intellectual disabilities in the UK (Seltzer, 1992). Bereavement is therefore a growing issue: the longer a person lives, the more likely it is that they will have experienced at least one death of someone of significance in their life.

We know that the loss of a significant other through death is psychologically traumatic. Engel argues that:

> ...grief represents a departure from the state of health and well-being, and just as healing is necessary in the physiological realm in order to bring the body back into homeostatic balance, a period of time is likewise needed to return the mourner to a similar state of equilibrium.
>
> (Engel (1961) cited in Worden, 1991, pp. 9–10)

For most people, bereavement leads to a period of grief that will gradually become less all-consuming. Mourning is a period during which people are often emotionally vulnerable. Without the support of others, or acknowledgment of the state of grieving, it is more likely that a person will experience a problematic bereavement. Unacknowledged grief is an emotional burden that can lead to mental ill health (Worden, 1983). For many people with intellectual disabilities, their grief can pass unacknowledged, or at the very least, can be played down. Sometimes they may not show any sign of grief at the beginning of a bereavement because it has taken them a while to understand the permanence of the situation. This can mean that when they are finally showing signs of grieving, this may not be recognised as such. There can also be secondary losses which can exacerbate the grieving process, such as loss of the family home, which may or may not include a move to live with paid carers.

There is increasing evidence to suggest that at least ten per cent of the general population will develop Complicated Grief in response to bereavement (Maccallum & Bryant, 2010). Characteristics of complicated grief are that the bereaved person appears to be stuck in a chronic state of mourning, with intense yearning and longing for the deceased continuing unabated (Prigerson, Vanderwerker & Maciejewski, 2008).

Bowlby (1980) interpreted pathological grief through attachment theory and linked it to childhood experiences. He hypothesised that there were disordered forms of attachment in childhood that could increase vulnerability following bereavement. This is significant when trying to understand the grief experience of people with intellectual disabilities because, for many, their early attachment has been complicated for a variety of reasons (Blackman, 2012; Minnis, Fleming & Cooper, 2010). For example, medical complications can arise from the birth of a disabled baby, resulting in procedures that prevent parents from holding their baby or taking him or her home straight away, and yet the first few days of a baby's life are a crucial time for parents and child to bond (Ainsworth, Bell, & Stayton, 1974; Bowlby, 1979; Schaffer, 1958). The mental health and emotional robustness of parents at the time of birth will affect the bonding process, as will the surrounding environment. Additionally, receiving news about their baby's disability in stark or insensitive ways will be traumatic. What Sinason identifies as the "trauma of disability" (1992, p. 138) can have a lifelong effect on a family and each individual within it. The mother, in particular, may become very depressed and withdraw from her child or she may respond by being overprotective. Either of these reactions will affect the bonding process and, consequently, the developing child. Without support and intervention, these responses can become established in the pattern of their relationships for the rest of their lives.

At a time of bereavement, whether we grieve healthily or not can be determined by the way in which we cope. This is determined, to some extent, by how we relate to others around us and how they respond, and this is significantly influenced by our early attachment experiences. Within the generic bereavement research, there has been a focus on trying to understand the environmental and personal characteristics that affect the bereavement outcome for individuals, in order to identify what it is that increases vulnerability in some bereaved people (Stroebe, Folkman, Hansson & Schut, 2006). The findings from this research have significantly shaped the national framework of bereavement response (Department of Health, 2008). Dodd and Blackman (2014) point out one significant study (Van Der Houwen, Stroebe, Schut, Stroebe & van den Bout, 2010) which focused on multiple potential risk factors which were simultaneously examined. These included the effects of attachment style and the development of depressive symptoms, in particular, the impact of social support on the expression of symptoms. This study seems particularly relevant to people with intellectual disabilities, given the high probability of insecure attachment patterns for this group (Clegg & Sheard, 2002; Penketh, 2011; Rutgers et al., 2007), combined with frequent lack of social support.

A further and more obvious reason that people with intellectual disabilities are at a greater risk of developing complicated grief is due to living life with an intellectual disability. This would make it more likely that there may be communication challenges as well as cognitive difficulties in achieving an understanding of the full implications of the loss. The literature review carried out as part of my own PhD study (Blackman 2011), highlighted several authors who made reference to the fact that people with intellectual disabilities have an increased vulnerability to atypical or complicated grief (Brickell & Munir, 2008; Dodd et al., 2008; Dowling, Hubert, White & Hollins, 2006; Kloeppel & Hollins, 1989). Recent studies in the bereavement experience of people with intellectual disabilities show that there is a difference between supporting normal grief and supporting the abnormally high incidence of complicated grief (Brickel & Munir, 2008; Dodd & Guerin, 2009). Kloeppel & Hollins (1989) suggest that many people with intellectual disabilities might experience death as sudden if they have not understood that the death was expected. This is a significant proposition as generic bereavement research highlights that recovering from the experience of sudden death is linked with complicated grief.

Kloeppel and Hollins (1989) make the first reference to the double taboo of death and disability, and how the fear and avoidance that they each elicit in carers and professionals can contribute to the complication of grieving. It could be considered that the double taboo makes it difficult for carers and professionals to think clearly in response to bereaved people with intellectual disabilities. For example, carers may feel overwhelmed, anxious, and unsure how best to communicate (Kitching, 1987; Murray, McKenzie & Quigley, 2000; Read, 2000) or they may overlook the possibility of any impact at all (Emerson, 1977; Hollins & Esterhuyzen, 1997). Additionally, there may be collusion in protecting the person from the death and any associated pain of grief (Kennedy, 1989; Lynggaard, 2002; MacHale & Carey, 2002). Indeed, one study found that people with intellectual disabilities often did not "bother" (Gilrane-McGarry & Taggart, 2007) to communicate their feelings to front-line staff, and that the staff did not ask any questions or follow-up news of the people's bereavements. The researchers argue that this passivity on the part of the person with intellectual disability could be perceived by staff as the person adjusting well to the bereavement. Another similar study (Murray, McKenzie & Quigley, 2000) suggests that one explanation for lack of engagement could be explained by staff members' lack of skills and confidence to indicate a willingness to talk about, or listen to, the bereaved people with intellectual disabilities.

Hollins and Sinason (2000) describe three secrets held by people with intellectual disabilities: they state that as well as loss through death, they are likely to experience other profound losses connected to living life with a disability, including the loss of sexual knowledge, and the loss of a welcomed, valued role in society. I consider this in more depth below.

The setting up of a specialised loss and bereavement service for people with intellectual disabilities

In the mid-1990s I began working within an NHS Trust which provided training to direct care staff working with people with intellectual disabilities. We were situated in an old ward of a long-stay hospital which was in the process of resettling people with intellectual disabilities into the community as directed by the UK National Health Service and Community Care Act 1990. I was working for the Trust as a trainer and not as a therapist at the time. However, as a newly trained dramatherapist, I was extremely aware of the overwhelming feelings of loss that were being stirred up within the whole organisation by this process (Obholzer & Zagier Roberts, 1994). People with intellectual disabilities, many of whom had been placed into the hospital during their childhoods by their families on the advice of their doctors, were now being moved into small houses in the community, away from all that had become familiar. As preparations were put in place for individuals to move out, the original history that had led to them moving into the hospital, often thirty years or more before, became rekindled. Strong feelings were often aroused, if not always expressed directly, in the people with intellectual disabilities, the staff working with them, or in members of their remaining family. This gave me the opportunity to write and run a training course on loss and bereavement. It was for staff in the community as well as for those still working in the hospital. The course addressed resettlement and the losses that accompanied this, as well as bereavement following a death. I found that staff members were concerned that when people with intellectual disabilities experienced difficulty grieving, and needed more support than they felt that they could offer, there was a paucity of specialist services that could help. It was in response to this that the Loss and Bereavement Service was created. It is the only service of its kind in the United Kingdom and is still open today.

Running a long-term, slow-open loss and bereavement group within an abuse service

In 1991 Valerie was an important figure in the founding of Respond, a national charity based in London. As described by Alan Corbett and Tamsin Cottis in their chapter in this book, it provides both one-to-one and group psychotherapy to people with intellectual disabilities who have experienced abuse or trauma. It also provides training and support to staff. In 2003, I came to work at Respond and I established the Respond Elders Project. Its aims were to provide a range of emotional support to people with intellectual disabilities confronted with ageing, death, and dying. The project offered training, consultancy, and supervision for staff teams who were supporting a person at the end of their life, or when someone close to them was dying. We also offered a bereavement psychotherapy group to people with intellectual disabilities. The group ran for ten years, with a total of fifteen people passing through the group. Members stayed for an average of three years each.

Many bereaved people with intellectual disabilities may not have had the chance to share how they feel about a person who has died, or about their experience surrounding the death. They may also not have been able to draw on social support. Bereavement research (Palletti, 2008; Van Der Houwen, Stroebe, Schut, Stroebe & van den Bout, 2010) highlights these factors as being important in the ability to grieve healthily. In my experience, I have found that a group approach to bereavement therapy offers the chance for people to normalise their grief experience by recognising that others have experienced something similar.

Prior to joining the group, each potential member was offered an assessment. For some people individual therapy was felt to be appropriate. Our assessment criteria were: cognitive ability; communication; previous experience of being in a group; the complexity of grief or the circumstances of the death; willingness to talk about loss and to listen to others. Each person joined the group for a minimum of six months and it was agreed they could stay for as long as they needed. This meant that there was a slow flow of people both leaving and joining the group, but importantly, there was a continuity of core members of the group. This was important for the building of trust, and also for the continuing development of thinking and reflection within the group itself.

The group met for one hour, once a week, and was led by two therapists. There were usually four or five members in the group and there was an expectation that each person would be supported by an escort to the clinic for at least the first few months. We found that, at first, people could feel very anxious, both before and after the group. The support of an escort provided emotional containment for participants: just knowing that their escort was in the waiting room could be supportive.

The therapists provided containment within the group by holding the "therapeutic frame" (see Georgina Parkes' chapter in this book), which consisted of: having uninterrupted time; being in the same place at the same time; having a consistency of approach; and allowing a space for feelings to be expressed consciously or unconsciously. Rather than reacting to the feelings, the therapists allowed time to think about and try to understand the feelings expressed, and they encouraged the group to do this also. In this way, over time, each member of the group became a little more curious about feelings and thoughts, both their own and those of others. The therapists were also mindful of their own feelings, in the form of countertransference, in understanding what was being expressed by group members. Valerie's insights helped us here too. She refers to Bion's (1959) concept of the analyst as a container. She says:

> The younger the child or the more severely handicapped the child or adult, the greater the need to work more by understanding the counter-transference or the nature of the communication the patient has sent to the therapist to be held.
>
> (1992, p. 80–81).

The group used a mixture of approaches including talking and discussion, watching DVDs, making family trees and other biographical material, and doing creative exercises. We encouraged each group member to tell their story when they first joined the group and this was referred to regularly throughout the life of the group. Members added to their stories and, over time, told them from new perspectives. Each group member was encouraged to consider how other group members were feeling and why they were thinking or expressing themselves in particular ways. This way of working enabled group members to become curious and supportive of one another whilst simultaneously becoming more aware and reflective about their own internal world. This shared opportunity aimed to provide each participant with the ability to process their grief and to strengthen their inner relationship to the deceased person through creating a shared dialogue about them.

Each participant had a review at six-monthly intervals in order to establish whether the group was still useful to them or whether they had reached a point where they felt ready to leave. The whole group took an active part in the review of each group member, sometimes gently challenging the person's view of themselves, and often adding positive comments about changes that they had noticed about them. Each time a group member made a decision to leave the group it served to illustrate the idea that bereavement can be survived. Each departure signified a loss and we used this as an opportunity to plan a positive goodbye and to celebrate the time the person had spent in the group. This process offered members a positive experience of an ending. During the course of the group it was our observation that, as well as deepening their understanding about their own grief experience, participants developed a capacity to reflect more deeply on their own thoughts and feelings. They were also able to empathise more with others, and they were more able to communicate this. We also witnessed a development in people's abilities to draw on a wider range of coping skills than when they had first joined the group.

In the group we did not only talk about loss through death. The trust and intimacy provided by the group enabled conversations about other kinds of losses. Many of these had not been talked about before and, in some cases, had not hitherto been contextualised as a loss. These were sometimes as painful as, or even more painful, than the loss through bereavement. A recurring theme was that of sex and relationships. One member of the group, in particular, who was an older man who had lived with his mother all of his life until her death three years earlier, often talked longingly of the wife he wished he had had. He yearned for a sense of belonging and had a deep desire for intimacy. These painful experiences of lack were felt by many other group members. This issue is especially poignant within a group of people whose lives are often lonely, and for whom there can be so many obstacles to making meaningful relationships (Mencap, 2017).

In talking about this difficult subject, group members often touched on the "difference" they felt due to their living with an intellectual disability. It was perhaps the most difficult issue to talk about, or even think about. It is well-documented that people will often develop defensive reactions to the insight into their own disability (Bicknell, 1983; Marks, 1999; Sinason, 1992; Thomas, 1997). This is not surprising when there is rarely the opportunity for people with intellectual disabilities to reflect on their experiences of difference and identity with others in a supportive environment. These defences can then further disable the person.

One man in the group always arrived late to the group despite not living far away. This began to feel like a deliberate act and perhaps his only way to show some sort of assertiveness or anger in his life. He would arrive in the group with a huge smile on his face and would rarely speak without being asked; he just sat quietly smiling. This would fit well with Sinason's concept of the handicapped smile (1992). It can take a long time to get beyond these defences, but it is important to find a balance between allowing space for the expression of very difficult feelings within the therapeutic space whilst also appreciating the enormous pain and shame that can be evoked by this process. The group, encouraged by the therapists, would think out loud together as to why this man would always be late. As he grew more trusting in the group, he would think with us and share snippets of his life in which he clearly had had decisions made for him. He described a life with little room for him to have control over even the smallest things. He was able to hear the group think about his lateness as being, perhaps, his way of exercising his control. Gradually he became a little less smiley and passive, and more able to be authentic to his feelings which were quite often feelings of frustration at his powerlessness.

Sometimes, in the groupwork, it was too painful to tackle experiences such as these directly, and at such times, the use of stories or enactments were safe and effective techniques to use, as they allowed for the projection of the painful feelings into an imaginary character or situation.

Valerie's direct influence on me as a therapist and researcher

During the time that Valerie supervised me, I was working with a woman with intellectual disabilities and a disorganised attachment style (Main & Solomon, 1986) for long-term bereavement psychotherapy (Blackman & Curen, 2013). During the often silent sessions of our first year of treatment, I was aware of the powerful transference I felt. The silence was often hard to endure. However, Valerie helped me to understand it as an unconscious expression of feelings associated with the woman's early experiences of being with a neglectful mother. Indeed, Valerie has described how infants may learn to survive the experience of feeling frightened daily, due to the absence of an emotionally available mother, saying they may give up, "all hope of communication and become quiet, sleep a lot, and become deeply depressed" (1992, p. 189).

This client eventually began to speak about the appalling abuse and neglect in her childhood. I then understood that the many attacks she made on herself were a combination of self-punishment and a tool with which she sometimes tried to find out who, if anyone, could keep her safe. Sinason describes what she terms "opportunistic handicap" in which "every destructive aspect of the self finds a home in the disability" (1992, p. 2). In the course of my work with this client, I was planning to go on a three-week holiday. Knowing that she could be so self-destructive, I felt anxious about leaving her for so long. Valerie supported me in an unusual decision which was that I should keep contact with her via a weekly telephone call at the same time as our usual session. This became a turning point in the therapy: my client internalised being remembered even in my absence. It changed our therapeutic relationship profoundly. This led to her gradually developing the ability to reflect a little more and to her becoming more curious and interested in thinking about and noticing things with me.

There were still sessions, however, where it was hard for me to experience her as an active presence in the room. I would say, for example, "I feel as though there are times when I am with you that you have switched off your brain, making thinking very hard. Sometimes, when you switch it on again, it feels as though I am with a different person." This very direct but non-persecutory style of speaking to clients is something that Valerie does so well, and I have been inspired by that. For my client, such interventions seemed very helpful. We became able to talk about this absence or dissociation as something that we could notice together. She described not only how tiring it was to keep her brain switched off and how hard it made it to cope with even the simplest things, but also how frightening it was sometimes to allow herself to think. She began to notice herself switching off and making a choice in the session to switch on. This became an exciting point in our work and I noticed in myself how much less tired I felt in the sessions. This is an example of another defence mechanism that Sinason describes as "secondary handicap". She describes how, "It can be easier to behave like the village idiot and make everyone laugh than to expose the unbearable tiny discrepancy between normal and not normal on the human continuum" (1992, pp. 20–21). Perhaps my client's switching off and appearing more stupid than she clearly was, had become an important coping mechanism.

Through this client, and with the different lenses that Valerie has shown me, I have discovered that the biggest complication in grief can be connected to the developing self. Many of the bereaved people with intellectual disabilities who I have supported over the years have had a very fragile sense of themselves, and this is connected to their attachment history: the more complex their attachment history, the more fragile their sense of self. We all learn about ourselves in relation to others, and if the relationship with our primary carer is complicated by disability, this can affect the emerging individual identity. Relational-based psychotherapy offers an opportunity to gain a stronger sense of self, making this form of psychotherapy imperative as an instrument of profound change.

Without Valerie, I think I would not have written my book (Blackman, 2003) or undertaken my PhD research (Blackman, 2011). From Valerie I have learned not to be afraid of my vulnerability or feelings of "stupidity", but instead to be courageous and learn from these states. She has helped me to recognise that my own experience, history, and ancestry are integral to my work. Valerie has emboldened me not to be afraid to make these connections between the personal and the professional, and to be open in doing so.

References

Ainsworth, M. D. S., Bell, S. M., & Stayton, D. J. (1974). Infant–mother attachment and social development: 'socialisation' as a product of reciprocal responsiveness to signals. In: M. P. M. Richards (Ed.), *The Integration of a Child into a Social World* (pp. 99–136). London: Cambridge University Press.

Bicknell, J. (1983). The psychopathology of handicap. *British Journal of Medical Psychology*, 56: 167–178.

Bion, W. R. (1959). Attacks on linking. *The International Journal of Psychoanalysis*, 40: 308–315. Available at: www.pep-web.org/document.php?id=ijp.040.0308a [last accessed 16.10.2017]. [reprinted in: Bion, W. R. (1967). Attacks on linking. *Second Thoughts* (pp. 93–109). London: William Heinemann Medical Books.]

Blackman, N. (2003). *Loss and Learning Disability*. London: Worth Publishing.

Blackman, N. (2011). *The Use of Psychotherapy in Supporting People with Intellectual Disabilities who have Experienced Bereavement*. PhD thesis, June 2011. University of Hertfordshire, Hatfield. https://core.ac.uk/download/pdf/9839917.pdf [last accessed 16.10.17].

Blackman, N. (2012). Bereavement and People with Intellectual Disabilities: A Critical Review of the Literature. Paper presented at the S. Raffaele-Tosinvest JPPID Special Symposium at the *2012 IASSID (International Association for the Scientific Study of Intellectual Disabilities) World Congress July 9–14*, World Trade Convention Centre, Halifax, Canada, 11 July. [unpublished].

Blackman, N., & Curen, R. (2013). Psychoanalytical approaches in practice 2. In: P. Heslop & A. Lovell, (Eds.), *Understanding and Working with People with Learning Disabilities who Self-injure* (pp. 99–108). London: Jessica Kingsley.

Bowlby, J. (1979). *The Making and Breaking of Affectional Bonds*. London: Tavistock.

Bowlby, J. (1980). *Attachment and Loss, Vol. 3: Loss – Sadness and Depression*. London: The Hogarth Press and The Institute of Psychoanalysis.

Brickell, C., & Munir, K. (2008). Grief and its complications in individuals with intellectual disability. *Harvard Review of Psychiatry*, *16*(1): 1–12.

Clegg, J., & Sheard, C. (2002). Challenging behaviour and insecure attachment. *Journal of Intellectual Disability Research*, *46*: 503–506.

Department of Health. (2008). *End of Life Care Strategy: Promoting High Quality Care for Adults at the End of their Life*. London: Central Office of Information. Available at: www.gov.uk/government/uploads/system/uploads/attachment_data/file/136431/End_of_life_strategy.pdf [last accessed 16.10.17].

Dodd, P., & Blackman, N. (2014). Complicated grief. In: S. Read (Ed.), *Supporting People with Intellectual Disabilities Experiencing Loss and Bereavement: Theory and Compassionate Practice* (pp. 59–70). London: Jessica Kingsley.

Dodd, P. C., & Guerin, S. (2009). Grief and bereavement in people with intellectual disabilities. *Current Opinion in Psychiatry*, *22*: 442–446.

Dodd, P., Guerin, S., McEvoy, J., Buckley, S., Tyrrell, J., & Hillery, J. (2008). A study of complicated grief symptoms in people with intellectual disabilities. *Journal of Intellectual Disability Research*, *52*: 415–425.

Dowling, S., Hubert, J., White, S., & Hollins, S. (2006). Bereaved adults with intellectual disabilities: a combined randomized controlled trial and qualitative study of two community-based interventions. *Journal of Intellectual Disability Research*, *50*: 277–287.

Emerson, P. (1977). Covert grief reaction in mentally retarded clients. *Mental Retardation*, *15*(6): 46–47.

Engel, G. L. (1961). Is grief a disease?: a challenge for medical research. *Psychosomatic Medicine*, *23*(1): 18–22.

Gilrane-McGarry, U., & Taggart, L. (2007). An exploration of the support received by people with intellectual disabilities who have been bereaved. *Journal of Research in Nursing*, *12*: 129–144.

HMSO. (2017). *National Health Service and Community Care Act 1990*. www.legislation.gov.uk/ukpga/1990/19/contents [last accessed 16.10.17].

Hollins, S., & Esterhuyzen, A. (1997). Bereavement and grief in adults with learning disabilities. *British Journal of Psychiatry*, *170*: 497–501.

Hollins, S., & Sinason, V. (2000). Psychotherapy, learning disabilities and trauma: new perspectives. *British Journal of Psychiatry*, *176*(1): 32–36.

Kennedy, J. (1989). Bereavement and the person with a mental handicap. *Mental Handicap Bulletin*, *78*(1): 11.

Kitching, N. (1987). Helping people with mental handicaps cope with bereavement: a case study with discussion. *British Journal of Learning* Disabilities, *15*: 60–63.

Kloeppel, D. A., & Hollins, S. (1989). Double handicap: mental retardation and death in the family. *Death Studies, 13*(1): 31–38.

Lynggaard, H. (2002). Issues across the life path: managing change, transition and loss. In: S. Carnaby (Ed.), *Learning Disability Today: A Reader for the Certificate in Working with People with Learning Disabilities*). Brighton: Pavilion Publishing.

Maccallum, F., & Bryant, R. A. (2010). Social problem solving in complicated grief. *British Journal of Clinical Psychology, 49*: 577–590.

MacHale, R., & Carey, S. (2002). An investigation of the effects of bereavement on mental health and challenging behaviour in adults with learning disability. *British Journal of Learning Disabilities, 30*: 113–117.

Main, M., & Solomon, J. (1986). Discovery of a new, insecure-disorganized/ disoriented attachment pattern. In: T. B. Brazelton & M. W. Yogman (Eds.), *Affective Development in Infancy* (pp. 95–124). Norwood, NJ: Ablex Publishing.

Marks, D. (1999). *Disability: Controversial Debates and Psychosocial Perspectives.* London: Routledge.

Mencap. (2017). Learning disability explained. Available at: www.mencap.org.uk/ learning-disability-explained/research-and-statistics/friendships-and-socialising-research-and [last accessed 16.08.2017].

Minnis, H., Fleming, G., & Cooper, S. (2010). Reactive attachment disorder symptoms in adults with intellectual disabilities. *Journal of Applied Research in Intellectual Disabilities, 23*(4): 398–403.

Murray, G. C., McKenzie, K., & Quigley, A. (2000). An examination of the knowledge and understanding of health and social care staff about the grieving process in individuals with a learning disability. *Journal of Learning Disabilities, 4*(1): 77–90.

Obholzer, A., & Zagier Roberts, V. (Eds.) (1994). *The Unconscious at Work: Individual and Organizational Stress in the Human Services.* London: Routledge.

Office for National Statistics. (2015). Life expectancy at birth and at age 65 by local areas in England and Wales: 2012 to 2014. Available at: www.ons.gov.uk/ peoplepopulationandcommunity/birthsdeathsandmarriages/lifeexpectancies/ bulletins/lifeexpectancyatbirthandatage65bylocalareasinenglandandwales/2015-11-04 [last accessed 26.6.18].

Oswin, M. (1971). *The Empty Hours: A Study of the Week-end Life of Handicapped Children in Institutions.* London: The Penguin Press.

Oswin, M. (1991). *Am I Allowed to Cry? A Study of Bereavement amongst People who have Learning Disabilities.* London: Souvenir Press.

Palletti, R. (2008). Recovery in context: bereavement, culture, and the transformation of the therapeutic self. *Death Studies, 32*(1): 17–26.

Penketh, V. J. (2011). Attachment in adults with intellectual disabilities: the examination of the psychometric properties of the Manchester Attachment Scale – Third Party Observational Measure (MAST). PhD thesis. University of Manchester, 2011. Available at: www.escholar.manchester.ac.uk/api/datastream?publicationPid=uk-ac-man-scw:132883&datastreamId=FULL-TEXT.PDF [last accessed 16.10.17].

Prigerson, H. G., Vanderwerker, L. C., & Maciejewski, P. K. (2008). A case for inclusion of prolonged grief disorder in DSM-V. In: M. S. Stroebe, R. O. Hansson, H. Schut,

& W. Stroebe (Eds.), *Handbook of Bereavement Research and Practice: Advances in Theory and Intervention* (pp. 165–186). Washington, DC: American Psychological Association.

Read, S. (2000). Bereavement and people with learning disabilities. *Nursing and Residential Care, 2*: 230–234.

Rutgers, A. H., van IJzendoorn, M. H., Bakermans-Kranenburg, M. J., Swinkels, S. H. N., van Daalen, E., Dietz, C., Naber, F. B. A., Buitelaar, J. K., & van Engeland, H. (2007). Autism, attachment and parenting: a comparison of children with autism spectrum disorder, mental retardation, language disorder, and non-clinical children. *Journal of Abnormal Child Psychology, 35*: 859–870.

Schaffer, H, R. (1958). Objective observations of personality development in early infancy. *British Journal of Medical Psychology, 31*: 174–183.

Seltzer, M. M. (1992). Aging in persons with developmental disabilities. In: J. E. Birren, R. B. Sloane, & G. D. Cohen (Eds.), *Handbook of Mental Health and Aging* (2nd edn) (pp. 583–599). San Diego, CA: Academic Press.

Sinason, V. (1992). *Mental Handicap and the Human Condition: New Approaches from the Tavistock*. London: Free Association Books.

Stroebe, M. S., Folkman, S., Hansson, R. O., & Schut, H. (2006). The prediction of bereavement outcome: development of an integrative risk factor framework. *Social Science & Medicine, 63*: 2440–2451.

Thomas, K. R. (1997). Countertransference and disability: some observations. *Journal of Melanie Klein and Object Relations, 15*(1): 145–161.

van der Houwen, K., Stroebe, M., Schut, H., Stroebe, W., & van den Bout, J. (2010). Mediating processes in bereavement: the role of rumination, threatening grief interpretations, and deliberate grief avoidance. *Social Science & Medicine, 71*: 1669–1676.

Worden, J. W. (1983). *Grief Counseling and Grief Therapy: A Handbook for the Mental Health Practitioner*. New York: Springer Publishing.

Worden, J. W. (1991). *Grief Counselling and Grief Therapy: A Handbook for the Mental Health Practitioner* (2nd edn). Abingdon: Routledge.

Chapter 6

Forensic groupwork and *Books Beyond Words*

Valerie Sinason as colleague, co-author, and friend

Sheila Hollins

Introduction

I have known Valerie for more than thirty-five years and our professional paths have frequently been joined. This chapter describes some of our most notable work together, and offers a perspective on our mutual engagement with the developing field of intellectual disability and psychotherapy since our initial meeting in 1981. We have been co-facilitators of a long-term group for men with intellectual disabilities; academic colleagues, writing papers and delivering presentations together; and co-authors at *Books Beyond Words* (2017).

The Tavistock Workshop

Valerie and I met at the Tavistock Clinic in 1981, at Neville Symington's seminars on psychotherapy and intellectual disability. I had completed my training as a psychotherapist and child and adolescent psychiatrist with a strong interest in childhood disability and I had joined Joan Bicknell at St George's Hospital Medical School as a senior lecturer in the psychiatry of mental handicap. After my appointment, Joan had introduced me to colleagues as a psychotherapist, and had been positive about my being the mother of a child with a severe intellectual disability. It had felt a somewhat strange new world for me compared to the established speciality of child psychiatry but it also felt exciting and somehow right.

I had always enjoyed seminars at the Tavistock as a trainee, but now the focus was on my own clinical interest. I remember well that first disability seminar and Neville's recently published paper about his therapy sessions with an adult with an intellectual disability (Symington, 1981). It is a shame that Neville did not continue long in this work but he certainly sowed a few important seeds and served to bring some like-minded people together. I remember Susanna Isaacs Elmhirst taking the workshop on, briefly, when Neville emigrated to Australia, and the focus switching to autism. I had met Susanna in 1970 during my first house job as a doctor at Paddington Green

Children's Hospital where her work had introduced me and other trainees to the horrors of child abuse. Attendance at the seminars dwindled until they were reinvigorated by Dr Jon Stokes from the Tavistock Adult Department, working with Valerie from the Children's Department. The workshop was then led by Valerie for ten years or more. She was soon joined by Sheila Bichard; she eventually handed on to Dr David Simpson, the workshop at last being properly funded by the Tavistock Children's Department. Although Valerie worked in the Children's Department, she worked with both children and adults with severe intellectual disabilities, as Dr Judith Trowell, Head of the Children's Department, was concerned that there was no provision for either group. During this period, Valerie also wrote her seminal work, *Mental Handicap and the Human Condition* (Sinason, 1992).

The St George's group

In the mid to late 1980s, whilst developing my own therapeutic work at St George's Hospital in south-west London, I was in the very fortunate position of having a research staff budget that I could use as I wished. In 1988, I invited Valerie to come to St George's to co-lead an adult psychotherapy group with me with the hope that we would be able to evaluate it. I had already run a number of therapy groups for community clients, usually conducted with a senior psychiatry trainee as co-therapist, but I was keen to learn from Valerie in this new group, which I had offered for men who were showing very concerning, sexually abusive behaviour.

We had some exploratory meetings with consultant colleagues in the Adult Psychotherapy Department at St George's. There was some polite interest but no one felt that they had any expertise with our patient group or any interest in acquiring some. The idea of providing us with supervision or an ear to listen to our experiences was anathema too. However, we were offered one of their group rooms once a week at a time that we could both manage.

Then Valerie gained an introduction to Dr Murray Cox through Estela Welldon from the Portman Clinic. Murray was a forensic psychiatrist and psychotherapist at Broadmoor and also had a clinic in Stratford in the East End of London. So began our fortnightly visits to Stratford for supervision. Murray was quite an enigma: in addition to his clinical expertise as one of a small band of forensic psychotherapists, he was also a Biblical and a Shakespearean scholar. He was known as "Mr Shakespeare" at Broadmoor (Cox, 1992), having invited the Royal Shakespeare Company (RSC) there to perform Shakespeare's Macbeth and other plays. Murray was also the psychiatric advisor to the RSC. Perhaps he agreed to work with us, in part, because we were also breaking new ground. I thought he recognised a kindred spirit in Valerie, who was a published poet and psychoanalyst. We were impressed by the depth of his philosophical and literary understanding of the human predicament, and he was not afraid of disability. During our supervisions he would alternately take down the Bible or a volume of Shakespeare to find a quote that had been sparked by some of the dialogue and interactions we were reporting from our group. We also used a recording sheet from one of Murray's books about transference (Cox, 1988; Cox & Theilgaard, 1987) and continued this method of recording throughout the group's eighteen-year life. We were two women working with a male group of offenders and we particularly valued our supervision from a male therapist.

One reason we felt our work and supervision proceeded so harmoniously was that our skills were complementary and we benefited by each other's differences and similarities. One of the ideas that we had explored together in supervision was that the experience of having an intellectual disability could be a trauma itself. Valerie explored this idea further in her PhD (Sinason, 2003) and I wrote about it too (Hollins, 1999).

Setting up this group took some time but we did have six patients at our first session, with anxious nurse escorts sitting outside for two of our group who were detained in hospital under Section 3 of the 1983 Mental Health Act (UK Government, 2017). One of the men, who I shall refer to as P, spent the first session lying on the floor sobbing. However, everyone came back the following week. Gradually the members helped to think about and manage the "rules" of the group, and a respectful group ethos was established. The rules included that everyone should sit down during the group, and that no one would touch anyone else. Valerie suggested another rule that I heartily approved of: that no one could hurt themselves or anyone else, thus showing the group that the self was valued and acknowledged as a potential victim of harm as well as a perpetrator. During the years of the group, neither Valerie nor I felt any personal threat from the members, and there were no violent incidents or disturbances. Today the members would be described as "challenging" but any challenges they presented to us were around their needs to communicate and to be heard.

We agreed with the group that we would share any letters or phone calls that we received about them. This led to some interesting transactions. We would start a session together noticing any empty seat and wondering where the absent person was. After everyone had settled, Valerie or I would read out any letters that had been received. We learned how to multitask in the group by formulating a letter, perhaps in response to one we had received, writing it down, taking it out to a secretary to be typed, and then signing it, all within group time. This was a totally novel experience for Valerie with her more formal Tavistock experience. We also started a waiting room group for escorts, who were usually support workers who needed some support and understanding themselves.

On one occasion, P's psychiatrist had written to ask if there was any point in P continuing to attend as he was still on Section 3 and therefore not at liberty to harm people outside his secure setting. We discussed this in the group and agreed a reply which was typed during the session and then signed by all the members. In the letter we asked the consultant how much medication P was taking, how many staff injuries there had been, and whether he was causing much harm to himself, to others, or to his few possessions. The next week we had a reply saying that all of those things had changed for the better, and that he and the nurses recognised that P was less troubled in himself. P actually stayed in the group for nearly ten years, the longest of any group member, and his clinical team and P himself accepted that he would almost certainly remain on a Section 3 for the rest of his life. One week, one of our patients arrived very late and told us that he had walked because he did not have money for the bus fare. We knew that he usually came by bicycle, but he explained that he had lost his glasses and could not see well enough to ride safely. He had been to the opticians to ask for a new pair and had been told that he would not be allowed another pair until the following year. It so happened that I had been asked to speak about intellectual disability healthcare on Radio 5 Live the next day and, with our patient's permission, I told his story. His optician happened to hear me speaking and contacted our patient with an apology. The group members were very impressed!

Another variation to group analytic practice was our decision to invite outside professionals to attend a session, to help the members connect their therapeutic experience with their real worlds. Such visitors included one member's social worker and a policeman.

After a while, we decided to hold the group for fifty weeks a year, and added a third therapist, usually a psychiatry or art therapy trainee, so that we could ensure there were at least two therapists for every session. Amongst those who joined us for a year or so were Dr Raj Attavar and Dr Georgina Parkes (see Chapter 7 in this book), both consultant psychiatrists who are still very active in this field and providing next-generation leadership to ensure that psychotherapy is provided for more people with intellectual disabilities.

Gradually, the focus of our work changed. We had found that we could not begin to develop empathy amongst the group members without first recognising the victim inside each of the men. It was the first time that these men's own trauma had been recognised and understood. Valerie had also started a group for women, with a trainee as co-therapist, and we decided to try to amalgamate the two groups. This was very difficult to achieve but the group did become a mixed group; the members changed and the culture of the group changed to reflect the more diverse needs of the members. There was no shortage of people referred to us for assessment and Valerie provided group supervision to a multidisciplinary group of trainees and others who were willing and able to offer individual psychotherapy or art therapy on a weekly basis. An interview study about the group was published in 2003 (Macdonald, Sinason, & Hollins, 2003).

Sadly, when Valerie and I both retired, a new model for psychotherapy referrals in the NHS Trust was introduced. This effectively excluded people with intellectual disabilities. All referrals to the psychotherapy service had to be made by Community Mental Health Teams (CMHTs) after a trial in the new Improving Access to Psychological Therapies (IAPT) service. The contracts for the locums who had taken on "our" group were not renewed and the group was closed at just three weeks' notice and with no follow-up for the members. Also, to our knowledge, no referrals to adult psychotherapy were accepted from people with intellectual disabilities. It seemed that so little had changed in the attitudes of adult mental health services over more than twenty years. In my view, the abrupt cessation of established therapeutic treatment programmes continues to speak of a devaluing and disrespect for the psychological needs of people with intellectual disabilities.

Books Beyond Words, the three secrets, and five mutative factors

In 1989 I had my first book published in what is now known as the *Books Beyond Words* (2017) series. My first books, co-authored with a psychiatrist and bereavement expert, were called *When Dad Died* (Hollins, Sireling, & Webb, 1989a) and *When Mum Died* (Hollins, Sireling, & Webb, 1989b). My research focus for many years was in death and dying in relation to people with intellectual disabilities. I will return to *Books Beyond Words* but first I will give a little more background about the insights that led me to create therapeutic picture books for people with intellectual disabilities.

Two years earlier in 1987, whilst lecturing in Rome at the International L'Arche Federation meeting, I had first spoken about "the three secrets" (Hollins & Grimer, 1988; Hollins & Sinason, 2000). I identified the "secrets" that family carers, teachers, and others try to keep from people with intellectual disabilities. These are the secrets of death and dying, of sexuality, and of disability and long-term dependency. In my clinical work with both children and adults with intellectual disabilities, I had been struck by the frequency with which these key aspects of life were ignored and, even worse, were considered irrelevant. The idea that people with intellectual disabilities who could not speak about their feelings actually had an inner, emotional world was beyond the comprehension of their carers and even some of their families. It seemed that it would be too painful to contemplate the possibility that the intellectually disabled person was also grieving when a family member died, or that they might have unfulfilled sexual feelings, or aspirations for an adult life that had no chance of materialising.

Valerie recognised and added another "secret" in her "five mutative factors" (Sinason, 1992; Sinason, 1999, p. 453), one that so many of her disabled patients had revealed to her. This was the fear of annihilation (the fear that other people wished they were dead). All of these ideas were being discussed in all too infrequent seminars and workshops at the time, but we were too busy to write much or to do any systematic research. My responsibilities now included being acting Head of Department at St George's: I was responsible for both postgraduate and teaching programmes, as well as having a heavy burden of service development and clinical work. This was in addition to my own family commitments. At times it felt an impossible load and I seriously considered leaving St George's. It was a joy to have a colleague like Valerie to support my work at this time.

In 1998 Valerie left the Tavistock and Portman clinics and was able to increase to four her consultant research psychotherapist sessions at St George's and in the Joan Bicknell Centre in Wandsworth. Our psychotherapy service developed more elements with assessments, supervision, and consultation groups for staff from the local NHS, care providers, and social services. Valerie's ties with the Tavistock may have come to an end but our own work was thriving.

Valerie always refers to *Books Beyond Words* as books without words, which they are, of course. Given the nature of our work together, it was only a matter of time before we would decide to co-create some books about the experience of sexual abuse. *Jenny Speaks Out* (Hollins, Sinason, & Webb, 1992b) and *Bob Tells All* (Hollins, Sinason, & Webb, 1992a) sold very well. Valerie spoke about them in her numerous speaking engagements and, in our series of now nearly fifty books, I think they are still two of our best books. We introduced much of our learning from our adult group into these stories, including pictures illustrating self-injury, in order to show that self-injury is a re-enactment of hurt inflicted on the person.

Valerie has continued to co-author books from time to time and remains a strong advocate of the series, although her own clinical interest moved away from intellectual disability as she became more in demand for her expertise in dissociative disorders. In our shared clinical work with the group, we often read some of our books that seemed relevant to our patients. We would read the colour roughs as new stories were being developed and the members learnt to listen respectfully to each person's interpretation of the pictures. Sometimes a group member would ask to read a book that they had particularly enjoyed or that had touched them at that moment.

With Valerie's early involvement, I think it is fair to say that the *Books Beyond Words* series developed something of a reputation, for bravely confronting some of the difficult topics we had raised in earlier writing regarding the "five mutative steps" (Sinason, 1992; Sinason, 1999, p. 453) and "the three secrets" (Hollins & Grimer, 1988; Hollins & Sinason, 2000). The theory underpinning the series has not been written about explicitly but was assumed by the early authors to draw hugely from psychoanalytic principles, drawing on attachment theory in particular. As an aside for interested PhD students, there is a rich source of material available from the development of these titles, and the sessional material from our eighteen-year forensic group has also been carefully preserved for possible future study. Perhaps Murray Cox also influenced the theoretical basis of *Books Beyond Words*, with his theological insights. My work in intellectual disability has been rewarded with honorary doctorates in a variety of fields including theology, science, medicine, and humanities, reminding me that the whole of human experience can be found and examined in the lives of people with intellectual disabilities.

Valerie's PhD

Books Beyond Words books are also based in a thorough understanding of trauma, which was the focus of Valerie's PhD (Sinason, 2003). I must admit to being somewhat daunted when Valerie asked me to supervise her PhD as she had a degree in English, not in science or psychology. As her father's daughter, she was accustomed to being in the public spotlight, and her father would often come to her talks. I can remember him sitting on the front row and always asking the first question. His pride was obvious and justifiable. He did not have a PhD himself. Stan Segal was one of seven children and Valerie once commented to me that his family experience of poverty and racism had brought them all together. Stan joined the print trade straight from school and at the age of fifteen he received the Tolpuddle Medal for his trade union work and for leading a strike when he was only fourteen years old. After the war, he studied education at Goldsmiths, and always hoped that Valerie would follow in his footsteps and become an educational psychologist. She did set out in the right direction by going to Goldsmiths, but to study English, soon followed by child psychotherapy, and finally psychoanalysis.

On completion of her PhD, three eminent people from different disciplines ensured a rigorous viva. I had been worried that Valerie would not get a good hearing if the examiners were, themselves, too narrow in their focus. The theoretical fields she had covered included: the history of disability; linguistics, or rather, language analysis and how it changes during therapy; trauma, including intellectual disability, itself, as trauma; individual case studies, and the use of projective tests. In the end, one of her examiners commented that it was really four separate theses rolled into one, and although they did not agree with all of her ideas, they were highly complimentary about them. There was just one hypothesis that did not gain agreement, with one examiner saying that Valerie had shown that intellectual disability could be a major contributor to trauma but not that it constituted trauma in itself, as the qualitative evidence she had provided was insufficient. Thankfully, she persevered and completed her PhD in 2003, including in it a case series and data regarding clinical outcomes.

I did not have a PhD myself and I felt that I, as well as Valerie, was also somewhat under scrutiny during the examination process. The truth is that the 1980s and 1990s were pioneering years and we were trying to find our way as we sought to establish disability psychotherapy as the important field of study and practice that we passionately believed it to be. I saw a PhD, primarily, as an advanced introduction to research methods in which the student would learn to apply established methodologies to a research question in which they had a sustained interest. In the process, they would become known as "the" expert in their particular, very specialised area and would publish papers and even books on their subject, and would often go on to do further research. Valerie was already well known as "the" expert in her field and had shown little interest in publishing scientific papers. Her publications were primarily clinically based books and papers and were already in great demand. We had different theoretical backgrounds but found we were able to synthesise our ideas, both being concerned with loss and dependence, and interested in attachment theory and relational approaches before they were much used, as demonstrated in our co-authored papers (Carlsson, Hollins, Nilsson and Sinason, 2002; Hollins & Sinason, 1998; 2000).

Our twenty-minute psychotherapy assessment relied on what was theoretically implicit, and focused on learning what was important to the patient. This often led us into an advocacy role on behalf of our patients with social services when it was clear that a patient's ordinary needs were not being met. It was Dr Deborah Marks, now a child psychotherapist, who coined the term "Psychoanalytic Advocacy Therapy" for what we did (Marks, 1999, pp. 111–112). Our trainees, observing this, often remarked on the way in which we did our assessments and advocated for our patients, commenting that this was one of the most revolutionary and non-hierarchical ways of effecting change for our patients (Bradley & Hollins, 2005).

Sharing our work with others

At a presentation at the Institute of Group Analysis in London, we presented a group session in which P, the man who had spent his first session crying, told the group that he had strangled a baby the previous day. He said, "I've done it, I've done it, the police are coming…" It is relevant that in his own history, in addition to many other incidents of physical, emotional, and sexual abuse, P was thought to have been strangled by a family member. We also learnt that P had attempted to take a baby out of a pram whilst its mother was inside a shop. The group had understood and reminded P that he was on a locked ward and could not hurt a baby and that he was safe. One member told him, "You are upset because Christmas is coming and you'll miss Sheila and Valerie." Valerie commented that he did not feel safe when there was a holiday from the group. P responded by saying, "If I heard a baby crying now, I wouldn't hurt it. If I was in the community, I would. That's why I am on a Section." Incidentally, some years later, P adopted the role of co-therapist and would comment constructively if another member was preparing to leave the group.

Valerie linked up the European psychoanalysts and psychoanalytic psychotherapists undertaking disability psychotherapy by booking space at the Tavistock for an international conference where we both spoke (Hollins, 1998). Valerie did not have the capacity for organising ongoing meetings and it was Dr Johan de Groef from Belgium who took up this mantle and has continued to do so since. Although he admired our clinical and theoretical writing, I remember him expressing some disappointment at our highly clinical presentation and lack of theory. We enjoyed hearing Professor Simone Korff Sause raising thought-provoking ideas about how things would be so different if disability were not perceived as a tragedy. We felt in tune with the French approach to disability and psychoanalysis. At another European meeting, this time in Belgium in 1994, there was a wonderful esprit de corps and a great social programme. I remember taking my sixteen-year-old daughter with me, and that she was both shocked and inspired by Valerie's paper about her work at the Tavistock Children's Day Unit.

At the IASSID (International Association for the Scientific Study of Intellectual and Developmental Disabilities) conferences in Montpelier 2004 and Cape Town 2008, we presented our work to groups in which many of the researchers present were behavioural psychologists (Hollins & Sinason, 2008; Parkes et al., 2004). We did not think that presenting attachment-based, psychodynamic offender work would go down well with behavioural psychology researchers so we realised how important it was to strive to be "bilingual" across professional disciplines and to try to present our work and research in a way that was meaningful. There is still unfinished evaluation work we could provide on this group in our retirement but, reflecting on our work over the past thirty-plus years, there have been many conferences where we have presented this work, both separately and together. As this book itself attests, I know that Valerie's powerful and effective teaching style has influenced generations of young clinicians from many different theoretical disciplines.

Concluding thoughts

As my own leadership positions took me further from day-to-day clinical work, the highlight of my week was Thursday afternoons. These were kept sacrosanct (as much as possible) because this was when Valerie and my joint assessments, consultations, and therapeutic work took place. Neither of us would miss the ninety-minute group session unless completely unavoidable. It was not just the satisfaction derived from an outstanding programme of work, it was also the pleasure of working with such a loyal, empathic, and skilled colleague. Valerie's warmth and sense of humour brought real joy into our work which touched such painful human stories. Our partnership has meant a huge amount to me.

References

Books Beyond Words. (2017). https://booksbeyondwords.co.uk [last accessed 3.12.17].

Bradley, E. & Hollins, S. (2005). Assessment of persons with intellectual disabilities. In: D. S. Goldbloom (Ed.), *Psychiatric Clinical Skills* (pp. 235–253). St Louis, MO: Mosby.

Carlsson, B., Hollins, S., Nilsson, A., & Sinason, V. (2002). Preliminary findings: an Anglo-Swedish psychoanalytic psychotherapy outcome study using PORT and DMT. *Tizard Learning Disability Review*, 7(4): 39–48.

Cox, M. (1988). *Structuring the Therapeutic Process: Compromise with Chaos*. London: Jessica Kingsley.

Cox, M. (Ed.) (1992). *Shakespeare Comes to Broadmoor: "The Actors are Come Hither" The Performance of Tragedy in a Secure Psychiatric Hospital*. London: Jessica Kingsley.

Cox, M., & Theilgaard, A. (1987). *Mutative Metaphors in Psychotherapy: The Aeolian Mode*. London: Tavistock Publications.

Hollins, S. (1998). Bereavement and grief in people with mental retardation. *Psychoanalysis and Mental Retardation: On Life and Death*. Conference talk presented at the Tavistock Clinic,

Hollins, S. (1999). Remorse for being: through the lens of learning disability. In: M. Cox (Ed.), *Remorse and Reparation* (pp. 95–104). London: Jessica Kingsley.

Hollins, S., & Grimer, M. (1988). *Going Somewhere: People with Mental Handicaps and Their Pastoral Care*. London: SPCK Publishing.

Hollins, S., & Sinason, V. (1998). Learning disability and developmental disorders. In: D. Tantam (Ed.), *Clinical Topics in Psychotherapy* (pp. 180–191). London: Gaskell.

Hollins, S., & Sinason, V. (2000). Psychotherapy, learning disabilities and trauma: new perspectives. *British Journal of Psychiatry*, 176(1): 32–36.

Hollins, S. & Sinason, V. (2008). Treatment approaches in forensic mental health services for people with learning disability. *People with Intellectual Disability: Citizens in the World*. Talk presented at IASSID World Congress, Cape Town, 2008, 25–30 August.

Hollins, S., Sinason, V., & Webb, B. (1992a). *Bob Tells All*. London: St George's Mental Health Library. [reprinted London: Gaskell and St George's, University of London, 2005].

Hollins, S., Sinason, V., & Webb, B. (1992b). *Jenny Speaks Out*. London: St George's Mental Health Library. [reprinted London: Gaskell and St George's, University of London, 2005].

Hollins, S., Sireling, L., Webb, B. (1989a) *When Dad Died*. London: St George's Mental Health Library in association with Silent Books. [reprinted London: Gaskell and St George's Medical School, 2004].

Hollins, S., Sireling, L., Webb, B. (1989b) *When Mum Died*. London: St George's Mental Health Library in association with Silent Books. [reprinted London: Gaskell and St George's Medical School, 2004].

MacDonald, J., Sinason, V., & Hollins, S. (2003). An interview study of people with learning disabilities' experience of, and satisfaction with, group analytic therapy. *Psychology and Psychotherapy: Theory, Research and Practice*, 76: 433–453.

Marks, D. (1999). Disability: *Controversial Debates and Psychosocial Perspectives*. London: Routledge.

Parkes, G., Mukherjee, R., Karagianni, E., Perisetti, A., Attavar, R., Sinason, V., & Hollins, S. (2004). Characteristics and outcomes of referrals to a psychotherapy service for people with intellectual disabilities. Paper presented at IASSID World Congress, Montpelier, 2004 [Reprinted in: *Journal of Intellectual Disability Research*, *48*: 311].

Sinason, V. (1992). *Mental Handicap and the Human Condition: New Approaches from the Tavistock*. London: Free Association Press.

Sinason, V. (1999). The psychotherapeutic needs of the learning disabled and the multiply disabled child. In: M. Lanyado & A. Horne (Eds.), *The Handbook of Child and Adolescent Psychotherapy: Psychoanalytic Approaches* (pp. 445–456). London: Routledge.

Sinason, V. (2003). *Learning Disability as Trauma and the Impact of Learning Disability on Trauma*. PhD thesis. University of London.

Symington, N. (1981). The psychotherapy of a subnormal patient. *British Journal of Medical Psychology*, *44*: 211–228.

UK Government. (2017). *Mental Health Act 1983*. Norwich: The Stationery Office. Available at: www.legislation.gov.uk/ukpga/1983/20/section/3 [last accessed 6.11.2017].

Chapter 7

The best of both worlds

The making of a disability psychiatrist

Georgina Parkes

My experience as a supervisee of Valerie is that, as a clinician, she is not just ready to believe, she is *already* believing in you. I was her supervisee and I also worked for a time as her co-therapist in a psychodynamic psychotherapy group with people with intellectual disability. Seeing her "live", observing her practise at close hand, as it were, I realised she was the rock on which the group was anchored. She was always reliable: seemingly never ill or on holiday or drawn away by other commitments. The members of the group had no trouble feeling that they were held in her mind between sessions. She was encouraging, warm, and containing. This approach has had a lasting influence on me and on how I approach patients, trainees, and colleagues alike. It particularly helps me when I am supervising trainee psychiatrists, helping them juggle the endless, all seemingly urgent, demands placed upon them whilst they are simultaneously undertaking a mandatory, training psychotherapy case.

As a medical student and later a fully-fledged doctor and psychiatry trainee, I was interested in the developmental and social aspects of medicine. I was attracted initially to paediatrics, child psychiatry, and medical psychotherapy before choosing – in large part due to Valerie – to specialise in learning disability psychiatry (now renamed psychiatry of intellectual disability). I decided that this discipline encompassed all my interests and would provide a potentially challenging and satisfying career. Valerie was my supervisor for psychoanalytic psychotherapy cases for more than four years. She was always smiling, warm, and genuinely interested in me in a way I had never experienced before during my training.

I am now a consultant psychiatrist in intellectual disability and our faculty has recently changed its name to Intellectual Disability. Valerie was the person who taught me that, despite all the name changes, the stigma attached to intellectual disability, sadly, does not go away. I run a supervision group in the NHS and my co-facilitator is David O'Driscoll (see Chapter 8 in this book), an adult therapist and former social worker. Our group members are psychiatry trainees who are undertaking weekly psychotherapy with a patient with intellectual disability. David and I have also, at various points, been co-therapists in a weekly group for people with intellectual disability.

As discussed in the Royal College of Psychiatrists' council report (2004), modern psychotherapy models do not distinguish between people with intellectual disability and the general population, and trainings in these modalities usually offer no specific training. People with intellectual disability are still excluded, for the main part, from both therapy and from being seen as training cases. The more recent British Psychological Society report (Beail, 2016), which updates the Royal College of Psychiatrists' report and describes the models of therapy used in more detail, states that whilst a broader range of therapies are offered to people with intellectual disability, these are still within specialist rather than mainstream services. This is at odds with government policy which says that people with intellectual disability need to be "mainstreamed". A case in point is IAPT (Increasing Access to Psychological Therapies) which is a government initiative for people to self-refer for therapy within primary care services. This could present a barrier to access for people with intellectual disability as they are more often referred to services by others (Beail & Jahoda, 2012). As Dodd, Joyce, Nixon, Jennison & Heneage (2011) identify, IAPT services would need significant modifications to enable increased access for people with intellectual disability. In my experience, even when local intellectual disability services step in to help facilitate these modifications, patients end up going through IAPT a couple of times and then back into our specialist intellectual disability services. I see this, in part, due to the way that people with intellectual disability need longer-term therapy and, in general, make smaller improvements in short timescales. This does not sit well with such a target-driven service as IAPT.

Whilst we at Hertfordshire Loss and Bereavement psychodynamic psychotherapy service are trying to bridge the gap in a small way by offering psychotherapy placements to psychiatric trainees who are not specialising in intellectual disability psychiatry, we are still met with stigma and ignorance. A consultant colleague recently asked me about a trainee being assigned a training patient with Down's Syndrome. He described the patient as "a girl who can't talk". He was clearly not happy about it, although managed to stop himself from actually saying so. In fact, the patient in question was very much able to talk. Also, she was not a girl at all, but a young woman in her twenties. I was taken aback and surprised by how little had changed. People with intellectual disability are often treated as being younger than they are and described as being unable to talk. Such attitudes mean that people with intellectual disability are spoken to loudly, or their carers and parents are spoken to rather than themselves. I took the opportunity to try to change my colleague's perceptions.

From knowing to not knowing

Trainees find the lack of specific instructions before starting psychodynamic therapy difficult. It can be anxiety provoking. Some trainees will ask many questions about what they are meant to say and about the format and aim of the sessions. Their prior professional training experience has been that they work with a set of questions to ask: in psychiatry most interactions with patients revolve around specific psychiatric history taking. Many versions for this are available, such as that by Carlat (1998). The Mental State Examination (MSE), developed as a shortened version of the Present State Examination (PSE) (Wing, Cooper & Sartorius, 1974) is part of this lengthy history-taking process. The art of psychiatry can be boiled down to interview skills for eliciting symptoms and then clustering symptoms together and making a diagnosis.

I have found, however, that also drawing on psychodynamic thinking adds an extra dimension which I find enormously valuable. Such thinking aids me in seeing the patient as both a human being, and part of a complex system. It can help me to see through the mass of information and to derive a greater understanding of the person. Unfortunately, for a trainee who is attempting to master the psychiatric way of thinking and formulating, it is difficult to then let go of this and to sit back in a place of silence and open questions. A trainee in psychiatry is an already-qualified doctor. He or she provides a high level of service to the Trust in which they work, including working night shifts. When they begin seeing a patient for psychodynamic psychotherapy under my supervision, nearly every aspect of their job seems to constitute a test to their ability to provide a reliable therapeutic framework, by which I mean: the timing, the therapy room, the reliability of the session and of the therapist to be there, every week, thinking about the patient.

When I first met Valerie, conflicting demands on my time were constantly drawing me in different directions. I went to her once a week to try to puzzle out in detail what was really going on; it was an opportunity for me to take some time to think more deeply about what I was doing. Working with Valerie like this, I came to understand how the therapeutic framework is the structure that supports the face-to-face therapy session. The cancellation of sessions is a significant issue in the working life of a psychiatrist. I therefore did all I could to avoid cancellations for my intellectually disabled patients. I think this helped them to stick with me, to remain committed to the therapy, and to continue to attend.

I always discuss this issue with the trainees I supervise, before they take on a patient for weekly therapy. I would never ask them to stay late after a night shift or to come in on a day off or during a week of study leave before an exam. However, I share my experience that if they are able to offer an extra level of commitment, especially in the early stages of treatment, they will find that the therapy treatment endures: that patients are more likely to keep attending and to be more able to withstand any ruptures, such as cancellations or absences, that may occur further down the line.

However, the passage of a psychotherapy treatment is not always straightforward. One patient of mine, a woman with intellectual disability, told me all about her terrible experience of sexual abuse in the very first session. She then never turned up again, leaving me for some weeks in a state of constant worry about her. It seemed she had passed on to me her shame and hurt and had moved on, possibly relieved for a little while. This woman was not ready to begin therapy and, in that instance, I needed supervision from Valerie to help me feel less guilty and anxious about her and to help me reflect on why she had not come back. Valerie helped me to see that a good experience of being listened to might have enabled her, in the future, to seek help when she was more ready.

At this time, in the early days of being a supervisee of Valerie's, I was an experienced practitioner. I had been signed off for long and short cases in different psychotherapy modalities. I had also completed a postgraduate certificate at the Tavistock Centre, and had undertaken infant and nursery observations. Despite this, I was shocked to discover the powerful impact that disability had on me as a therapist. I can now understand the power of the "disability transference" (Corbett, 2014): at times I felt completely useless, as if I could not communicate or understand.

With my first patient with intellectual disability, I would meticulously write out my session verbatim and wait for a miracle from Valerie to help me understand it. To begin with, at times, I found her responses equally baffling. How could that statement from a patient, or this one, or this, mean this, or that? I can see that, with Valerie's help, I was learning to inhabit the world of the patient. Valerie was always encouraging, despite me feeling clueless. With my first patient, I could not understand what he was saying to me. Try as I might, I just could not tune in to him. I would smile and nod, because repeating, "I didn't catch that. Could you say that again?" too many times just became irritating for us both. I felt anxious about this, and also anxious for him. How could he make himself understood in the world outside? I really felt that I had the problem, as I could not understand, try as I might. He was very lonely although that was not apparent at first; he was putting on a brave face for me so that I would keep seeing him. Over time, his repetition possibly helped me; he repeated the same things over and over about his dog and his day, and gradually I could work out what he was saying. Later, when he repeated his experiences of the trauma he had suffered, I was also more able to hear him, and not search for the facts but stay with the emotion. I was able to keep going and eventually I reached a shared understanding with the patient. I even reached the point where I had stopped noticing his very real speech impediment. I cannot say that I know what happened, but as a result of that therapeutic time, I can tune in better to what people are saying, and really concentrate and hear them.

Communication skills

Open questions can lead to very short responses, or no meaningful responses, in people with intellectual disability and there are often high levels of compliance and acquiescence. Patients either want to agree with the therapist as they want to please, or they see the therapist as someone in a position of power who has to be agreed with. For doctors in training used to using pro formas of endless, often closed questions, falling back on these familiar patterns is a way out of the silence and awkwardness, especially when there have been a few failed attempts with open questions. When I started out under Valerie's supervision, I was no different. She used to give me very practical examples of what I could say and how to phrase my comments; I would eagerly write the notes down and then wait for opportune moments in the sessions to ask these gems. In those early days, this approach certainly helped to relieve my anxiety around what was happening in the sessions.

Another aspect of my psychotherapy work with people with intellectual disability that I was not prepared for, was the frequency with which I was asked direct, personal questions, such as about my family, whether my parents were alive or dead, about my religion and marital status, and whether or not I had children. Valerie helped me to understand that a question about me might also be a communication about what was on the patient's mind. For example, she would suggest that in response to the question, "Do you have a dad?", it might be helpful for me to say, "I'm really glad you've asked me that question. Perhaps you are missing your dad?"

Valerie's ideas and teaching have been invaluable to my understanding of how to work with people with intellectual disability. Two in particular, which I outline below, have been incredibly helpful. First, her idea, which she developed from traditional psychotherapy, that there are three stages of therapy, consisting of secondary handicap reduction or elimination, the depressive stage, and resolution (Graeme Galton's chapter in this book; Sinason, 1992). Second, her thoughts about modifications to therapy for people with intellectual disability (Sinason, 2003).

The three stages of therapy (Sinason, 1992)

Carlsson (2000) asserts that psychotherapy has been shown to reduce secondary handicap. An example of a secondary handicap is seeming to be more disabled that you are, such as the case of a fifty-year-old patient of mine who used to come to the clinic with her eighty-year-old mother, wearing long socks, an Alice band, and trousers that were too short.

The idea of handicap itself being exaggerated as a form of secondary handicap is explored and evaluated further in research in which Valerie participated (Bichard, Sinason & Usiskin, 1996), which used the Draw-a-Person test (Goodenough, 1926; Harris, 1963) as an outcome measure for children who had had two years of psychoanalytic psychotherapy. At the end of the two years the children showed an increase in mental age (when actual age was accounted for) although it was not a significant result. The

WAIS (IQ) score (Carlsson, 2000) did not change although many subjective differences, as well as an increase in attention (see Graeme Galton's chapter in this book), were noted as improvements after eighteen months of therapy.

More recent research (Shepherd & Beail, 2017) also explores outcomes of therapeutic interventions, including psychodynamic and psychoanalytic approaches, for people with intellectual disabilities. It is to be hoped that such research, though not without its challenges, will continue.

The depressive stage is not clinical depression as psychiatrists would understand it; rather, it is a stage when some of the defences, previously used to ward off painful and difficult feelings, are starting to break down with the result that the patient may go through a difficult patch, with their behaviours worsening or their mental state dipping. The depressive stage can begin at any time during therapy and can take longer to achieve in people with intellectual disability. Valerie would comment that once it is achieved, a further minimum of three months of therapy is needed to achieve resolution. Some patients never achieve resolution of the depressive stage, but need the ongoing containment of support from another person, and it may be that this support could be provided by experienced care staff. A therapist may need to work with the staff to prepare them for the depressive stage when the patient may become worse and staff may decide not to bring the patient to therapy anymore, thus ending the therapy prematurely.

Modifications to therapy for people with intellectual disabilities (Sinason, 2003)

Valerie highlighted the following:

* the need for warmth and friendliness
* to attend to the possibility of silence feeling persecutory to the patient with learning disability
* to recognise that real life difficulties can intrude into the therapy and this may necessitate slightly looser boundaries
* that part of the therapist's role is to act as a therapeutic facilitator with the outside world
* that having a disability can lead to direct psychological consequences such as: more fragile emotional attachments; a slower development of a sense of self; and the realisation of a lifelong dependency.

Over the years, Valerie's voice has become internalised in my head, to the extent that it is as if I can hear her speaking to me from time to time. This experience is, in itself, a reflection of the psychotherapeutic process, by which the patient internalises the relational experience they have had with their therapist, and can draw on this as a resource to support them in their everyday life.

Assessment

After about two years of having Valerie as a supervisor, she asked me to join her in assessing patients for psychotherapy prior to their commencing therapy. Unfortunately though, these patients were then usually placed on a waiting list for an available therapist unless the patient was happy to attend a group, in which there were usually one or two spaces available.

If, as sometimes happened, the patient arrived alone for his or her assessment, I would have the following experience: although the patient lived alone, and was, to all intents and purposes, self-sufficient, I would find them unable to explain coherently why they were there or who had referred them, or any clear narrative about their day or week. They might also launch into a story about people who constantly bullied them. I would think: How did they get to the appointment? Who was looking after them to stop them from being bullied? Were they really being bullied? Could any of what they say be true? My thoughts could spiral into a need to know facts.

Beside me, Valerie would sit calmly, nodding and encouraging. She would tell the patient they were brave to come on their own and see us when they had not met us before. She would say, for example, "It sounds like you're worrying a lot about these people who hurt you, and would you like some help to think about that?" It was only later that she might ask how they had travelled to the appointment, and how they were planning to get home, and whether or not there was a carer waiting for them outside. Valerie was able to accept and bear the not knowing, and respond instead to the emotional needs of the patient; this was her first task.

New trainees in initial therapy sessions often experience what I experienced above, where they get stuck trying to verify facts and establish whether things have really happened or not. In these situations, trainees ask lots of questions and patients often speak very little. The patients can often get flustered and anxious, and can be confused by questioning and misunderstand what is happening. When their emotional needs are met, however, this feeds into building the trusting therapeutic relationship, making the patient more likely to engage in therapy and want to come back to sessions.

Premature endings

Endings are an important part of therapy. I have often found, and some-times acknowledge in myself, a strong wish for therapy to end. Sessions can feel repetitious; this is a key feature of therapy with someone with intellectual disability and often a necessary coping strategy for them to deal with memory or attention difficulties. Also, it can be a way for the patient to check that the therapist understands, as they may feel that the therapist has not understood or listened to the emotional needs behind their statements, so the patient needs to repeat these until the therapist does understand. In well-established therapy, I have heard more senior trainees, who are more confident and able to question, say things like, "I can't see how I am helping him. He is so keen, turning up early. He tells me it's helping but he just repeats the same things every week. I can't understand what he is saying half the time anyway. I think we should finish." I can understand my senior trainees' point of view as it can be frustrating work requiring intense concentration. It can also be incredibly painful for the therapist and wanting to end therapy can be a powerful response to the feeling of helplessness and the sense of uselessness. Countertransference feelings can be very powerful, particularly in work with those who have reduced verbal communication. Feelings of helplessness and confusion can be so overwhelming that therapy may end prematurely. The result of this can be that patients who are thought to be doing fine and not needing any more support, continue turning up for help.

David O'Driscoll and I have observed that the psychotherapy supervision group we run brings about personal and professional changes in the doctors who attend. Their experience of being with a patient week after week, listening and thinking and then getting a new perspective from us about what is going on, can support them in finding a way through the confusion and feelings of inadequacy. It can be a humbling and profound experience. It also makes doctors less anxious and fearful of working with people with intellectual disability, and improves their communication skills generally.

Group therapy

As a co-therapist with Valerie and Sheila Hollins (see Sheila Hollins' chapter in this book) in a group for men and women with intellectual disabilities, I learnt the value of being a therapeutic facilitator in the real world, outside of the therapy space. For example, I would write letters for individuals from the group. All the group members would then sign their name or make their mark at the end of these. Everyone from the group enjoyed sticking up for each other, and helping to voice concerns. The letters were, for example, to the local optician to request new glasses for someone who had both lenses broken and taped up, or to a social worker to request to move house, or to voice the experience that someone in somebody's life was shouting at them. The letters produced amazing results and helped the group to feel powerful in a way that they were not usually, as individuals who could not make themselves understood outside of the group.

Whilst the group was going on, Valerie would often make a phone call on behalf of the group or an individual from the group. Everyone enjoyed these calls; they appreciated that she would do this for them, and that they could hear what was being said and that they were not being excluded. I have learnt never to underestimate the power of a letter expressing the patient's own words, or a telephone call made in front of a patient, voicing their concerns.

Valerie would often go out of her way to explain to me and other colleagues her view of therapy, and to set out clearly the aims and processes of group therapy for people with intellectual disability. These were:

- to assist emotional maturation
- to reduce secondary handicaps: usually people improve in their ability to relate to others and in their ability to share time and attention
- that the stages of therapy take longer to reach than in individual work
- that therapists have to be more active in ensuring understanding and making connections
- that, if possible, it is best to have two therapists facilitating a group, as this helps when people arrive late or need the toilet, so that the rest of the group are not left alone. Also, this means that the group can continue with fewer breaks over difficult holiday periods.

I learnt so much from my experience being a co-therapist in the group with Valerie and Sheila (for Sheila's influence on my professional career and outlook, I would need to write another chapter). For example, a member who I shall call Amy for confidentiality reasons, joined our mixed gender group from her previous women-only group which had ended (I had also been a therapist in this previous group with another doctor at the same stage of his training as myself). Amy had rarely spoken in this previous group, although she had turned up every week without fail, and had generally arrived early. We did wonder, though, whether this was because the carers were bringing her because they thought they should, rather than because she actually wanted to be there. Consent to treatment is not always clear when a patient has intellectual disability, as discussed in Beail (2016). Most importantly, assent and willingness to attend the sessions is needed. When Amy was asked directly if she wanted to join the new group, she would clearly nod and, again, turned up regularly and on time.

Valerie succeeded where others had not: as Amy experienced Valerie's unconditional, positive warmth and her regard for her, she became able to voice her thoughts aloud. Valerie would say, for example, "You really want to be here; it means a lot to you to be in this group." In response, Amy would nod vigorously and smile. "You are so courageous even to come here. You can't say what's on your mind at the moment, but you will be able to when you get to know us all better and can trust us." As the weeks passed, Amy began to speak in the group and I remember how amazed I was and how grateful; because of her previous silence, my doubts about her consent had been a burden I had not even realised I was carrying. Amy had been taken into an institution at the age of four and had never gone back home to live with her family again. This had led to a profound acquiescence and an inability to voice her own thoughts and feelings, or possibly even to identify her own feelings and put a name to them. She had just been a vast, sad, unknown inside, with a smiling face (the handicapped smile) on the outside. Valerie's empathic and supportive approach helped her feel safe enough and valued enough to begin to use her own voice, and to connect with her own feelings, and believe that, after all, it could be worthwhile to share these.

Another elderly man, Martin (again, a pseudonym), who had been deprived in a different way, also benefited from the group. He had been kept at home rather than being put into an institution; however, he had grown up with so many siblings that he had often had no decent clothes and had had to share a bed with five or six other children. It had always been cold and he had often wet the bed, incurring the anger of his siblings. Even though now he no longer had to be cold or wear dirty clothes or many layers, he still kept the heating off and wore such clothes, and also continued to put up with things that were broken. As a result, people complained about the state of his flat and his personal hygiene.

Martin gradually began to enjoy being in the group and being able to advocate for others when he often found this difficult to do so for himself. We also came to see his lovely sense of humour. Gradually, we noticed that he had started to take time with his appearance and had begun, in little ways, to smarten up, wearing new clothes and having better personal hygiene. He was proud of being in the group and gradually he also took a small pride about the way he looked, although, there were still times when he would slip back into familiar patterns.

Change

When I became a consultant, and, as such, began to operate as an independent practitioner, I thought about how I had been changed by my experience of working with Valerie. I wanted to obtain more concrete evidence of how being a group co-therapist can develop one's skills as a mental health practitioner. I wanted to start a group and asked the community team if anyone would be interested in being a co-therapist. A community nurse and an occupational therapist came forward. Both were experienced in their professional roles but neither had engaged in psychoanalytic psychotherapy before. I asked them to keep reflective diaries and we had supervision from a group analyst for a short time before moving into more peer group supervision.

When they came to look at their reflective diaries after a year of our working together, both colleagues declared that it had changed their clinical practice. One said she had learnt to bear the pain of someone being acutely distressed and crying, and was even able to listen to suicidal feelings, alone, without rushing out to seek help immediately, which she would have done previously. She realised that what she had been looking for, in fact, was help to relieve her own feelings of impotency, inadequacy, and anxiety. She was initially surprised when sometimes nothing further needed be done other than listening, and that people then stopped crying and sometimes came up with ways forward for themselves.

My other colleague described situations in which she had always sprung into action, problem-solving and finding solutions for people who had come to her for help. She explained that she had felt responsible for them and that she had needed to sort things out. Now, however, she was able to sit back and listen, and work with the person to come up with solutions of their own. She was aware that these were much more likely to work because the person was empowered by the process and invested in it.

I often wish I had kept a reflective diary of my own when I had first begun to work with Valerie. I could definitely identify that it changed me; it allowed me to move into the position of not knowing and to be comfortable with that, of realising that there is time and that if I do not understand what a patient is saying to me this time, maybe the next time I will, or that eventually I will. In this work each of us finds different parts of ourselves that change, and we find different capacities and tolerances. I remember Valerie's example of this was when she told me that she could never tolerate spitting: she could cope with other bodily fluids, but not this one. I found it strange at the time, as Valerie could tolerate so much and had such a large capacity for seeing positives. In fact, I have never met anyone else who can genuinely compete with her in this regard. Now I look back on this, however, and see that she was right when she said that we can all tolerate different things in varying amounts.

I feel that now in my career I have the best of both worlds: combining and balancing the world of intellectual disability psychiatry with psychodynamic thinking and practice. I am very fortunate to be able to carry the voices of my supervisors in my mind. It is my privilege to have had the opportunity to work with Valerie so closely, and to have learnt so much from her. To paraphrase Allan Schore, who used the phrase in his book's title, I see her as a truly great practitioner of the "art of psychotherapy" (2012).

References

Beail, N. (Ed.) (2016). Psychological therapies and people who have intellectual disabilities. *Commissioning Team for the Faculties for Intellectual Disabilities of the Royal College of Psychiatrists and the Division of Clinical Psychology of the British Psychological Society*. Leicester: The British Psychological Society.

Beail, N., & Jahoda, A. (2012). Working with people: direct interventions. In: E. Emerson, C. Hatton, K. Dickson, R. Gone, A. Caine, & J. Bromley (Eds.), *Clinical Psychology and People with Intellectual Disabilities* (2nd edn) (pp. 121–140). Chichester: Wiley-Blackwell.

Bichard, S. H., Sinason, V., & Usiskin, J. (1996). Measuring change in mentally retarded clients in long-term psychoanalytic psychotherapy. 1. The Draw-A-Person test. *National Association for Dual Diagnosis (NADD) Newsletter*, *13*(5): 6–11.

Carlat, D. J. (1998). The psychiatric review of symptoms: a screening tool for family physicians. *American Family Physician*, *58*: 1617–1624.

Carlsson, B. (2000). Psychoanalytic psychotherapy with intellectually disabled adults – evaluation by using projective tests: a collaboration project between a psychiatric clinic and the services for mentally handicapped. *National Association for Dual Diagnosis (NADD) Bulletin*, *3*(5): Article 3.

Corbett, A. (2014). The disability transference: transference and countertransference issues. *Disabling Perversions: Forensic Psychotherapy with People with Intellectual Disabilities*. London: Karnac.

Dodd, K., Joyce, T., Nixon, J., Jennison, J., & Heneage, C. (2011). Improving access to psychological therapies (IAPT): are they applicable to people with intellectual disabilities? *Advances in Mental Health and Intellectual Disabilities*, *5*(2): 29–34.

Goodenough, F. L. (1926). *Measurement of Intelligence by Drawings*. New York: World Book Company.

Harris, D. B. (1963). *Children's Drawings as a Measure of Intellectual Maturity: A Revision and Extension of the Goodenough Draw-a-Man Test*. New York: Harcourt, Brace and World.

Royal College of Psychiatrists. (2004). *Psychotherapy and Learning Disability (Council Report CR116)*. London: Royal College of Psychiatrists.

Schore, A. N. (2012). *The Science of the Art of Psychotherapy*. New York: Norton.

Shepherd, C., & Beail, N. (2017). A systematic review of the effectiveness of psychoanalysis, psychoanalytic and psychodynamic psychotherapy with adults with intellectual and developmental disabilities: progress and challenges. *Psychoanalytic Psychotherapy*, *31*(1): 94–117.

Sinason, V. (1992). *Mental Handicap and the Human Condition: New Approaches from the Tavistock*. London: Free Association Books.

Sinason, V. (2003). *Learning Disability as Trauma and the Impact of Learning Disability on Trauma*. PhD thesis. University of London.

Wing, J. K., Cooper, J. E., & Sartorius, N. (1974). *The Measurement and Classification of Psychiatric Symptoms*. Cambridge: Cambridge University Press.

Chapter 8

Building insight and changing lives

The contribution of Valerie Sinason to the history of disability psychotherapy

David O'Driscoll

When I was a team leader in a residential unit for adults with intellectual disabilities, we had a service user called "Fred" (not his real name). My team and I struggled to understand him. Most of the time Fred was fine and got on with his life. He would potter around the house waiting for his money to get cigarettes, or he would go for a pint. He declined any offers of alternative activities. Every now and then, seemingly out of nowhere, Fred would fly into a rage, threatening violence to anyone within his range. These rages could last up to eight hours and were very difficult to be with and to manage. A striking feature of these episodes was the fact that the focus of Fred's rage was males, either male members of staff or other male residents. The only way we could contain Fred was to isolate him within his part of the house. We looked for support from the local intellectual disability service but they offered little. Their treatment suggestions focused on changing his medication, which could be administered "as needed" (prn), or using a behavioural strategy. We needed extra assistance in understanding and helping him and this is when I first came across Valerie Sinason.

In this chapter I will attempt to put Sinason within her historical context. Today, she is recognised as the main innovator of a psychoanalytic approach for people with intellectual disabilities, a group of patients who, historically, have attracted only intermittent psychological interest. In my view, she is a true pioneer in the field of psychoanalysis and has not yet obtained the wider recognition she is due. Indeed, I find it bewildering that her contribution has not been acknowledged in recent histories of psychoanalysis (Schwartz, 1999; Zaretsky, 2004). Her work with Fred and with his support network, of which I was a part, reflected her open, inclusive, generous, and concerned approach. It had a big impact on me at the time. I had just finished my social work training in 1994, and could not see how psychoanalytic ideas could be of relevance. If pressed to define the way in which I thought about psycho-logical support for people with intellectual disabilities, I would have described myself as a "person-centred, Rogerian" practitioner (Rogers, 1967). Rogers was a hugely influential founder of the humanistic approach to psychology. I often struggled with the professional focus on behavioural interventions that I experienced at that time, when there was no such thing as "disability psychotherapy".

Fred had a mild intellectual disability and Fragile X syndrome. This syndrome has a number of features including very distinctive physical characteristics such as an elongated face, large or protruding ears, and behavioural characteristics which included stereotypic movements such as hand-flapping and social anxiety. Fred was conscious of the way his condition made him look, and this added to the awkwardness he felt in social situations. He had experienced much trauma in childhood, having been abandoned by his family. There was also some anecdotal evidence that he had been abused although Fred made no mention of this. Since childhood, Fred had lived in specialist local authority accommodation. He had no contact with his family and we knew nothing about them. He had been living with the same group of residents for some time and had a settled team of staff supporting him. The high point of his day was going to the pub. It was an opportunity to be with men, and he often tried to join in, laughing at jokes he did not fully understand or talking about football even though he was not interested in it. "Did you see the game last night? Wasn't it good?" he would ask. It seemed to me that his questions acted as a kind of pseudo-social exchange, belying the emptiness beneath. On the whole, Fred had a settled pattern of living; his various routines centred round the pub, cigarettes, and watching the television. As a team leader I was concerned when he flew into his rages, not only because of the awful impact of his rage upon Fred himself, but also because of the significant stress and anxiety it caused the staff team. I noticed how we tiptoed around Fred at times, pandering to his every need, because of our fear that he might "kick off" or that we might "set him off". We had the option of medicating Fred if he did become enraged and we did use it despite the fact that I felt uncomfortable about this. Levitas and Hurley (2007) studied the ways in which support staff use medication in these situations. They discuss countertransference as a factor in the over-medication of people with intellectual disabilities, suggesting that support workers are often driven to administer medication by their own anxieties and fear, rather than through responding to any medical need in the service user.

One day, looking through Fred's file, I came across a note from Valerie Sinason, who had seen him when he was a child, and had described him as traumatised. This was the first time "trauma" had been used in a diagnostic context in relation to Fred. I subsequently arranged an appointment for Fred to see Valerie but he refused to go. At that point, Valerie invited me, as a trainee psychotherapist, to attend the Mental Handicap Workshop at the Tavistock Clinic (Stokes & Sinason, 1992) to talk about Fred there. This was a multidisciplinary group which met weekly to listen to case presentations. I agreed rather nervously. I was struck by the diversity of the professionals in attendance at the workshop: psychiatrists, nurses, teachers, and social workers. Valerie explained her view to me that, in this field, all staff shared a common goal which was concern for their patients. She said she simply wanted to see if she, too, could help. This underlined her philosophy for the workshop.

In my presentation on Fred, I included some background information and some examples of dialogue with him which showed his wariness and distrust. For example, I had asked him to have a private one-to-one discussion in the office with me but he had refused to even come in, saying, "Some dogs are out to bite me." He had laughed as he said this. There was always something deeply uncomfortable about his smiling and laughing. This concern about dogs seemed to symbolise an anxiety that I later came to understand as annihilation anxiety (Sinason, 1992). Valerie initially focused on Fred's anxiety: she spoke about the dog-biting and wondered aloud what Fred might be frightened about losing. Maybe, she ventured, it was to do with a "castration anxiety". I remember this because, as a staff team, we were all conscious of Fred's masculinity and tried to find ways of supporting this. In his rages, he would threaten anyone within his vision, although, as mentioned above, he was mainly focused on the men. This helped us to recognise the fear he felt about the male workers. It can be difficult as a support worker to recognise such negative transference. Although the support worker is being helpful and kind, he or she may be experienced as threatening or malign, due to the past experiences of the service user.

Sinason's ideas on trauma are at the core of her thinking. She put forward the view that traumatic symptoms are significantly under-recognised in people with intellectual disabilities. There is nothing new about psychological trauma; indeed, Trigg (2016) recounts that Samuel Pepys writes in his diaries that, following the Great Fire of 1666, he was having difficulty sleeping as he kept seeing flames. In setting out diagnostic criteria for trauma, the *Diagnostic and Statistical Manual of Mental Disorders (DSM-5)* (American Psychiatric Association, 2013) identifies psychological trauma as occurring when a person experiences an event outside their normal range of experience that would be markedly distressing to almost anyone. This includes a serious threat of harm to life or one's physical integrity. Sinason is more influenced by Freud's view, drawing on his and Breuer's work, *Studies in Hysteria* (1895), to describe trauma as "a shocking experience that breaks through the protective shield of the psyche and cannot be processed. Freud saw it as a foreign body within the self" (Sinason, 1992, p. 327). In terms of people with intellectual disabilities, if there is no organic damage, trauma can be an actual cause of the intellectual disabilities, for example, via abuse or violence, substance abuse, or poverty.

Sinason also observed from her clinical work how the disability itself is experienced as a trauma:

> Opening your eyes ... to the realisation that you will not be an Austen, Einstein, Madonna or Picasso can be painful enough to the ordinary adolescent. Opening your eyes to admitting you look, sound, walk, talk,

move or think differently from the ordinary, average person … takes
greater reserves of courage, honesty and toleration of one's envy.

(1992, p. 20)

Perhaps Fred was protecting himself from the knowledge of his difference
when he would distance himself from other residents, rejecting any activities,
day services, or leisure outings. When he did participate, he would always put
himself apart from the other residents. The staff team often felt that he saw
himself as a staff member.

Valerie wondered if Fred was also traumatised by the fact that he had an
intellectual disability. This idea is a radical and provocative one, even today;
I noticed that it was a difficult concept for some of the staff team to think
about. Sinason (1986) discusses the role of unconscious guilt that the non-
disabled support worker may feel about not having a disability: they may try
to minimise the differences between the disabled client and themselves by
claiming that everyone is the same.

The staff team had conflicting views about what Fred could actually do.
We were never sure of his abilities. We tried to protect him from the shame of
failure by not pushing him to do things with which he might struggle. Sinason
is helpful here as she characterises intellectual disability as a fluid state: disability can vary greatly in individuals throughout the day, with emotions
greatly affecting state of mind and levels of competence. In services, there
is a tendency to ascribe emotional difficulties experienced by a person with
intellectual disabilities to the disability rather than to an emotional state or
to particular experiences. Sinason describes "secondary handicaps" (1986,
p. 135) as having a protective function in shielding the self from the unbearable memory of trauma. Valerie helped me to see that there were a number
of factors behind Fred's rages. Key was his hatred of his disability and his
envy of the male workers in particular. Understanding that the secondary
handicap further reduces the ability for thought, helped me understand why
it was difficult to get Fred to think about these painful matters.

Sinason wrote about the handicapped smile as a fixed grin: "People who are
close to grief and cannot bear it encourage happiness and smiling" (Sinason,
1992, p. 141). The staff team understood this concept easily as it was something they recognised from their work with people with intellectual disabilities. Fred had an ever-present smile – unsettling and uncomfortable at times,
even sickening. I often wondered about his experiences of abuse. I remember
feeling anxious and uncertain about how I, as a support worker, could possibly talk with him about this.

In discussing my presentation at the workshop, Valerie opened up a new
world of thinking to me: new possibilities and new insights, which I then fed
back to my staff team. This led to changes in their relationships with Fred.
They become more aware of his personal predicament, some of his inner
conflicts, and importantly, how they were experienced by him. While his rages

did not stop completely, we observed they were less intense and frequent. The team were able to reflect upon the fears and frustrations stirred by their work with Fred, so that they could contain such feelings, rather than project them. They were calmer and less anxious about him and, I believe, less likely to act on their own feelings. While there was no evidence of staff being abusive, I still remember the stress of being with Fred while he yelled into my face, jabbing his finger at me: "I'm going to do you. You fucking wanker. Wait and see. You wait and see, pal." Valerie's highlighting of Fred's rich internal world, and the rather revolutionary idea at the time that he had an unconscious world, gave the staff team an alternative to the sometimes sterile, behavioural thinking that, in my view, dominated disability services at the time (Stenfert Kroese, Dagnan, & Loumidis, 1997).

After some time, Fred agreed to see a therapist. It should be noted that he chose to see a male therapist which was perhaps a sign of his awareness that something needed to be worked on, not just in the context of his relationship to other men, but also in his relationship to himself as a man. Valerie's input was also hugely significant for me. I had just begun my psychotherapy training and she sparked something in me which resulted in me becoming one of the very few "disability psychotherapists" working in an intellectual disabilities team in the National Health Service today.

Disability psychotherapy

The idea of "disability psychotherapy" has been a long time coming. Several contemporary commentators have noted the historical reluctance of mental health specialists to provide psychotherapy treatment for people with intellectual disabilities (Beail, 1998; Bender, 1993), often referring first to Freud's paper, *On Psychotherapy* (1905) and his comment that, "Those patients who do not possess a reasonable degree of education and reliable character should be refused" (1905, p. 263), and then to the view of Tyson and Sandler (1971) that mental deficiency is generally regarded as a contra-indication for psychoanalysis. For Sinason, the key element is not intelligence but emotional responses. She says, "However crippled someone's external functional intelligence might be, there still can be intact a complex emotional structure and capacity" (1992, p. 74).

In the 1980s, Neville Symington was the first therapist of the modern era to try psychoanalytically oriented psychotherapy with people with intellectual disabilities. I have written elsewhere about the earlier history of this work, which I have experienced as characterised by "moments of curiosity" rather than a sustained, cumulative body of research (O'Driscoll, 2009; O'Driscoll & Walmsley, 2010). Symington's work coincided with an important policy change: the closure of long-stay hospitals for people with intellectual disabilities, which in turn led to the development of the self-advocacy movement in the UK. Symington (1981) honestly discusses his own anxiety and doubts about offering psychotherapy to this client group. He uses his own uncertainty to understand why there had previously been such measly psychoanalytic interest. He says, "There is a strong tendency for people to despair as soon as the word organic is mentioned ... Neurological growth can be stimulated and is not static. What remains static are people's expectations that change can occur" (1981, p. 199). At this time, the Tavistock was beginning to think about conditions not traditionally examined under the psychoanalytic lens. This meant that Sinason was able to develop her ideas with a group of like-minded professionals from a broad section of the learning disability community. One of the criticisms levelled at certain practitioners of psychoanalysis is that they can be insular in their thinking, reluctant to think outside of their own field. While Sinason was trained in the Kleinian tradition, she was not bound by its theory; she drew on many sources, in particular, literature. Indeed, this book is itself testament to her capacity to work alongside, to supervise, and to train a wide range of colleagues, nationally and internationally; it is also testament to the inclusive foundations she, along with Brett Kahr (2000), laid for membership of the Institute of Psychotherapy and Disability (IPD) (2017).

Historical academic perspectives

Sinason's book, *Mental Handicap and the Human Condition* (1992), centres around seven case accounts. The book has been reprinted almost yearly since 1992 and the second edition, with three further chapters, was published in 2010. It is clearly the "go to" book for disability therapists of all persuasions. It has also reached a more diverse professional audience (see Jan Walmsley's chapter in this book), and Sinason's thinking on language and terminology is still as relevant today as ever. Here is her response to the term, "challenging behaviour":

> Like all such words, this had an honourable genesis with a wish to describe the behaviour as a challenge to services rather being pejorative about the person. However, such psycholinguistic processes never succeed. Far from challenging the thinking of the services, the term can become a dustbin term that means "very difficult" so the unique individual emotional pain that is being expressed this way becomes disavowed and denied meaning.
>
> (Sinason, 2013, p. 89)

Mental Handicap and the Human Condition was well received at the time. It had reviews in major journals, including *The International Journal of Psycho-Analysis*, where it was respectfully reviewed by Paola Mariotti (1994). While Sinason was trying to develop interest in the psychoanalytic community, she was also trying to convince the wider mental health community that psycho-analytic psychotherapy could be a useful treatment option for people with intellectual disabilities. There have been a number of studies showing how mental health professionals downplay or ignore mental health problems in people with intellectual disabilities. The context for this is shown via a series of case-based studies with professionals (Reiss, Levitan, & Szyszko, 1982) in which they were told that one group had an IQ in the average range and another group was in the below average range (intellectual disabilities range of 60–70). The latter group was less likely to be diagnosed with an emotional disorder by the professionals and less likely to receive the same array of interventions (in particular, psychological interventions) than the former group. Today, the main intervention is still medication, as evidenced by a recent government report by Public Heath England: "The study shows antipsychotic and antidepressant drugs are being prescribed for people with learning disabilities in England in the absence of the conditions for which they are known to be effective" (Public Health England, 2015, p. 50).

At the time Sinason's book was published, a collection of psychotherapy papers outlining different therapeutic approaches was also published (Waitman & Conboy-Hill, 1992). Since then, however, only two of these approaches, psychodynamic and cognitive behavioural therapy (CBT), have been developed further. This book gave the first historical account of psychotherapy and intellectual disabilities and was the first serious account of our psychological attempts to support this client group. Historical interest of any sort was thin on the ground. It was not until Bender's seminal paper, *The Unoffered Chair* (1993), and the groundbreaking work of the Social History of Learning Disability research group at the Open University in the late 1990s (Atkinson, Jackson, & Walmsley, 1997) that there was some serious academic interest in this history. My own work came much later (O'Driscoll, 2009; O'Driscoll & Walmsley, 2010). Bender's explanation for this exclusion is "that psychotherapy involves intensely relating over quite a long period to another person – a certain kind of intimacy. The giving of this intimacy is more difficult, aversive and more energy consuming when that person is seen as unattractive" (1993, p. 11). American historian, James Trent, records that, "almost all psychodynamically oriented psychiatrists saw the retarded as hardly receptive to psychodynamic insight. Indeed, most psychiatrists … were quick to say, albeit privately, that the mentally retarded were boring" (1994, p. 245).

It is now established that the therapist needs to modify the psychoanalytic technique when working with this client group (Corbett, 2014; Jackson & Beail, 2013). Sinason (2000) addresses some of the challenges in technique. She believes that the therapist needs to work with greater flexibility and willingness to engage with the wider systems. This stands out against the idea of the psychoanalyst as a "blank screen". Sinason describes how the patient needs the analyst not to be the cold or abusive archaic transference figure of the survivor's history but for there to be transparency, warmth, and affect. This is an approach also advocated by her former supervisor and colleague, Anne Alvarez (1992; 2012). Sinason says that in terms of object relations therapy, Alvarez "has shown most forcefully that some deprived and disturbed children need to have presence mentioned as much as absence" (Sinason, 2010, p. 166). The therapist can be a valuable, reparative, and sometimes unique experience of a good object for the very disturbed or deprived client.

The first motto for the Institute for Psychotherapy and Disability was, "treating with respect". This was a mark of how, historically, patients with intellectual disabilities had not been treated with respect. Sinason describes the start of a psychotherapy session with a patient with intellectual disabilities in which the patient is consulted as to his wishes, thereby demonstrating the concept of "treating with respect":

> The therapist came to greet him at the appointment time. She said her full name, Dr Anna Alter (not her real name), and said he could call her Anna or Dr Alter and asked what would he like to be called? He was very excited and said he would like to be called Mr Manning, Mr Morris Manning (also a pseudonym). Dr Alter then asked Mr Manning if he would like the social worker to come in with him at the beginning to join her and the psychiatrist or whether he felt able to come by himself. Mr Manning said he would like his social worker, Ms Worker, to come in with him for the start.
>
> (Sinason, 2017, p. 16)

Neville Symington writes of his struggle to deal with the anxieties of his patient, Harry: "Harry walked round the consulting room. I did not feel at ease just sitting down in my normal chair and watching him, so I used to stand and walk around the room as well" (1986, p. 324). Symington, too, shows respect for his patient by mirroring his actions, thereby showing attunement to his emotional state.

Returning to Fred – when he went to see his male therapist, he was unsurprisingly wary and rather suspicious of him. Fred could not last the traditional fifty-minute session and so often left after twenty-five to thirty-five minutes. I remember feeling quite critical of this, believing Fred needed to be challenged a bit more; maybe this was more to do with my frustrations. Today, I agree with Corbett (2014) and others who talk about how the client should be free to leave although the therapist needs to be there for his or her allotted, agreed session time.

Sex and learning disabilities

Hollins and Sinason (2000) refer to sex as one of the "three secrets" of people with intellectual disabilities. It is a taboo for them in that the development of a healthy sense of a sexual self is often fraught with obstacles (Cottis, 2009b).

There may be an unconscious sense that the sexual act which led to the disabled life was in some way "bad". As Sinason says, "...there is unresolved anger and fear in some societies that the sexual and procreative connection between a man and a woman could lead to a damaged offspring" (1992, p. 257). Early attachment difficulties may make the forming of mutually satisfying relationships more difficult (Cottis, 2009b) and the opportunities for free and full sexual expression are often hampered by the facts of institutional care and supported living. It is a complex area and one which therapists in this field will almost always need to address.

Fred liked to buy "engagement rings", some cheap and some not so cheap, which he would keep in his room. Sometimes he would bring them out to show me, saying: "You seen this, Dave? She will like that." I would ask him who the ring was for but he could not or would not answer. Fred never had a relationship with a woman, nor did he seem to show much interest in having one, so this was a surprising development for us. We were always concerned that Fred had bought the rings for one of the female staff. We were mindful of the fact that we did not want to shame or humiliate him, so we always treated him and his fantasies with respect. We also wondered if the episodes of rage were linked in any way to his sexuality, feelings of sexual frustration, and lack of sexual contact. Again, the question arose of whether Fred had been sexually abused. This highlighted to us the dilemmas and challenges of supporting someone's sexuality.

Today, it seems sexual abuse is everywhere. It is a rare week when we do not hear of it and its prevalence in some of our powerful and trusted institutions, and even in some of its trusted individuals. This has not always been the case. 1992 saw the first significant research into the incidence of sexual abuse against people with intellectual disabilities (Brown & Turk, 1993). Through her work, Valerie has played a highly significant role in highlighting this issue and bringing it to greater attention. In her writing about the ways in which her psychoanalytically informed psychotherapy helps patients with intellectual disabilities who have been abused, for example in the case of "Ali" (1992, p. 104), Valerie opened the door to providing the kind of support and therapy to people with intellectual disabilities that is provided for others who have experienced the trauma of sexual abuse. It is her view that working psychoanalytically with people with intellectual disabilities is clinically important and also part of a wider struggle for equality, justice, and empowerment (Alan Corbett's interview with Valerie in this book; Cottis, 2009a).

Despite Valerie's work, though, there are many current risks to progress in the care of people with intellectual disabilities (Heslop & Lovell, 2013; Jan Walmsley's chapter in this book). My understanding is that the service now supporting Fred has been switched from local authority care to a private supplier. He has fewer hours of support and the pay of his carers is declining in real terms. In such circumstances one must wonder about the quality of support he is receiving. There is currently a mixed picture of care. A recently published UN Report outlines the UK's failure to uphold the Convention on the Rights of People with Disabilities (2016). The report shows that in the UK we are still struggling to find ways of supporting disabled people to live even "good enough" lives. There is also recent evidence that austerity has hit people with disabilities disproportionately hard (O'Hara, 2016). In addition, there have been the examples of scandals at Winterbourne View care home (Hill, 2012) and others (see Jan Walmsley's chapter in this book). Despite all of this, the place of people with intellectual disabilities in society has changed for the better in a number of ways. There have been advances in legislation pertaining to human rights, such as the Human Rights Act 1998 (UK Government, 2017c) and the implementation of the Disability Discrimination Acts of 1995 and 2005 (UK Government, 2017a; 2017b).

This varied picture is also reflected in the "disability psychotherapy" world. There is now a widespread acceptance that people with intellectual disability can use psychotherapy, and some research that people benefit from psychodynamic psychotherapy (Beail, 2016; Sinason, 1992). There is a growing catalogue of literature (Corbett, 2014; Cottis, 2009a; 2009b) but there is still uncertainty and fear. I was one of the co-authors of the MA in Psychotherapy and Disability at Hertfordshire University which could not run due to lack of applicants. This was hugely disappointing to me personally as we had been through an exhaustive academic acceptance process. Despite this, training in disability psychotherapy continues in other ways: for example, the Institute for Psychotherapy and Disability runs regular short courses and seminars; also, my NHS colleague, Dr Georgina Parkes, and I have set up clinical supervision groups in our NHS service, offering long and short courses to psychiatric trainees, and these are popular and successful (see Georgina Parkes' chapter in this book). The Bowlby Centre's (2017) four-year adult psychotherapy training also includes a mandatory module on "disability psychotherapy", which I teach.

One of the main dynamics underpinning the development of disability psychotherapy has been its stop–start nature. There have been brilliant pioneers across the decades, but very little development from one generation to the next, with little written theory with which to develop future thinking (Jackson & Beail, 2013). However, through her writing, Sinason has developed core theoretical concepts that are continuing to be developed by the next generation. As important, perhaps, is her highly relational therapeutic style which stems from her personal characteristics. She likes people and is a gifted communicator. Because of this, she has not continued in the tradition of brilliant, but isolated, disability pioneers. The impact of her thinking on Fred and those working with him is just one of hundreds of examples of how Sinason's theories are having a profound impact, both on how services are run, and more crucially, on how lives are led. Sinason (2010) has written that while the psychoanalytic pioneers may often get the blame for any exclusion criteria, such as the previously mentioned example from Freud's *On Psychotherapy*

(Freud, 1905, cited by Sinason, 2010, p. 51), and have arguably hindered the continuity of progress of psychotherapy for people with learning disabilities, it is the responsibility of the upcoming generation to question and develop this thinking. This is a philosophy that Valerie has never hesitated to put into practice herself and I remain hopeful that the coming decades will see a blossoming of the ethos of humanity, respect, and equality, that she has espoused through all her work with patients with disabilities.

References

Alvarez, A. (1992). *Live Company: Psychoanalytic Psychotherapy with Autistic, Borderline, Deprived and Abused Children*. Hove: Routledge.

Alvarez, A. (2012). *The Thinking Heart: Three Levels of Psychoanalytic Therapy with Disturbed Children*. Hove: Routledge.

American Psychiatric Association. (2013). *Diagnostic and Statistical Manual of Mental Disorders (DSM-5)* (5th edn). Arlington, VA: American Psychiatric Association.

Atkinson, D., Jackson, M., & Walmsley, J. (1997). *Forgotten Lives: Exploring the History of Learning Disability*. Kidderminster: Bild Publications.

Beail, N. (1998). Outcome of psychoanalysis, psychoanalytic and psychodynamic psychotherapy with people with intellectual disabilities: a review. *Changes, 13*: 186–191.

Beail, N. (Ed.) (2016). Psychological therapies and people who have intellectual disabilities. *Commissioning Team for the Faculties for Intellectual Disabilities of the Royal College of Psychiatrists and the Division of Clinical Psychology of the British Psychological Society*. Leicester: The British Psychological Society.

Bender, M. (1993). The unoffered chair: the history of therapeutic disdain towards people with a learning disability. *Clinical Psychology Forum, 54*: 7–12.

The Bowlby Centre. (2017). www.thebowlbycentre.org.uk/ [30.10.17].

Brown, H., & Turk, V. (1993). The sexual abuse of adults with learning disabilities: results of a two year incidence survey. *Journal of Applied Research in Learning Disabilities, 6*(3): 193–216.

Cottis, T. (2009a). Life support or intensive care? endings and outcomes in psychotherapy for people with intellectual disabilities. In: T. Cottis (Ed.), *Intellectual Disability, Trauma and Psychotherapy* (pp. 189–204). Hove: Routledge.

Cottis. T. (2009b). Love hurts: the emotional impact of intellectual disability and sexual abuse on a family. In: T. Cottis (Ed.), *Intellectual Disability, Trauma and Psychotherapy* (pp. 75–89). Hove: Routledge.

Corbett, A. (2014). *Disabling Perversions: Forensic Psychotherapy with People with Intellectual Disabilities*. London: Karnac.

Freud, S. (1905). On psychotherapy (1905 [1904]). *Mschr. Psychiat. Neurol., 8*(4 & 5): 285–310 & 408–467. [reprinted in: *The Standard Edition of the Complete Psychological Works of Sigmund Freud, Volume VII (1901–1905): A Case of Hysteria, Three Essays on Sexuality and Other Works* (pp. 257–270) (trans. J. Strachey). London: Vintage, 2001.]

Freud, S., & Breuer, J. (1895). *Studies in Hysteria*. Leipzig and Vienna: Deuticke. [reprinted London: Penguin, 2004. (trans. N. Luckhurst)].

Heslop, P., & Lovell, A. (2013). *Understanding and Working with People with Learning Disabilities who Self-injure*. London: Jessica Kingsley.

Hill, A. (2012). Winterbourne View care home staff jailed for abusing residents. *The Guardian*, 26 October. www.theguardian.com/society/2012/oct/26/winterbourne-view-care-staff-jailed [last accessed 30.10.17].

Hollins, S., & Sinason, V. (2000). Psychotherapy, learning disabilities and trauma: new perspectives. *British Journal of Psychiatry*, *176*(1): 32–36.

Institute of psychotherapy and disability. (2017). https://instpd.org.uk/ [last accessed 30.10.17].

Jackson, T., & Beail, N. (2013). The practice of individual psychodynamic psychotherapy with people who have intellectual disabilities. *Psychoanalytic Psychotherapy*, *27*: 108–123.

Kahr, B. (2000). Towards the creation of disability psychotherapists. *Psychotherapist Review*, *2*: 420–423.

Levitas, A. S., & Hurley, A. D. (2007). Overmedication as a manifestation of counter-transference. *Mental Health Aspects of Developmental Disabilities*, *10*(2): 1–5.

Mariotti, P. (1994). Mental Handicap and the Human Condition: by Valerie Sinason. *The International Journal of Psycho-Analysis*, *75*: 168–170.

O'Driscoll, D. (2009). Psychotherapy and intellectual disability: a historical view. In: T. Cottis (Ed.), *Intellectual Disability, Trauma and Psychotherapy* (pp. 9–28). Hove: Routledge.

O'Driscoll, D., & Walmsley, J. (2010). Absconding from hospitals: a means of resistance? *British Journal of Learning Disabilities*, *38*: 97–102.

O'Hara, J. (2016). Austerity has hit disabled people hardest – now they're fighting back. *The Guardian*, 24 February. Available at: www.theguardian.com/public-leaders-network/2016/feb/24/austerity-disabled-people-norfolk-council-care-act [last accessed 30.10.17].

Public Health England. (2015). *Prescribing of psychotropic drugs to people with learning disabilities and/or autism by general practitioners in England*. London: Public Health England. Available at: www.bild.org.uk/EasySiteWeb/GatewayLink.aspx?alId=6629 [last accessed 8.9.2017].

Reiss, S., Levitan, G. W., & Szyszko, J. (1982). Emotional disturbance and mental retardation: diagnostic overshadowing. *American Journal of Mental Deficiency*, *86*: 567–574.

Rogers, C. (1967). *On Becoming a Person*. London: Constable & Company. [reprinted London: Constable, 2004].

Schwartz, J. (1999). *Cassandra's Daughter: A History of Psychoanalysis in Europe and America*. London: Penguin.

Sinason, V. (1986). Secondary mental handicap and its relationship to trauma. *Psychoanalytic Psychotherapy*, *2*(2): 131–54.

Sinason, V. (1992). *Mental Handicap and the Human Condition: New Approaches from the Tavistock*. London: Free Association Books.

Sinason, V. (2010). *Mental Handicap and the Human Condition: An Analytical Approach to Intellectual Disability* (2nd edn). London: Karnac.

Sinason, V. (2013). Psychological approaches in practice 1. In: P. Heslop & A. Lovell (Eds.), *Understanding and Working with People with Learning Disabilities who Self-injure*. London. Jessica Kingsley.

Sinason, V. (2017). The breathing boundary. *British Journal of Psychotherapy*, *33*(1): 6–16.

Stenfert Kroese, B., Dagnan, D., & Loumidis, K. (Eds.) (1997). *Cognitive-Behaviour Therapy for People with Learning Disabilities*. Hove: Routledge.

Stokes, J., & Sinason, V. (1992). Secondary mental handicap as a defence. In: A. Waitman & S. Conboy-Hill (Eds.), *Psychotherapy and Mental Handicap* (pp. 46–58). London: Sage.

Symington, N. (1981). The psychotherapy of a subnormal patient. *British Journal of Medical Psychology, 54*: 187–199.

Symington, N. (1986). *The Analytic Experience: Lectures from the Tavistock*. London: Free Association Books.

Trent Jr., J. W. (1994). *Inventing the Feeble Mind: A History of Mental Retardation in America*. Berkeley: University of California Press.

Trigg, S. (2016). Samuel Pepys and the Great Fire of London: trauma and emotion, private and public. In: J. Spinks & C. Zika (Eds.), *Disaster, Death and the Emotions in the Shadow of the Apocalypse, 1400–1700*. London: Palgrave Macmillan.

Tyson, R. L., & Sandler, J. (1971). Problems in the selection of patients for psychoanalysis: comments on the application of 'indications', 'suitability' and 'analysability'. *British Journal of Medical Psychology, 44*: 211–228.

UK Government. (2017a). *Disability Discrimination Act 1995*. Norwich: The Stationery Office. Available at: www.legislation.gov.uk/ukpga/1995/50 [last accessed 8.9.2017].

UK Government. (2017b). *Disability Discrimination Act 2005*. Norwich: The Stationery Office. Available at: www.legislation.gov.uk/ukpga/2005/13/contents [last accessed 8.9.2017].

UK Government. (2017c). *Human Rights Act 1998*. Norwich: The Stationery Office. Available at: www.legislation.gov.uk/ukpga/1998/42/contents [last accessed 8.9.2017].

United Nations Convention on the Rights of Persons with Disabilities. (2016). *Inquiry Concerning the United Kingdom of Great Britain and Northern Ireland carried out by the Committee under Article 6 of the Optional Protocol to the Convention: Report of the Committee*. Geneva: United Nations. Available at: www.ohchr.org/EN/HRBodies/CRPD/Pages/InquiryProcedure.aspx [last accessed 8.9.2017].

Waitman, A., & Conboy-Hill, S. (Eds.) (1992). *Psychotherapy and Mental Handicap*. London: Sage.

Zaretsky, E. (2004). *Secrets of the Soul: A Social and Cultural History of Psychoanalysis*. New York: Alfred A. Knopf.

Chapter 9

Sharing our history, informing our future

Valerie Sinason and the development of training for frontline care workers and therapists

Pat Frankish

I would like to start with a bit of history. My first experience of using psychodynamic models with people with intellectual disabilities occurred when I was training to be a clinical psychologist in Liverpool in the 1980s. I worked with a young child who responded positively, after having previously resisted all attempts to help him. Having found him responsive to this way of working, I decided to try to make contact with other people working with similar models so I sent a letter into a couple of journals asking if there was "anyone out there". Nigel Beail and Valerie Sinason were among the people who responded and that was the beginning of some wonderful friendships, but also of the development of what we now know as disability psychotherapy. My previous experience before going to Liverpool, had not included anything much about psychodynamic approaches so I was very appreciative of the range of learning we were offered there, which included a psychotherapy supervision option in addition to the main training. It was all very new so I felt relieved to find that there were other people on a similar path.

Not too long after that, Nigel, I and others formed the Yorkshire Supervision Group. Its members were other people who had responded to the original search for like-minded people, as well as those who we met in our daily work. Nigel and I have both been gratified by the mostly positive response we have received when putting forward psychodynamic ideas. There will always be the very behaviourally and medically oriented practitioners who think it is not scientific and therefore useless, but there is a growing body of professionals and service users who recognise the need to always take account of the emotional world of our clients, and the potential for traumatic experiences to have featured in the lives of people with intellectual disabilities. We invited Valerie to come and provide us with her ten-session supervision course and we were so enabled by that course that most of us went on to do further work in the field of disability psychotherapy. Valerie was, and is, an inspirational teacher and gave us models of understanding that have stayed with us.

My own career has subsequently proceeded from this, to working in community and secure settings, to starting my own business in 2003. This business has grown into four separate companies, each with specific aims. There is a psychology and psychotherapy company, a training company, and a care company. There is also a holding company which owns various properties and manages capital assets. All of these are influenced, to a greater or lesser extent, by Valerie and her book, *Mental Handicap and the Human Condition* (1992). In all of my professional roles I have continued to build on this initial knowledge and experience and have taken a real interest in providing data that can make the evaluation of the impact of psychotherapy possible, and this is reflected in my publications (Frankish, 1989; 1992; 2013a; 2013b; 2013c; 2016). Nigel Beail has been even more prolific in the field and has made a significant contribution to the growing body of clinical-based evidence available (Beail, 1998; 2001). The opportunity to run a randomised controlled trial has not yet been possible despite our best efforts, but we persevere with gathering clinical evidence and it is very good to see its increasingly wide recognition and acceptance. Much of my more recent work has been in the field of training others and the influence of Valerie on this training will be explored in greater depth in this chapter.

Valerie has given us a deeper understanding of some key concepts and these have been incorporated into our training courses for direct support staff and therapists. In our training company we provide Levels 1 to 3 training for direct care staff, who we call support workers. They support people with intellectual disabilities in supported living environments, rather than in residential care, as these allow greater freedom and a better quality of life. Some have round-the clock support if required; others have fewer hours of support; and some share support with other people with similar needs. Included in the staff training is information from Valerie about her key concepts of secondary handicap, and the handicapped smile (1986). She also introduces trainees to her idea of the "pain of difference" (Sinason, 1992) and the necessity for all workers, at whatever level, to have the capacity to accept the individuality of everyone they meet.

Valerie's background is similar to my own in that we both grew up amid services for people with disabilities: my parents worked in an NHS hospital for people with "mental handicap" and Valerie's father set up a village community for a similar group. Thus, we were both relaxed in communicating with people with intellectual disabilities, but we also saw some practices that would be described today as inhumane.

Another similarity was the circuitous route we both took to becoming the people we are in the field in which we work. We both married and raised children before embarking on our careers. Valerie proceeded along an educational pathway before finding psychoanalysis for children, and then adults, and then specialising in difference. I took the route through psychology to clinical psychology and then to psychotherapy. For both of us, it was by chance that we found some very disturbed children who we were able to help; we found some other like-minded people who wanted to help; and then we found each other. We have worked well together and been mutually supportive.

We have also both gone on to extend our range of skills for helping people with dissociative identity disorder (DID). Valerie's work and influence in this field has been extended to our support staff who also support people with DID who have twenty-four-hour support services. I have valued Valerie's consistent support; she is always willing to respond to queries and is always an inspiration when she does so.

Topics covered in staff training

Some key topics are introduced in our training for direct support staff (Frankish Training, 2017) and these are presented as part of the section on Valerie. These are outlined below:

The handicapped smile

This is the phenomenon of people with disabilities smiling to ward off attack and to make themselves acceptable to non-disabled people. Addressing this in therapy can provide great benefits. Just knowing that the smile exists as a defence, and understanding about defences, is crucial learning, and something that had not been previously thought about. The change in the behaviour and understanding of direct support staff once they have this knowledge and insight is significant, and this enables them to work more effectively with clients, as well as to provide better informed support.

When we reflect on what has led to the development of the defence, we are taken into the early life experience of the individual. Valerie was one of the first people to speak openly about the abuse of disabled people. Martin, in his book, *Hospitals in Trouble* (1984), had highlighted the abusive practices in the old institutions, but in a more general way and with lots of emphasis on financial abuse and neglect. It was Valerie who spoke out about the sexual abuse of disabled adults and children and was ridiculed for doing so. She expanded this concept in her book, *Mental Handicap and the Human Condition* (Sinason, 1992), arguing that the defensive smile is often seen in abuse victims, where they have learned to be submissive to avoid pain; they have reached a position where they know they will not be believed so they have adopted this defence as a survival strategy.

We now know that such abuse has been widespread and the 1990s saw Valerie actively involved in campaigns to change the criminal justice system (Sinason, 1997) to take account of the needs of vulnerable witnesses. These changes have now been enshrined in the Youth Justice and Criminal Evidence Act 1999 (Home Office, 1999). Notwithstanding recent abuse scandals (see Jan Walmsley's chapter in this book), it is to be hoped that a drive towards eradicating such abuse within services is a priority in all present-day systems.

Support staff are trained to consider the meaning behind the constant smiling of an individual whom they support, and to ask themselves, "Is it because the individual is really happy or is the smile a defence against attack?"

Trainers do not expect the support staff to engage in therapy with individuals, but to be able to recognise when therapy should be sought, and to provide the right level and type of support for that therapy; together we consider whether the support worker is able to provide the level of support that is needed for an individual to feel safe and "seen" as the person they are. Staff attend support sessions where they can work through the effects of learning about the sometimes horrific life stories of the people they support. We have found that individuals who have therapy and learn to reframe what has happened to them, may want to talk to their direct support staff as well as their therapist, so it is essential that the support staff receive support themselves.

The pain of difference

Each person is different and unique, and a group of people with disabilities is likely to have more difference amongst them than a group of people without disabilities, yet they are expected to engage in group activities with each other all the time. The vast majority of disabled people know from a very early age that they are different: they have siblings who overtake them in ability; they see other children who can walk, talk, and do things that they cannot; and they find themselves in segregated services with strangers. Their lived experience will often be one of rejection for being different, but they may find it difficult to understand this. The emotional pain then experienced can be immense, and may be one factor leading to what is described as challenging behaviour. Consequently, there is a need to provide support staff with both an understanding and also a personal capacity to bear the fact of that pain of difference experienced by the person with intellectual disabilities. Avoiding it or belittling it will cause further emotional wounds and an increase of disturbed behaviour.

Emotional "intactness"

For many years there was an assumption that people with intellectual disabilities suffered similar levels of emotional deficit. Valerie (Sinason, 1992) has argued that there is no emotional deficit, that people remain emotionally intact even when there is severe cognitive impairment. This knowledge may once have been difficult for service providers and professionals to accept. It was too much to believe that people who were so different could have feelings and emotional inner worlds, as others did. Valerie's ideas, however, have been influential in changing the way that care and support is provided. The movement towards community care has been influenced by the work of social care leaders who have listened and learned. The humanity of services has changed hugely since my early memories of long-stay hospitals in which people were herded together anonymously. However, there are still too many individuals who are not heard, and their emotional pain is not recognised or accepted.

It was commonplace in the old, long-stay hospitals for staff to be told that they must not get emotionally involved with the "patients" and, if they did form any degree of attachment to someone, they would be moved to another ward to break it. We now know how important attachments are to everyone (Fletcher, Flood & Hare, 2016) and it was the recognition of this emotional "intactness" that has greatly influenced the improvements in provision. Direct care staff are now introduced to emotional developmental models and attachment needs so that they can recognise and accept the need to be emotionally available to the people they support. Their ability to meet people as who they are, is essential to the provision of support that offers individuals opportunities to grow in their sense of self to feel that they are of worth and value. Staff also need this opportunity to develop their sense of self and this is also why they receive the training and support sessions.

Protocols for support staff

In taking account of what Valerie has taught us, we arrive at some basic needs that must be met by the support staff. One of these is to recognise the attachment needs of individuals and, in relation to this, the need for a significant other to be present at all times. As it is not possible for this to be the same person continuously, changeover between staff needs to be as painless as possible. The individual being supported needs to know who is coming on duty next and the handover needs to happen in their presence. This is a very simple thing to do but rarely happens unless staff have been expressly instructed to do it. It is far more common for the handover to happen in the office and for the leaving staff just to disappear. Similarly, it is good if the same person can be present at going-to-sleep and waking-up times, but, if not, the individual needs to be told before they go to sleep who will be there in the morning, or in the night if they wake up.

Another important requirement for support staff is to treat everyone with respect: the people being supported, and each other. In a climate of mutual respect, there is positivity and warmth that enables the development and maintenance of self. People see each other as individuals and it becomes impossible to be neglectful, rude, or cruel. When we see abuse on our television screens, such as in the Panorama documentary which exposed abuse in the Winterbourne View care home (BBC, 2011), we know that respect has long gone from the services being exposed. Being enlightened about the emotional world of the people they support, and the trauma that they have already experienced, enables support staff to closely monitor their own behaviour so as not to add to the trauma of these individuals. Staff who have learned together will be able to support each other to maintain the necessary respect and appropriate behaviour.

Support staff need to feel confident in their practice. If they are being assaulted by the individuals they support, they need to be able to find, within themselves, the capacity to understand and not retaliate. In some secure settings, like the old hospitals, where there is a closed environment, staff can become emotionally blunted, and the neglect of their needs can lead to them neglecting the needs of their charges. In this situation it is management that is failing. The system requires input of a positive nature, with optimism and competence at all levels. Staff support groups and management supervision become key ingredients for the provision of emotionally nurturing support. Providing a nurturing environment is only possible when all members of the service know what they are doing and why. The provision of individual psychotherapy, whilst desirable and often necessary, cannot be enough if the distressed individual remains in an emotionally hostile environment.

Valerie demonstrated the power of supervision in the ten-session course that she delivered to us in the 1980s. It is a model I have used many times since in my own practice and I will be forever grateful to her for having modelled it so expertly. The sessions begin with each person speaking briefly about something that has happened or been seen or read in the previous week that has made them do a "double take", or in other words, has impinged on their consciousness. These events are then discussed and themes are identified. People attending the group deepen their awareness of their surroundings, and begin to notice what has an impact on them, hence also deepening their self-awareness. The second part of the session includes some teaching about ideas and ways of working, moving into case discussions brought by group members. The depth and breadth of what can be covered is huge and the learning is very powerful. These types of sessions have the safety of a therapy group and the learning potential of a seminar provided by an expert, yet the material comes mostly from the participants. This may be the model that is used in the Tavistock workshops, but they had not previously been accessible to us in the north of England. In bringing them to us, Valerie left a lasting legacy of skill for those of us who attended, and a valuable model that I, personally, have used many times since.

Staff training

The following is an example of one of the exercises from the Level 2 training provided for our direct support staff. Participants are given the poem below, written by Valerie in 1988, and are asked to respond to it.

HEADBANGER
The man kicked the telly right
so he smashed smashed
with his great fists
at the stubborn interference
in his brain.
His knuckles grew lumps

his forehead grew bumps
but the picture did not change.
'Birdbrain' cries his mother
feeding him plaster and flannels
helmets and hugs.
She could see
it was an injured eagle
that flickered
in the half light of his eyes
that would never be right
and when he let his eyes
open wide
he kicked the television
to pieces.

The instructions are:

> Stop and think about secondary handicap. Read the poem and think about what it means. You may need to read it through a few times. Give details of your thoughts.

With the permission of Amara Care workers, some example responses are given here:

1

The man definitely appears to be very frustrated and I think that the cause of this is due to a disability of his brain ('he smashed smashed with great fists at the stubborn interference of his brain)'. Punching the TV may be the way he communicates and releases the anger and frustration that he is experiencing.

'His knuckles grew lumps, his forehead grew bumps, but the picture did not change' – I think the man is trying to fix the disability and is hoping that by punching and banging his head on the TV he will remove the disability from his brain. He is trying to repair himself.

His mother is obviously used to this happening by the way she jokes calling him 'Birdbrain' and is on hand to give him 'plasters, flannels, helmets and hugs' following any injuries the man gets as a result of punching and banging his head. She is prepared for the situation.

In this case, the 'stubborn interference of his brain' is the disability and the upset and frustration causing the man to punch and bang his head on the TV as a result of the brain disability is the secondary handicap.

2

I wonder if the TV represents his view of himself. Then later in the poem, his view of how others (his mother) view him, and thus his experience of being different.

He views himself as someone who is disturbed in some way: 'the stubborn interference in his brain'.

His mother tries to soothe him but this is influenced by her views of him: 'never be right', 'Birdbrain'.

His distress is increased by his acknowledgement that his mother views him in this way: 'when he let his eyes open wide'.

3

I think this poem by Sinason would like to show us like still people have lack of understanding of the emotional lives of people with learning disabilities.

It is important to understand how things were for people with learning disabilities. Relation between both was felt that because of his disabilities was not affect by emotional events. It was felt that because of his disabilities he couldn't understand upsetting things and she didn't understand his needs therefore would not be distressed by her. His mother saw his behaviour as being part of his condition, or his learning disabilities rather than anything else.

From reading the poem, my interpretation is that there is a male who knows he is different from others, and perhaps he feels he needs 'fixing'. The male feels the frustration of not understanding why he is why he is. By hitting himself, abusing himself continuously, it is almost as if he is reliving a past experience. This is possibly a secondary handicap presenting itself within the male. The secondary handicap would potentially limit that individual and suppress his true potential.

4

I think that the poem relates to a young man who is damaged mentally by the father, when he was younger his father may have been abusive towards his mother and himself. He may have witnessed from a young age his father abusing his mother mentally or physically smashing up belongings, because he was witness this it may have a domino effect.

The young man loves his mother as she may have been his protector when he was younger taking the beatings to save him, this may of caused him to have mental health problems and frustration shown in the only form that he relates to the anger he has inside him by destroying things around him.

As can be seen above, there are a range of responses which represent the different staff and their different experiences or education. They all enter into the work with enthusiasm and want to learn. Many of them find the concepts hard and, at times, distressing, so they benefit from having this framework within which the issues can be addressed. As well as the on-line learning that they do, they have the opportunity for face-to-face discussion and regular support groups with a psychologist. These ideas are novel for most of them and they generally feel inspired to provide the emotional environment that is needed.

The next question that they are asked to respond to is about how they interpret their own distress. It is worded as follows:

Stop and think about times in your life when you have been stressed or distressed. Did you notice how this made it more difficult for you to think clearly or remember things? For someone who is distressed this is what can happen to their intellectual abilities. Now think about how it would have felt trying to hide those feelings of distress or upset you had – indeed you may have done this. For someone who is experiencing mild secondary handicap by trying to hide their pain and distress it is an almost permanent state like this. Although this is difficult – try to give some brief details.

Here are some examples of responses:

1
In my past I went through an experience that was very painful. I was still quite young. I felt it was too much for me to handle so I found it easier to pretend it never happened. I refused to talk about it. Eventually it was forgotten, but looking back I can see it wasn't, just covered over.
2
If we have to contain our stressful feelings it makes you feel excluded. The world carries on despite your pain.
3
A client I work with is in constant distress and anguish yet they attempt to continue with daily life as though nothing is wrong, but at times their thinking is not clear and gets muddled. They do not show this to other people.
4
They would be agitated and jumpy constantly fidgeting, when speaking to that person they would show interest in what your saying but not hear what has been said to them. They could show slight signs by being close to tears and not keeping eye contact with you as they was afraid that you may see their distress.

People vary in what they see in the question and this will reflect their own ability to look at their own issues and those of the people they support. What is clear is that they can think about the issues and this will inevitably stimulate further reflection.

The following case examples are composites. They demonstrate the changes in staff support following Valerie's training, and the impact of these changes on individuals being supported.

Case example 1

One gentleman, who had been supported for many years in a variety of environments and had a complex family history, was reaching a point where staff were saying they could not look after him. He was a constant trial to them with his demands, his destruction, his lack of ability to communicate, and his obvious lack of concern for them. After the training, the staff could see that he was very unhappy and that the destruction of property was representative of his despair about his disability, as well as being linked to abuse within his family. They were able to recognise that he had nothing "spare" emotionally for anyone outside of himself, because of his emptiness. He would often have a big smile on his face and this became accepted as a defence against his despair. This was confirmed when a happy, smiley phase was quickly followed by him trashing his room.

Staff became able to give and not ask anything in return, to be helpful in clearing up the mess without criticising, and to offer a range of meaningful activities that led to him learning to manage his own world to the extent that he could. The atmosphere changed and everyone felt better – the destruction of property reduced, and his quality of life improved. He did not speak so there was no talking therapy as such, but the provision of an emotionally nurturing environment enabled him to learn to trust and to grow.

Case example 2

A young woman with severe intellectual disabilities had lots of seizures, some of which were thought to be pseudo and some real, but it was difficult for staff to know the difference. Staff were encouraged to treat all the seizures as real, as suggesting that they were not, caused distress to the woman, as it implied that the woman's intention was to be manipulative in some way. Once staff could recognise, after the training, that people who appear to be manipulative are distressed and feeling unseen, it became possible for change to occur. As they recognised the pain of difference in the individual, who hated her epilepsy, they were able to feel and to show more compassion. This, in turn, enabled her to feel seen and supported and the pseudo seizures reduced in frequency. Staff were also able to see that an increase in pseudo seizures was a barometer of her emotional state, indicating a need for greater support and concern.

The benefits of training

Many other individuals have had similar experiences of not being seen or heard or both, like in these case examples above. Their difficulties mean they become hard to help and this leads to staff feeling inadequate and reluctant to do the job, which can then lead to a high staff turnover. It has been found that providing training to help staff manage their emotions reduces staff turnover, increases skill, and reduces breakdown in support packages. It has also been our observation that it generally contributes to a better quality of life for everyone. Indeed, one of the notable impacts of the training is on the well-being of the staff being trained. All benefit from connecting with their own life experience and comparing it with the lives of the people they support. Even when staff have experienced traumatic events themselves, they can see that they had a better chance of managing their distress because of their ability to think about what happened, because of their family support, and because of knowing how to seek out help when they needed it. People with disabilities are trapped in systems, may have limited cognition and communication skills, and develop defences in order to survive. We would all want our service users to do more than just survive, and enabling staff to understand individuals' distress, recognise their defensive symptoms, and tolerate their own feelings, benefits everyone in the system.

Humanity, respect for individuality, empathy, compassion, and enabling individuals to be supported and understood are all qualities which Valerie models in her professional and personal life. Through her writing and teaching, we have been inspired, informed, and supported in pursuing our commitment to giving these values and qualities a practical application in our own comprehensive services and training courses.

References

BBC. (2011). *Panorama. Undercover Care: the Abuse Exposed Behind Closed Doors.* BBC One Television, 31 May.

Beail, N. (1998). Psychoanalytic psychotherapy with men with intellectual disabilities: a preliminary outcome study. *British Journal of Medical Psychology, 71*(1): 1–11.

Beail, N. (2001). Recidivism following psychodynamic psychotherapy amongst offenders with intellectual disabilities. *British Journal of Forensic Practice, 3*(1): 33–37.

Fletcher, H. K., Flood, A., & Hare, D. J. (Eds.) (2016). *Attachment in Intellectual and Developmental Disability: A Clinician's Guide to Practice and Research.* Chichester: John Wiley & Sons.

Frankish, P. (1989). Meeting the emotional needs of handicapped people: a psychodynamic approach. *Journal of Mental Deficiency Research, 33*: 407–414.

Frankish, P. (1992). A psychodynamic approach to emotional difficulties within a social framework. *Journal of Intellectual Disability Research, 36*: 559–563.

Frankish, P. (2013a). Facing emotional pain: a model for working with people with intellectual disabilities and trauma. *Attachment: New Directions in Psychotherapy and Relational Psychoanalysis*, 7(3): 276–282.

Frankish, P. (2013b). Measuring the emotional development of adults with ID. *Advances in Mental Health and Intellectual Disabilities*, 7(5): 272–276.

Frankish, P. (2013c) Thirty years of disability psychotherapy: a paradigm shift? *Advances in Mental Health and Intellectual Disabilities*, 7(5): 257–262.

Frankish, P. (2016). *Disability Psychotherapy: An Innovative Approach to Trauma-Informed Care*. London: Karnac.

Frankish Training. (2017). www.frankishtraining.co.uk/ [last accessed 25.8.2017].

Martin, J. P. (1984). *Hospitals in Trouble*. Basil Blackwell: Oxford.

The National Archives: Office of Public Sector Information. (1999). *Youth Justice and Criminal Evidence Act 1999*. http://webarchive.nationalarchives.gov.uk/20080805025347/www.opsi.gov.uk/acts/acts1999/ukpga_19990023_en_1 [last accessed 25.8.17].

Sinason, V. (1986). Secondary mental handicap and its relationship to trauma. *Psychoanalytic Psychotherapy*, 2(2): 131–154.

Sinason, V. (1988). Poem: "Headbanger". *British Journal of Psychotherapy*, 5(2): 251.

Sinason, V. (1992). *Mental Handicap and the Human Condition: New Approaches from the Tavistock*. London: Free Association Books.

Sinason, V. (1997). A relationship with the law. *Bulletin of the Association of Child Psychotherapists*, 73: 22–28.

Chapter 10

Secondary handicap and a model for the supervision of nurses

Shula Wilson

Introduction

In May 2000, I went to the launch of the Institute of Psychotherapy and Disability (2017) where both Valerie Sinason and Alan Corbett were in attendance. My expertise is about people with physical disability so I raised my hand and asked if the word "disability" in the title referred to all disabled people? The answer was a resounding "Yes". At the end of the meeting I asked Valerie Sinason, "What next?" She responded in her warm, friendly, yet challenging way: she invited me to join, saying, "It is up to us. We are the adults. We need to make it work." Later I found myself working with Alan Corbett on the training committee. This was an inspiring experience as he was able to weave a coherent training programme for psychotherapists working with disabled people. When he invited me to write a chapter for this book, I questioned the relevance of physical disability to it. He answered that to celebrate Valerie's all-embracing view of the human condition, the physical aspect of disability should be included. Valerie Sinason is still leading the way towards respect for and inclusion of all disabled people. She taught me to always seek the person behind and beyond the physical damage, the professional title, or the uniform.

In *Mental Handicap and the Human Condition*, Sinason offers an interpretation of Shakespeare's portrayal of Richard III's deformity (Sinason, 1992, p. 267). She points to a link between Richard's angry and unhappy approach to life and his claim that the deformity he is burdened with, is the responsibility of his parents who conceived him through "bad intercourse". Sinason suggests that while this may have satisfied Richard's need to make sense of his affliction, it may also have created what Sinason termed a "secondary handicap" (Sinason, 1986; 1992) as Richard became consumed by anger and misery and a sense that he was unlovable. In *Mental Handicap and the Human Condition*, Valerie cites Richard's speech in Act 1, Scene 1:

> But I, that am not shap'd for sportive tricks,
> Nor made to court an amorous looking-glass;

I, that am rudely stamp'd, and want love's majesty
To strut before a wanton ambling nymph;
I, that am curtail'd of this fair proportion,
Cheated of feature by dissembling nature,
Deform'd, unfinish'd, sent before my time
Into this breathing world, scarce half made up,

> (Shakespeare, *Richard III*, Act 1, Scene 1, 14–21,
> cited in Sinason, 1992, p. 267)

Richard III feels cheated, unfinished, deformed. His misery for himself and others is his defence against the anxiety triggered by feeling unlovable and alone. If Richard III were in psychotherapy, the work would probably have revolved around his feelings, relationships, and self-image, allowing and enabling a change of perception and attitude. The issue is not the body but how the impaired individual and others relate to it.

My understanding of Sinason's concept of secondary handicap is as follows: the organic damage is the primary handicap; secondary handicap occurs when the individual or the environment struggle to accept difference, and find it difficult to contain, confront, and dissipate the anxiety and fear which are often triggered by impairment.

Secondary handicap is not a given, and can be minimised or even prevented. Inspired by Sinason's ideas, I believe that the main challenge for psychotherapy with disabled people is how to address the issues that lead to secondary handicap. It is my experience that one of the main obstacles to doing this is the fear triggered by the presence of impairment: it reminds us of our own fragility and mortality. This may result in the wish by therapists, carers, patients, and others to avoid or deny disability. For most disabled people, a great deal of their frustration, hurt, and pain results from the attitudes and reactions of other people to their impairment, ranging from denial and rejection to over-compensation (Wilson, 2003). In her book, *Disability: Controversial Debates and Psychosocial Perspectives*, Marks (1999) summarises Finkelstein's ideas (1980) by saying:

> ... our sense of normality and difference does not arise naturally from physical or mental differences between individuals, but rather is an effect of the way in which these differences are framed through an interaction between people in the context of work and society.
>
> (Marks, 1999, p. 82)

It may be useful at times for a therapist working with a disabled person to seek information about the client's condition. However, knowing about the condition does not mean knowing how this individual is affected. As Osler says, "It is more important to know what kind of patient has a disease than what kind of disease a patient has" (2016 [1905], p. 55).

In an attempt to protect his vulnerability, Richard III, consciously or unconsciously, chooses to become angry and miserable because of the wrong that he perceives has been done to him at birth. Was this the only way to live his life? Could he (and other disabled people, likewise) not be offered the opportunity to embrace and enjoy life while accepting their impairment as a given?

In his autobiography, Stephen Kuusisto writes about the experience of being born with severe sight impairment:

> Raised to know I was blind but taught to disavow it ... I couldn't stand up proudly, nor could I retreat... Still, I remained ashamed of my blind self. The very words "blind" and "blindness" were scarcely ... spoken around me.
>
> (1998, p. 7)

Little Stephen internalised his parents' denial of his impairment, saying, "I am three years old, and I've already buried my first pair of glasses" (1998, p. 10). As a result, he spent many years pretending to see, falling, and being continually hurt. Only in his late thirties did he admit that he was blind:

> Why should it take so long for me to like the blind self? I resist it, admit it, then resist again, as though blindness were a fetish, a perverse weakness, a thing I could overcome with the force of will power.
>
> (1998, p. 142)

Not until he was forty years of age did Kuusisto realise that it was possible to admit blindness and still be accepted in the world of sighted people: "I've needed help all my life. It's that simple" (1998, p. 143).

Unlike Richard III, who blames his parents for his primary disability, Kuusisto blames his parents for his secondary disability: they could not accept the blindness of their child so they used denial as a defence against the pain and disappointment of having a blind child. Many authors who have written about their own disability (Begum, 1996; Brown, 1954; Keith, 1994; 2001; Morris, 1996; Murphy, 1990; Oliver, 1996; Shakespeare, 1998; Williams, 1992; 1994) and those who have written about them (Erskine & Judd, 1994; Jureidini, 1988; Lussier, 1960; Taylor, 1987) seem to agree on one elementary point: that the major cause of emotional distress for disabled people is not the actual physical impairment but the effect that the impairment has on their relationship with others, and on their ability to manage the environment. In Western society we have appointed professionals (who operate in a medical way) as gatekeepers, protecting the rest of us from fears triggered by disability. In doing this job, they may unintentionally be contributing to secondary disability.

In the following pages, I present a model of supervision for health professionals (particularly nurses) that may help to avoid, or at least minimise, secondary handicap in institutions. This model is based on the idea that through encouraging reflection in caregivers, and in raising awareness of their own needs and reactions, individuals and teams in institutions will be enabled to achieve a balance between encouraging their patients' freedom of choice and its consequences, and respecting and accepting their responsibilities within the limitations of reality.

Developing the supervision model

Many years ago when I was taking my first steps as a psychotherapist, I had a conversation with an Australian psychiatrist on sabbatical in London. He told me he was shocked by how little care was given to nurses in the UK. He had been on placement in a children's leukaemia unit in a London teaching hospital and had noticed that sometimes a nurse would go to the toilet and, after a while, would come out with red eyes, looking as if she had been crying. He had asked another nurse what was happening and she explained that one of the children in the leukaemia ward had died and that the nurse who had taken care of him for the last months of his life was very upset and would go to the toilet to cry. The psychiatrist was shocked that there was no dedicated place for the nurse to go to, and no person to turn to. The nurse shrugged her shoulders and said, "That is how it is for us." The psychiatrist told me he could not believe that nurses, who have the lion's share of care for dying children, are being left alone with no one to support them through the grief and pain of losing them.

Unfortunately, the neglect of nurses' needs, as described here, may seem all too familiar to many who are at the coalface of patient care. This kind of neglect leaves nurses feeling alone, isolated, and unappreciated. The need for support, when the institution fails to provide it, may lead nurses to seek, and even to become dependent on, approval and human kindness from their patients. Sometimes, nurses may find themselves going above and beyond their duty, partially driven by the need to gain this needed love from patients. If, for example, a nurse makes herself available for calls at all times of the day and night, both the nurse and his or her patients may become confused about their relationships, their roles, and their mutual expectations. In these cases, a nurse's ability to keep clear professional boundaries and maintain a healthy balance between offering adequate support and looking after his or her own needs, can be impaired.

The life and environment of a person with significant illness or disability will include many health professionals and medical institutions. To try to reduce secondary handicap, we need to understand the relationship between the disabled person and his or her environment.

The supervision model

This supervision model has been developed through working with people who have Epidermolysis Bullosa (EB) and those who care for them in St Thomas' and Great Ormond Street Hospitals. EB is a currently incurable genetic skin disorder. In its most severe form, it is fatal in infancy and can cause fatal skin cancer in young adults. However, in its mildest form it can cause lifelong disability and pain. EB causes a breakdown in the natural protein that holds the skin and internal membrane, causing blistering and sores at the slightest touch, or even spontaneously. Skin blisters have to be lanced and dressed frequently, a painful procedure taking up to three hours. Excessive blistering can create scar tissue which can cause toes and fingers to fuse together. Scar tissue can also cause the oesophagus to narrow, making eating difficult. People with EB are often fighting infection, both internally and externally. One person in 227 carries the recessive EB gene. There are 5,000 people in the UK living with EB and about 500,000 worldwide. This means that 1 in 17,000 births are affected by EB (DEBRA, 2017).

It is my view, as illustrated by the following case example, that in the support and training of nurses, the focus should be to reflect on and question the meaning of the wish to "fix things" and to "find a cure", and to address the tension between genetic determination and freedom of choice.

In 1995, soon after I had founded Skylark, a psychotherapy service for people affected by disability, I received a call from Sally (all names in this case-based material have been changed), a nurse seeking counselling for one of her patients. When we met, Sally told me about her role as a nurse specialist for EB and about one patient in particular called Cathy. Cathy had told Sally that she was lonely so Sally organised carers to come and help her. Cathy still felt left out, alone, and frustrated so we at Skylark allocated a therapist for her. A week later, Sally phoned to thank us, and asked if I would be willing to supervise her in her work with Cathy and other EB patients. Never having worked with nurses before, I was intrigued. I knew nothing about EB but, admitting my lack of specific knowledge and experience, I agreed to give it a try and Sally and I started to meet for individual supervision. Eventually, I came to supervise the whole team of consultants and nurses for adults and, a few years later, I began supervising the EB paediatric team.

Our work focused on both the actual and the symbolic meaning of damaged skin and the conscious and unconscious ways in which it may affect patients, their families, and the health professionals who treat and support them. EB means that the sufferer's skin cannot be touched; babies and adults alike have to be treated with care. Hugging and cuddling are restricted and are often not possible. As Bick (1968) writes, the skin contains the body and gives it the essential sense of being held together, intact. Physically and emotionally, the skin is our first line of defence against injury and hurt. Winnicott explains that when all is well, the skin marks the separation between "me" and "not-me" (1965, p. 57). Through touch, the skin is also an important source of pleasurable sensations. Therefore, when the skin is damaged, fragile, and painful, as it is in EB, parents could be perceived, both by themselves and by their child, to have failed in their protecting and containing role. To navigate this delicate yet stormy path, care providers need to work hard to reflect on their own, as well as on their patients', experience of being in the world, and also to develop the ability to observe, through heightened self-awareness, their own thinking and perceptions in regard to that experience.

Supervision creates a space away from patients, whilst still focusing on the relationships with patients. The experience of taking a step back in order to gain better insight and understanding, also mirrors the distance between the patient as sufferer and the nurse as observer. This distance enables the disclosure of the patient's effect on the nurse's consciousness. Through developing the ability to reflect and think about the internal and external experience, seeds of security are sown for the nurse. This creates in him or her the ability to negotiate choices which then allows for the possibility of change to occur.

On being a nurse

The nurse is always in the middle. In our health care system, nurses have to respond to patients and family on the one hand, and doctors and the hospital on the other. While paying attention to those who need their care, nurses will be carrying an awareness of the complex tapestry of which they are a part, and will be sensitive to how it is impacting on their practice. The nurse is a part of the system: influencing, and being influenced by it. As a carer of people with high levels of need in a highly pressured work environment, self-care is also critical. Dures, Morris, Gleeson & Rumsey (2010) list three main issues confronting EB health and social care professionals:

1   *Intensity and depth of involvement*: the emotional demands of long-term relationships and palliative care; frustration at the limited effectiveness of treatment; difficulties switching off
2   *Managing with limited resources*: liaising with other professionals and service providers; the additional demands of a rare condition; isolation (The fact that the treatment of those affected by EB is not widely understood has resulted in many professionals working on their own.)
3   *The need for self-care*: learning self-care strategies.
            (adapted from: Dures, Morris, Gleeson & Rumsey, 2010, pp. 218)

Keeping the impact of the professional role in check and maintaining well-being is made more difficult by working in isolation. This is illustrated in the following vignette involving Sally, the EB nurse specialist mentioned above, and her patient Lynn (also a pseudonym). In our first session, Sally recounted Lynn's story:

Sally told me that Lynn had been born with EB. Lynn is in her early forties and lives with her thirteen-year-old son, Ray, in a small town in the Midlands.

She is a woman who has fought hard to minimise the effects of the pain and the restrictions of her impairment. Amongst other achievements, she found a job at a local firm, and she loved the independence and sense of worth it gave her. However, about a year before, due to the economic recession and cuts to the work force, Lynn had been the first to be made redundant. She had felt rejected and betrayed and became angry and bitter.

Sally, along with the entire EB team, admired Lynn's courage in having had a child despite her EB. They also admired her striving to work and her independence. Yet they all felt sad and worried as they knew that Lynn's condition was getting worse, and that she was alone and struggling. They really wanted to support her so when she hesitated about coming to see her consultant in London, they did not think twice about using their own cars and time to bring her to London for appointments.

In the long term, however, it became impossible for the team to sustain this extra time for the long drive as it was impacting on their ability to care for other patients and was an inappropriate use of resources. Lynn's life became more difficult, perhaps due to her lack of work and her EB worsening through developing an aggressive cancerous growth. She began to behave as if it were her right to have the nurses supporting her in this way, and she refused to accept alternative transport arrangements, such as the ambulance.

After consulting with the rest of the team, Sally had to tell Lynn that, unfortunately, she could no longer bring her to appointments, and she offered to organise hospital transport for her. Lynn would not hear of it, and became angry and aggressive in response. Although Lynn would not say it openly, Sally felt that Lynn was angry at her "failure" to give her what she felt she needed. Lynn had always found attending the hospital difficult and she now refused to come to her appointments unless she was taken there and back by one of the team. As her condition worsened, however, she did eventually agree to come by NHS transport although she was adamant that she would attend on a day of her choosing rather than when her appointment was made.

Sally told me that, in her view, Lynn was clearly extremely fearful of the cancer's rapid growth, and angry and frustrated by the long wait. Her fury and pain were directed both at Sally and the hospital system. She referred to everyone as "f-----g stupid and hopeless". In addition, Sally found that she had become a go-between between Lynn and the hospital and whilst Lynn was exasperated by the hospital not being able to meet her demands, the hospital staff could become equally exasperated with her behaviour. This was very hard for Sally as she had to suppress her own frustration and feelings of anger in order to remain professional and support Lynn. Yet, because Sally could not communicate her feelings, this created a wall, and Sally felt as though she were in a battle with Lynn. Lynn could be her charming self when other nurses were around, but she directed all her frustration and rage at Sally. Sally felt as if she were failing Lynn as a nurse and as a human being.

Lynn was her patient yet she was not getting what she wanted; she was so unhappy. Sally was confused and was experiencing an internal battle between her professional role and her personal feeling of simple human affection and friendship.

In my role as her supervisor, I could see that Sally was in internal turmoil. In order to defend against her anxiety and fear of failure she was (in my view) holding on to the sense of power and respect conferred on her by her professional role as a nurse. She wanted to take care of Lynn but was, at the same time, feeling pushed away and hurt by her. She felt stuck, and constrained by all her conflicting emotions. She came to supervision flustered, upset, and confused. Whilst listening to her story, I acknowledged and validated the complex entanglement of her feelings. Then, together, we identified the elements of her experience and started to untangle them. These seemed to be:

- her need to feel needed, which may have played a role in her choice of profession
- the deep-seated, though irrational, human fear of contamination, triggered by damaged skin such as in EB
- survivors' guilt that may lead to bargaining: "If I am giving my time and energy and going out of my way to help, perhaps the EB will ease off or even disappear, and my patient and I will survive."
- the unconscious, omnipotent fantasy of curing the EB (mending the broken skin) – the nurse's defence against her helplessness in the face of the incurable EB
- her role as the one in the middle – between the patient and the medical environment. Sally may be representing the skin function, the separation between outside and inside. Failure in her role could be experienced, unconsciously, as the damaged, failing EB skin.

After identifying these as possible elements in Sally's state of mind, we explored how emotions could affect Sally's relationship with Lynn. Sally recognised her dependency on Lynn's willingness to accept and contain these emotions in the form of appreciating Sally's efforts. As she was inappropriately looking for the patient's love and approval to compensate for the lack of emotional understanding and support from the institution, this dependency increased Sally's initial insecurity.

To paraphrase Holland, who writes about this (although in reference to doctors rather than nurses):

A ... [nurse] ... may defend herself [sic] by attempting to deny reality and climb onto a pedestal labelled 'Excellent carer'. She may make herself busy with excessively full care for the patient but, in the process, take over many of the responsibilities of the patient or of the patient's family, even to the extent that her patient is left holding all the feelings of incompetence and powerlessness, while the ... [nurse] ... becomes vulnerable to the patient's projection that she be all powerful.

(Holland, 1995, p. 161)

In addition to these identified elements, it was also important for Sally and myself to be aware of accumulative secondary, or vicarious trauma (McCann & Pearlman, 1990). This can result when fear and anxiety, triggered by an ongoing involvement in life-threatening situations, are not recognised and processed. This kind of trauma can cause a person to defend against continuous exposure to unbearable experiences by "encapsulating" the experience and endeavouring to keep it out of the conscious mind. As McCann and Pearlman explain, there is a "transformation that occurs within the caregiver as a result of emphatic engagement with the patients' trauma, experience and their sequels" (1990, p. 131–149). I would argue that this transformation may be resisted by caregivers and, if left untreated, the "capsule" of experience, such as Sally experienced, can erupt and destabilise a nurse's physical or mental health, to the detriment of both themselves and their patients.

Supervision can offer a space to work with this trauma, where the frightening, unbearable experiences can be unwrapped, acknowledged, appreciated, and validated. For an EB nurse, avoidance is not an easy option. The risk of not addressing this second-hand trauma is that the nurse may suffer burnout, stemming from identifying with what they perceive as the patient's "unjust" fate or punishment, and the unconscious wish or fantasy of becoming the saviour, the hero, who will fight against this. The supervisor's role is to facilitate ways of thinking that will enable nurses like Sally to feel secure enough to confront and let go of those defences which are unhelpful and often damaging.

The first step is to support the nurse in setting clear boundaries for his or her practice. By defining their role and its limits, these boundaries will provide a workable structure for the nurse. As Sally became aware of her defences and accepted the reality and the limitations of her role, she was also able to understand and appreciate Lynn's reactions as a cry for help rather than a threat. She became ready to ask herself, "Why is Lynn so angry with me?", and to recognise that a possible answer was, "Because you have confused her by making her special and not keeping the boundaries. You have allowed her to hope that you would do the impossible: that you could save her". As Sally let go of her omnipotent fantasy and became aware of her limitations, she felt more in control. When I asked her, "What do you want to say to Lynn?", she was able to say, "I want Lynn to know that this is too much for me; I can't take it any more". Sally did not need to hide behind the wall anymore. She did not need to pretend that she could do the impossible. She could be open and truthful with Lynn.

In subsequent supervision sessions, Sally reported that Lynn had changed. In fact, she seemed relieved to be able to let go of her rage against the nurse and welcomed Sally's closeness. In my view, Sally's admission of her limitations freed Lynn from having to worry about Sally's unrealistic perception of her own omnipotence. This enabled Lynn to attend to her own needs by accepting Sally's help, knowing that Sally was taking care of her own emotions rather than projecting them into the nurse/patient relationship.

Sometimes the fantasy of an EB nurse is that she should be the whole, perfect skin. So when Sally was finally able to say, "I cannot do it any more", the imaginary, whole skin cracked. Sally admitted her own limitations, or disability, both to herself and to Lynn, and this admission and acceptance of it restored trust and put an end to the battle. This allowed both nurse and patient to have, in Sally's words, "a simple, human friendship", safely contained within clear professional boundaries. Lynn was now able to allow the professionals to take care of her.

Nurses as part of a team

However much we want to believe in our independence and self-reliance, in most aspects of life we do depend on others to various degrees. Winnicott (1964) described the infant's initial relationship as being a part of a triangle, which consists of the mother–baby dyad at the base and the father holding them, supporting and protecting the mother. Winnicott saw the mother as the main and constant caregiver, directly responsible for the wellbeing of the baby, for most aspects of physical care and emotional support. He saw the father as the holding agent, ensuring physical and emotional support for the mother–baby dyad by breaking the isolation and loneliness of the mother through accepting, listening, and encouraging. The father also provides a framework for the family, with clearly structured boundaries. Although, perhaps, out of step with contemporary thinking regarding gender roles and responsibilities, this triangle is a useful basic model for the dynamic of roles, relationships, and needs in most care systems. This includes the supervisory relationship, as Hawkins and Shohet (2000) explain, where Winnicott's triangle of mother–baby–father is translated in a nursing context into nurse–patient/family–supervision/team. In the context of EB, it is clear that, due to the severity and fragility of some patients' conditions, the nurse–patient attachment often resembles the mother–baby dyad. However, what is not always clear is who, if anyone, fulfils the father's role.

As my Australian psychiatrist colleague noted, it seems that most hospitals rarely accept, or even recognise, the need to support nurses (Menzies Lyth, 1988). Rather, the hospital care system encourages the formation of nurse–patient dyads, in which the nurse is expected to be very closely involved with the critically ill patient and their family, often sharing and sometimes having to take over, the mother's role. Yet this system seems oblivious to the effects that such a level of involvement might have on the nurse. It can leave them, as I described earlier, without the much-needed support of a holding agency.

The missing element is the understanding and acceptance by the medical system that where there is an expectation for ongoing output by nurses, there is a need to ensure adequate input for them. Nurses, like mothers, are often seen as givers with infinite inner resources. The assumption is that their willingness to give is enough to sustain them. However, in order to carry on giving adequately, the giver has to be held and supported. People who choose caring for others as a profession are rewarded when they see the people they care for getting better. Unfortunately, working with patients who have incurable conditions such as EB, means that alleviation of pain and suffering is minimal and temporary. Rarely, therefore, do nurses experience satisfaction and a sense of achievement and success. Helplessness, frustration, and sadness are part of their everyday work. This is hard enough, but there is another aspect of being an EB nurse: due to the rarity of the condition, there are only a few specialist nurses who operate in the community, mainly alone and often far away from colleagues and medical resources. Support must be given to these nurses.

At St. Thomas', we have attached a group supervision session to the monthly clinic so that the nurses who live and work in different parts of the country, can gather to discuss their patients with the multidisciplinary team. In order to help the nursing team to function well, we have created a container in which members feel secure enough to think and reflect. All aspects of the group operation are negotiated and agreed by all participants. This includes meeting arrangements, content, and issues of confidentiality. In order to build and maintain such a structure, there is a need for a third party, a group leader, who is not directly involved and has no managerial power or authority over the members, and yet is sufficiently informed about the team's work. In my experience as a supervisor in a medical setting, this creates a secure frame within which members feel safe to share concerns as well as new ideas and initiatives. It allows members the freedom to respectfully disagree about issues and to question or complain about issues within and outside the group. It also enables members, as much as possible, to congratulate each other and to know that they are valued and heard. Most importantly, it enables them to feel they are in it together, thereby helping to overcome the loneliness. Taking care of the caregivers seems a natural step towards including and integrating disabled people in the human quest for life worth living.

References

Begum, N. (1996). Doctor, doctor... disabled women's experiences of general practitioners. In: J. Morris (Ed.), *Encounters with Strangers: Feminism and Disability* (pp. 168–193). London: The Women's Press.

Bick, E. (1968). The experience of the skin in early object relations. *International Journal of Psycho-Analysis*, *49*: 484–486. [reprinted in: Harris, M., & Bick, E. (1987). *Collected Papers of Martha Harris and Esther Bick* (pp. 484–486). Strathtay, Perthshire: Clunie Press.

Brown, C. (1954). *My Left Foot.* London: Martin Secker & Warburg. [reprinted London: Minerva Press, 1994].

DEBRA. (2017). Epidermolysis bullosa. Available at: www.debra-international.org/what-is-eb.html [last accessed 2.10.2017].

Dures, E., Morris, M., Gleeson, K., & Rumsey, N. (2010). 'You're whatever the patient needs at the time': the impact on health and social care professionals of supporting people with epidermolysis bullosa. *Chronic Illness, 6*: 215–227.

Erskine. A., & Judd, D. (Eds.) (1994). *The Imaginative Body: Psychodynamic Therapy in Healthcare.* London: Whurr.

Finkelstein, V. (1980). *Attitudes and Disabled People: Issues for Discussion.* New York: World Rehabilitation Fund.

Hawkins, P., & Shohet, R. (2000). *Supervision in the Helping Professions* (2nd edn). Buckingham: Open University Press.

Holland, J. W. (1995). *A Doctor's Dilemma: Stress and the Role of the Carer.* London: Free Association Books.

Jureidini, J. (1988). Psychotherapeutic implications of severe physical disability, *American Journal of Psychotherapy, 42*: 297–307.

Keith, L. (Ed.) (1994). *Mustn't Grumble: Writing by Disabled Women.* London: The Women's Press.

Keith, L. (2001). *Take up Thy Bed and Walk: Death, Disability and Cure in Classic Fiction for Girls.* London: The Women's Press.

Kuusisto, S. (1998). *Planet of the Blind.* London: Faber and Faber.

Lussier, A. (1960). The analysis of a boy with congenital deformity. *Psychoanalytic Study of the Child, 15*: 430–453.

Marks, D. (1999). *Disability: Controversial Debates and Psychosocial Perspectives.* London: Routledge.

McCann, L., & Pearlman, L. A. (1990). Vicarious traumatization: a framework for understanding the psychological effects of working with victims. *Journal of Traumatic Stress, 3*(1): 131–149.

Menzies Lyth, I. (1988). *Containing Anxiety in Institutions: Selected Essays (Volume 1).* London: Free Association Books.

Morris, J. (1996). *Encounters with Strangers: Feminism and Disability.* London: The Women's Press.

Murphy, R. F. (1990). *The Body Silent: The Different World of the Disabled.* New York: Norton.

Oliver, M. (1996). *Understanding Disability: From Theory to Practice.* Basingstoke: Palgrave Macmillan.

Osler, W. (2016). *Counsels and Ideals from the Writings of William Osler [1905].* South Yarra, Australia: Leopold Classic Library.

Shakespeare, T. (Ed.) (1998). *The Disability Studies Reader: Social Science Perspectives.* London: Continuum.

Sinason, V. (1986). Secondary mental handicap and its relationship to trauma. *Psychoanalytic Psychotherapy, 2*: 131–154.

Sinason, V. (1992). *Mental Handicap and the Human Condition: New Approaches from the Tavistock.* London: Free Association Books.

Taylor, G. J. (1987). *Psychosomatic Medicine and Contemporary Psychoanalysis.* Madison, CT: International Universities Press.

Williams, D. (1992). *Nobody Nowhere: The Remarkable Autobiography of an Autistic Girl.* London: Doubleday.

Williams, D. (1994). *Somebody Somewhere: Breaking Free from the World of Autism*. London: Doubleday.

Wilson, S. (2003). *Disability, Counselling and Psychotherapy: Challenges and Opportunities*. Basingstoke: Palgrave Macmillan.

Winnicott, D. W. (1964). The Child, the Family and the Outside World. London: Pelican.

Winnicott, D. W. (1965). Ego integration in child development (1962). In: *The Maturational Process and the Facilitating Environment* (pp. 56–63). London: The Hogarth Press. [reprinted London: Karnac, 2007].

Chapter 11

Labels, death-making and an alternative to Social Role Valorisation

Valerie Sinason's influence on my work

Jan Walmsley

I was surprised and not a little pleased to be asked by the editors to write about ways in which Valerie Sinason's work has influenced my thinking. I have never met Valerie but she has had a profound influence on my work. It is timely to reflect on her contribution at a time when many of the gains I thought we had achieved for people with intellectual disabilities appear to be unravelling. This has been seen in the United Nation's recent condemnation of the UK's failure to sustain its commitment to uphold the United Nations Convention on the Rights of Persons with Disabilities (UN Convention on the Rights of Persons with Disabilities, 2016). Writing this chapter has been an interesting exercise, entailing a review of the influence of Valerie's ideas on my own work since I began my academic career in the 1980s. As I reflected, I identified the following three themes, which I use to structure this chapter:

1. Initially, in the 1980s, Valerie offered an alternative and compelling perspective to the then dominant Social Role Valorisation (SRV) to explain the continuing rejection and devaluation of people with intellectual disabilities (Sinason, 1986). SRV is a theory which argues that to counter "devaluation" it is important that people with learning disabilities have valued social roles, such as householder, or paid worker; that they use mainstream, not "special" services; that their relationships are with non-disabled people; and that positive imagery is promoted in all circumstances (Wolfensberger & Tullman, 1989). SRV has been criticised as meaning people with learning disabilities need support in passing as "normal" (Brown & Walmsley, 1997, p. 232).

2. Subsequently, Valerie's view was that the ever-changing labels, and the bitter conversations accompanying these debates, are a means to hiding our discomfort about "learning disability" (Sinason, 1992). Even as I began writing this chapter, "learning disability" nurses in England were discussing on Twitter (WeLDNurses, 2016) whether they should be called "intellectual disability" nurses.

3. Finally, as I wrote this chapter, I found that Valerie's views on "death-making" (to use Wolf Wolfensberger's term (Sinason, 1992; Wolfensberger, 1980a)), in which she says, "The damaged child is written off as pre-born or pre-human and therefore the value of his or her life is under threat" (Sinason, 1992, p. 12), helped me think about, and perhaps better understand, both the continual depressing stories about people dying carelessly unheeded in the hands of health and social care services (Justice for LB, 2014; 7 Days of Action, 2017), and the reported practice of keeping families at arms' length. These practices relate particularly to people whose so-called challenging behaviour has led to their confinement in Assessment and Training Units, or secure services, sometimes for many years. This has been extensively reported in blogs written by family members and their allies, such as Mark Neary (2017), Finola Moss (2017), and Sara Ryan (2017).

An alternative to Social Role Valorisation

I first encountered Valerie's work in the 1980s when I was new to a field then known as "mental handicap". By a series of happy accidents, I managed to secure myself a job at the Open University, working with a fantastic team of academics who, in 1985, produced the celebrated "Patterns for Living" pack (Open University, 1986), an open learning, non-accredited course to encourage better communication between professionals and family members through studying together. It was a great success, reaching well in excess of 30,000 people, and remembered by many who were around then. It was a great course but, as a newcomer, I remember being struck by how inward-looking this field was. It was as if the rest of the world of academia did not exist: we were in a "handicap bubble", talking only to one another.

After launching and marketing "Patterns for Living", I had my first opportunity to edit a book (Brechin & Walmsley, 1989), a course reader for a follow-on undergraduate course, *Learning Disability: Changing Perspectives* (Open University, 1990). We were looking for new angles to the, by then, well-worn track of normalisation and SRV so we could live up to the "Changing Perspectives" title. We came across Valerie's groundbreaking work on psychotherapy and were determined to include a chapter on this in the reader. It was our view that her work really did "change perspectives". Other than the work of Neville Symington, on which Valerie had built, the application of psycho-therapeutic insights to intellectual disability was at that time and remains, I would suggest, despite the fantastic work reported in this book, little known or little used. The insights from psychotherapy that we take for granted in working with people without intellectual disabilities, had been denied to those with intellectual disabilities; this was part of the dehumanising and distancing to which the latter are subject. We felt it was vitally important to bring this different perspective to the attention of the professionals and family carers who were the intended audience for the course. We managed to obtain Valerie's permission and included in the book a chapter on "Barry" (Sinason, 1989), a case study from her paper *Secondary Mental Handicap and its Relationship to Trauma* (Sinason, 1986). This brought Valerie's work to a wider audience than might have encountered it otherwise, as this was a course studied by a thousand or so students a year over its six-year life.

On re-reading the chapter, I am struck anew by Valerie's patience, courage, and insight into the world of this lonely boy. She used case studies like Barry's to develop the idea of "secondary handicap" (Sinason, 1992), the defensive and often destructive behaviour which compounds the pain of having an intellectual disability, and she shows how this is a further, additional disadvantage.

I began writing this chapter during the week of 7 Days of Action (2017), a Twitter campaign to draw attention to the plight of young people incarcerated in secure units (7 Days of Action, 2016). These young people need Valerie's insight and understanding. Instead, their "challenging" and, like Barry's, frequently violent behaviour, is treated with antipsychotic drugs, restraint, and seclusion. Valerie was writing about treating Barry in the early 1980s. Over thirty years – a generation – later, notwithstanding increased understanding of psychotherapy and the significance of an individual's emotional world on his or her behaviour, Valerie's lessons continue to be unheeded. The manifest distress and unhappiness of people with severe intellectual disabilities and mental health problems forced to live apart from their families and communities is treated not as a cry against loneliness and rejection, but as behaviour to be managed (Heslop & Macaulay, 2009). The rejection and marginalisation of people with intellectual disabilities continues. I am struck by how, in her pioneering work, Valerie did not reject people with intellectual disabilities as others did, but worked tirelessly to understand their communication.

Euphemistic labelling

A second area in which Valerie influenced my thinking is around labelling. I cannot count the number of hours I feel I have wasted discussing the correct terminology for what we now call intellectual disability.[1] If as much energy had been devoted to actually changing attitudes, the world would be a better place. Valerie waded in, in characteristically heedless and courageous fashion, refusing to change the title of her 1992 book, *Mental Handicap and the Human Condition*, at a time when the ferment over language was very strong. It was around 1990 that the UK Department of Health officially dropped "mental handicap" and replaced it with "learning disability" (Sinason, 1992). What is the reason for this continual relabelling? Valerie's argument is that the labels we use are euphemistic; that we change language, not to reflect changed attitudes, but to distance ourselves from the discomfort engendered by the condition – of retardation, sub-normality, mental handicap – and to disguise that discomfort (Sinason 1992). This extract from *Mental Handicap and the Human Condition* particularly influenced me when thinking about history:

> Each worker introducing a new term hopes that the new word brings new hope and a new period of historical change. Each time the new word is coined, it is coined honourably ... Each such chapter praises itself for a hopeful new term. It is therefore doing a grave disservice to past pioneers to point contemptuously to their chosen term.
>
> (Sinason, 1992, p. 40)

Valerie also drew attention to the superficiality of our dreams for people with intellectual disabilities. They are pictured, smiling, in their hygienic and tidy, modern kitchens, alone. She explains the smiling thus: "Some handicapped people behave like smiling pets for fear of offending those they are dependent on ... When people depend for their lives on cruel regimes, they need to cut their intelligence and awareness" (Sinason, 1992, p. 21). In fact, as Deborah Marks says, they are all too aware of messages from the environment that they should not exist (Marks, 1999).

This set me thinking about what I would term "visual laundering": it was happy, smiling faces that adorned *Valuing People* (Department of Health, 2001) and *Valuing People Now* (Department of Health, 2009), replacing the grim, freakshow approach in older publications such as Tredgold's *Mental Retardation* (Craft, 1979).[2] But how real were the smiles? As Valerie writes, "the new beautiful community homes provide an even more disconcerting backdrop for communications of despair" (Sinason, 2003, p. xvi).

Thanks to Valerie's insights, in the book I wrote with Kelley Johnson and Marie Wolfe, *People with Intellectual Disabilities: Towards a Good Life?* (2010), we developed the argument that the prevailing understanding of the history of intellectual disability has been one of Whiggish progress, darkness to light. Each generation rejects, not only the labels of the past, as Sinason argued (Sinason, 1992), but also its practice and beliefs, its language and visual imagery. We lurch from one perfect "solution" to the next, from institutions to community care to supported living to personalisation, and refuse to accept that change is incremental and that some of our predecessors may actually have had honourable intentions, and may have done some things well. This shows we do not learn from the past; we reject and deny it. This is similar to the way that people leaving long-stay hospital were told to move on and, literally, leave their past behind. I recall visiting a recently closed ward which had housed men with so-called "challenging behavior". They had been locked away, and then later moved to a smaller house, though still confined behind a high fence on the same campus. Amongst the scattered possessions left in the deserted ward were photograph albums showing the individuals who had lived there. I felt these albums symbolically represented lives discarded.

Just as no group has had its label changed so frequently, a point made by Valerie (Sinason, 1992), there can also be no other group in society who has been subject to so many dramatic changes in policy. It is true that things have improved for many since the institutional era, but there has been much less change in the challenges faced and the underlying attitudes. In recent focus groups for self-advocates in two Australian states, every single participant of the thirty, mildly impaired adults, reported that they had been bullied and name-called (Strnadová, 2017[3]). This is where Valerie's strength lay: she saw beyond the visual laundering, the hollow, empty posturing around the correct labels to use.

Death-making

My final theme is death-making, one I have only just begun to write about (Dale & Walmsley, in press). As I mentioned above, back in the late 1980s we were struggling to find voices other than those of Wolfensberger and his allies (Wolfensberger & Tullman, 1989), who espoused SRV to the exclusion of all other possibilities. This was a bit like the ubiquity of Positive Behaviour Support (APBS, 2017) or RAID (APT, 2017) today. However, like Valerie, Wolfensberger is the other major thinker on intellectual disability who has highlighted death-making. In the 1980s I tended to dismiss death-making but recent events have caused me to revisit Wolfensberger's writings, and compare them with Valerie's.

Wolfensberger's view was that death-making is one of the functions of intellectual disability services. His writings on this topic are conveniently grouped in Chapter 6 of a collection of his writings edited by David Race (2003). It is powerful stuff. He used case studies to show how medical services fail disabled people because their lives are perceived to have low quality and value. He wrote: "Handicapped people are given massive doses of psychoactive drugs, so that they die from drug effects – even though the death certificate will list only the complications, such as cardiac arrest, pneumonia…" (Wolfensberger, 1980a) p. 171, reprinted in Race, 2003, p. 190). Wolfensberger also targeted abortion. He drew parallels between Nazi Germany's extermination practices and contemporary practice of aborting disabled foetuses (Wolfensberger, 1980b, reprinted in Race, 2003, pp. 191–193). Wolfensberger says:

> I think that the liberalisation of abortion is one of the expressions of the lowering of human life and I do believe we will soon see legalised euthanasia. We will see it applied to the aged and the retarded first …. We will have to see that you can't have this part way; that once you break through a qualitative barrier of defining human life and its value, then there's no stopping.
>
> (Soeffing & Wolfensberger, 1974, reprinted in Race, 2003, p. 186–187)

Back in the 1980s, I had dismissed death-making as far-fetched. I was, after all, a supporter of a woman's right to choose abortion. Even now, I recognise it as contentious – but recent events and reports have made me think again. The abuse of people at Winterbourne View (BBC, 2011); or the death of Connor Sparrowhawk due to "neglect" (Mazars, 2015); the poor health care offered to people with learning disabilities revealed in Mencap's "Death by Indifference" campaign (Mencap, 2007); the findings of the University of Bristol's *CIPOLD* (*Confidential Enquiry into Premature Deaths of People with Learning Disabilities*) (University of Bristol, 2013), and the failure to investigate unexpected and premature deaths, to which the *Mazars Report* (2015) drew attention, reinforced by the Care Quality Commission's findings (2016a; 2016b), all point to the low value accorded to the lives of people with learning disabilities.

One of Valerie's most powerful insights is that "the understandable widespread wish for medical science to eradicate intellectual disability means that those born and living 'with it' are not emotionally welcomed nor included" (Sinason, 2003, p. xiii). How can you feel welcome in the world when you know that if your defects had been detected in utero, you would never have lived? She argues that at a primitive, unspoken level, mothers are blamed for producing defective children (Sinason, 2003), and that this can manifest, however well it is hidden, in a parental death wish: that this child had never been born. This unspoken, deeply taboo wish, transfers itself to the child, who may well protect him or herself with behaviour intended to keep the world at bay, and protect the self from even more hurt and rejection ("secondary handicap" in Sinason's language (1992). I can do no better here than to quote Deborah Marks, another fan of Valerie's:

> The pain of rejection is often suppressed in order to survive and function under a barrage of rejecting messages. Appropriate feelings of rage regarding the everyday oppression and abuse they endure are often directed inwards, through self-abuse ... or in a self-defeating way, outwards in challenging behaviour.
>
> (Marks, 1999, p. 46)

Even as I write this, I feel the opprobrium of families I know well; they would vehemently reject Valerie's interpretation that they wish any ill on their relatives. There can be no doubt, too, that lack of service support exacerbates the more primitive pain of families. As Corbett says:

> Having a child with a disability inevitably tests how solid the foundations of a family are. To have a child with a disability involves a complex process of grief for the loss of the imagined baby ... a process that requires an optimal mixture of good internal working models on the part of parents, and an equivalent robust system of support and care on the part of society. It is rare that the two phenomena co-exist.
>
> (2014, p. 106)

Yet, I am drawn to Valerie's interpretation as a way of understanding a phenomenon that is otherwise inexplicable: the rejection and vilification of families by service providers. I have struggled to understand this. This is more than professional hubris being challenged by lay people who know better as far as their relatives are concerned. Why else was Sara Ryan (mother of Connor Sparrowhawk) labelled "toxic" for trying to draw staff attention to the need to manage her son's epilepsy (Ryan, 2017)? Why are families barred from visiting their relatives? This is from the 7 Days of Action archive:

> Parent-blaming is still widespread, as shown in the exchange recorded at 12.56 on day 7 https://whobyf1re.wordpress.com/2015/10/13/lbs-inquest-day-7-session-1/ [(Kara, 2008, 2015)] of Connor's inquest. Families are blamed for 'upsetting' their incarcerated young people and banned from visiting or have their visits arbitrarily curtailed. Visits from under-age family members are generally forbidden and such children actually have less contact with their relatives who reside in ATUs, than they would if those people were in prison.
>
> (7 Days of Action, 2016)

I would argue that we need to consider Valerie's insights as a way of understanding the otherwise inexplicable rejection of families by services.

Like Valerie, Wolfensberger's starting point for arguing that we are on a slippery slope to discarding lives perceived by others to be of low value, was the widespread practice of aborting foetuses identified through pre-natal testing as disabled. His argument is not unlike Valerie's, although it is articulated more at a societal rather than an individual level:

> People who refuse to acknowledge that all of the forms of 'death-making' are related, and who believe that they can contain a legitimated form of death-making to narrow and specific circumstances, and to a highly restricted range of human life, are deluding themselves; at least they seem to ignore some important lessons from history.
>
> (Wolfensberger, 1980b, reprinted in Race, 2003, p. 193)

It seems interesting to me that Valerie and the late Wolfensberger would have seen eye to eye (although coming from very different starting points) on the significance for disabled people of the easy assumption that it is acceptable to get rid of them as long as the condition is detected before birth. Recent medical "advances" open up the real possibility that Down's Syndrome will be eradicated entirely by early detection in utero, followed by abortion. This possibility was aired in Sally Phillips' documentary, *A World Without Down's Syndrome?*, first broadcast in 2016 (BBC, 2016). Sally is, herself, the mother of a young man with Down's. Her point that this was happening without significant public debate as to its desirability, drew sharp rejoinders from people who rejected her views because of the fact that she is wealthy and her son only mildly impaired (McVeigh, 2016). It was argued that bringing the debate into the mainstream media was unhelpful for families struggling with difficult decisions. This point about eradicating Down's Syndrome, however, is an example of how medical practice consistently sidelines and discards people with intellectual disabilities, as documented in painful detail by both *CIPOLD* (University of Bristol, 2013) and the *Mazars Report* (2015), as previously mentioned.

Both Wolfensberger and Sinason were developing these ideas in the 1970s and 1980s. As far as I know, they never communicated, but the parallels are striking. Both seek, from different starting points, to understand the consistent, societal rejection of people with intellectual disabilities, and their families. Taken together, their arguments are compelling, and I am not sure that contemporary theory and practice, which has largely chosen to overlook their insights, whether consciously or unconsciously, has taken us any further.

Conclusion

It has been an interesting, and thought-provoking experience to write this chapter and has enhanced my already high regard for Valerie Sinason, one of the most original and most courageous thinkers about intellectual disability. Compared to other authors, she has written comparatively little, but what she has written packs more into a short paragraph than most of us manage in lengthy tomes. At the time of writing, we are faced with a denuded and dehumanised health and social care system reeling under the constraints of austerity (UN Committee on the Rights of Persons with Disabilities, 2016). It is certainly worth revisiting Valerie's ideas at a time when I and others are struggling to understand, and resist, the undermining of what we saw as progress.

Notes

1 Ironically, my original terminology of "learning disability" used in this chapter was altered by the editors to "intellectual disability". I wonder what Valerie would say.
2 Alfred Tredgold's *Mental Deficiency (Amentia)* was the standard medical and nursing textbook from the time of its first publication in 1908 up until the 1980s. It went through numerous editions and even the updated twelfth edition, *Tredgold's Mental Retardation*, published in 1979, contains grotesque photographs of individuals to highlight their "defects".
3 This data will be cited in a paper to be authored by Iva Strnadová, Kelley Johnson, and the author of this chapter, but as this has yet to be submitted to a journal, no more details are available at the time of writing.

References

APBS (Association for Positive Behavior Support). (2017). What is Positive Behaviour Support? Available at: www.apbs.org/new_apbs/genintro.aspx#definition [last accessed 15.8.17].

APT (Association for Psychological Therapies). (2017). What does RAID stand for in mental health? Available at: www.apt.ac/what-does-raid-stand-for-in-mental-health.html [last accessed 30.12.2017].

BBC. (2011). *Panorama. Undercover Care: the Abuse Exposed Behind Closed Doors.* BBC One Television, 31 May.

BBC. (2016). *A World Without Down's Syndrome?* BBC Two Television, 5 October.

Brechin, A., & Walmsley, J. (1989). *Making Connections: Reflecting on the Lives and Experiences of People with Learning Difficulties.* London: Hodder & Stoughton.

Brown, H., & Walmsley, J. (1997). When 'ordinary' isn't enough: a review of the principle of normalisation. In: J. Bornat, J. Johnson, C. Pereira, D. Pilgrim, & F. Williams (Eds.), *Community Care: A Reader* (pp. 227–236). London: Palgrave Macmillan.

Care Quality Commission. (2016a). *Learning, candour and accountability: a review of the way NHS trusts review and investigate the deaths of patients in England.* Newcastle upon Tyne: Care Quality Commission. Available at: www.cqc.org.uk/publications/themed-work/learning-candour-and-accountability [last accessed 15.8.2017].

Care Quality Commission. (2016b). *Report on Southern Health NHS Foundation Trust, following Independent (Mazars) Report Commissioned by NHS England exploring failure to investigate and learn from deaths of patients accessing services for mental health, learning disability and older people.* London: Care Quality Commission.

Craft, M. (Ed.) (1979). *Tredgold's Mental Retardation* (12th edn). London: Ballière Tindall.

Corbett, A. (2014). *Disabling Perversions: Forensic Psychotherapy with People with Intellectual Disabilities.* London: Karnac.

Dale, P., & Walmsley, J. (in press). Should we be asking questions about deaths at the old institutions? *Community Living.* Lancashire: CI Initiatives Ltd.

Department of Health. (2001). *Valuing People: A New Strategy for Learning Disability for the 21st Century* (A White Paper). London: Central Office of Information.

Department of Health. (2009). *Valuing People Now: A New Three-year Strategy for People with Learning Disabilities* (A White Paper). London: Central Office of Information.

Heslop, P., & Macaulay, F. (2009). *Hidden Pain? Self-injury and People with Learning Disabilities.* Bristol: Bristol Crisis Service for Women.

Johnson, K., & Walmsley, J., with Wolfe, M. (2010). *People with Intellectual Disabilities: Towards a Good Life?* Bristol: Policy Press.

Justice for LB. (2014). 23 February. https://twitter.com/justiceforlb?lang=en [last accessed 15.8.2017].

Kara, 2008. (2015). LB's inquest: day 7, session 1, *Who By Fire – High Ordeals and Common Trials* (blog), 13 October. Available at: https://whobyf1re.wordpress.com/2015/10/13/lbs-inquest-day-7-session-1/ [last accessed: 15.8.2017].

Marks, D. (1999). *Disability: Controversial Debates and Psychosocial Perspectives.* London: Routledge.

Mazars. (2015). *Independent Review of Deaths of People with a Learning Disability or Mental Health Problem in Contact with Southern Health NHS Foundation Trust April 2011–March 2015.* Available at: www.england.nhs.uk/south/wp-content/uploads/sites/6/2015/12/mazars-rep.pdf [last accessed 15.8.2017].

McVeigh, T. (2016). Sally Phillips's film on Down's is 'unhelpful' for families, warns antenatal specialist. *The Observer*, 2 October. Available at: www.theguardian.com/society/2016/oct/01/downs-syndrome-screening-jane--fisher-expert-criticises-sally-phillips-bbc-documentary [last accessed 7.5.2017].

Mencap. (2007). *Death by Indifference*. Available at: www.mencap.org.uk/sites/default/files/2016-06/DBIreport.pdf [last accessed 15.08.2017].

Moss, F. (2017). 'Best interests': no choice, no oversight, no accountability – the sad story of MN. *My Life with an Autistic Daughter* (blog), 6 May. Available at: https://finolamoss.wordpress.com/2017/05/06/best-interests-no-choice-no-outcomes-no-accountability-the-story-of-mn/ [last accessed 6.5.2017].

Neary, M. (2017). *Love, Belief and Balls* (blog). Available at: https://marknearyldotcom1.wordpress.com/ [last accessed: 6.5.2017].

Open University. (1986). *Mental Handicap: Patterns for Living*. Milton Keynes: The Open University.

Open University. (1990). *Learning Disability: Changing Perspectives*. Milton Keynes: The Open University.

Race, D. G. (Ed.) (2003). *Leadership and Change in Human Services: Selected Readings from Wolf Wolfensberger*. London: Routledge.

Ryan, S. (2017). Summary. *MyDaftLife*. Available at: https://mydaftlife.com/summary/ [last accessed 15.8.2017].

7 Days of Action. (2016). Just want to go home. *7 Days of Action: Life for a Learning Disabled Person 2016* (blog), 25 April. Available at: https://theatuscandal.wordpress.com/2016/04/ [last accessed: 30.12.2017].

7 Days of Action. (2017). Official Twitter Account, 30 May. Available at: https://twitter.com/7days_campaigns?lang=en [last accessed: 15.8.2017].

Sinason, V. (1986). Secondary mental handicap and its relationship to trauma. *Psychoanalytic Psychotherapy*, *2*: 131–154.

Sinason, V. (1989). Barry: a case study. In: A. Brechin & J. Walmsley (Eds.), *Making Connections: Reflecting on the Lives and Experiences of People with Learning Difficulties*. (pp. 140–146). London: Hodder & Stoughton.

Sinason, V. (1992). *Mental Handicap and the Human Condition: New Approaches from the Tavistock*. London: Free Association Books.

Sinason, V. (2003). Foreword. In: D. Niedecken. *Nameless: Understanding Learning Disability* (pp. xv–xvii). Hove: Brunner-Routledge.

Soeffing, M. Y., & Wolfensberger, W. (1974). Normalization of services for the mentally retarded: a conversation with Dr Wolf Wolfensberger. *Education and Training of the Mentally Retarded*, *9*: 202–208. [reprinted in: D. G. Race (Ed.) (2003). *Leadership and Change in Human Services: Selected Readings from Wolf Wolfensberger* (pp. 185–187). London: Routledge.]

Strnadová, I., Johnson, K., & Walmsley, J. (2017). … but if you're afraid of things, how are you meant to belong? What belonging means to people with intellectual disabilities. *Journal of Applied Research in Intellectual Disabilities*. doi: 10.1111/jar.12469.

Tredgold, A. F. (1908). *Mental Deficiency (Amentia)*. London: Ballière, Tindall & Cox.

United Nations Convention on the Rights of Persons with Disabilities. (2016). *Inquiry Concerning the United Kingdom of Great Britain and Northern Ireland carried out by the Committee under Article 6 of the Optional Protocol to the Convention: Report of the Committee*. Geneva: United Nations. Available at: www.ohchr.org/EN/HRBodies/CRPD/Pages/InquiryProcedure.aspx [last accessed 21.2.2017].

University of Bristol. (2013). *CIPOLD (Confidential Inquiry into Premature Deaths of People with Learning Disabilities)*. Bristol: Norah Fry Research Centre. Available at: www.bris.ac.uk/cipold/reports/ [last accessed 31.12.2015] [reprinted in: Heslop, P., Blair, P. S., Fleming, P., Hoghton, M., Marriott, A., & Russ, L. (2014). The Confidential Inquiry into Premature Deaths of People with Learning Disabilities: A Population-based Study. *The Lancet*, *383*(9920): 889–895. Available at: www. thelancet.com/journals/lancet/article/PIIS0140-6736(13)62026–7/fulltext   [last accessed 15.8.2017].]

WeLDNurses. (2016). Twitter Account, 26 April. http://twitter.com/WeLDNurses [last accessed: 26.4.2016].

Wolfensberger, W. (1980a). A call to wake up to the beginning of a new wave of 'euthanasia' of severely impaired people. *Education and Training of the Mentally Retarded*, *15*: Guest Editorial, 171–173. [reprinted in: D. G. Race (Ed.) (2003). *Leadership and Change in Human Services: Selected Readings from Wolf Wolfensberger* (pp. 189–191). London: Routledge.]

Wolfensberger, W. (1980b). Extermination: disabled people in Nazi Germany. *Disabled USA*, *4*(2): 22–24. [reprinted in: D. G. Race (Ed.) (2003). *Leadership and Change in Human Services: Selected Readings from Wolf Wolfensberger* (pp. 191–193). London: Routledge.]

Wolfensberger, W., & Tullman, S. (1989). A brief outline of the principle of normalisation. In: A. Brechin & J. Walmsley (Eds.), *Making Connections: Reflecting on the Lives and Experiences of People with Learning Difficulties* (pp. 211–219). London: Hodder & Stoughton.

Chapter 12

Valerie Sinason, South Africa, and the politics of seeing

Leslie Swartz

As befits a glamorous international city and playground of the rich, famous and beautiful, Cape Town has a smart, modern airport. A problem with Cape Town for these pleasure-seekers, however, is the fact that the view from the highway on the short drive into the city is anything but glamorous – one can clearly see impoverished shanty towns, and the grim reality of bare life which confronts most people living in and around Cape Town. On one of her more recent visits to Cape Town, as she tells it, Valerie Sinason was in a taxi on her way to the city from the airport. Trying to be kind to an English tourist, the taxi driver said, "Don't look – that is not the real Cape Town." He was speaking to quite the wrong person: looking is what Valerie Sinason does most.

I first met Valerie in 1994. I had heard about her from Trevor Lubbe, a Cape Town psychoanalytic psychotherapist who had trained in London, and I had read something of her work. At the time, I was director of the Child Guidance Clinic at the University of Cape Town, at a time when we, as psychologists, were trying to develop new ways of engaging with the pressing issues facing our fractured society (Swartz, Gibson, & Gelman, 2002). We invited Valerie to Cape Town, and the rest, as they say, is history. Valerie has worked with many of us on the long haul of trying to develop services and practice which are appropriate and helpful in a context far removed from London.

South Africa is one of the most unequal societies in the world, as the spatial inequality of Cape Town continues to attest so graphically (McDonald, 2009). It is extremely violent (Prinsloo, Matzopoulos, Laubscher, Myers, & Bradshaw, 2016), with high rates of gender-based violence and femicide (Joyner, 2016); there are also intersections between other forms of violence and exclusion, and the abuse and exclusion of disabled people (van der Heijden, Abrahams, and Harries, 2016). South Africa has the highest HIV prevalence rate globally (Makusha et al., 2017), and, once again, there appear to be intersections of risk, with disabled people forming a population of particular concern (Groce et al., 2013). It is also the case that people who care for vulnerable people – formally trained healthcare workers, community healthworkers, and informal carers, amongst others – are themselves affected by poverty, inequality, oppression, and violence, and hence may struggle to provide care (Frenkel, 2002; Gibson & Swartz, 2008; van der Walt & Swartz, 1999). This is a world away from the Tavistock Clinic and the British health and care system, notwithstanding how concerned some may be about attacks on care in the UK at present (Bates, Goodley, & Runswick-Cole, 2017).

It would not be possible in this space for me to outline each and every contribution Valerie has made to our work in South Africa. Much of it I do not even know about (such is the nature of the contacts Valerie, through her generosity, has been able to make), despite having been her formal host for many of the years that she visited, before I moved to Stellenbosch University. I will try, instead, to offer some ideas as to what has made Valerie's contribution so valuable and unique.

In order to provide some context for this, I will give a brief description of some of the challenges of our work here. There is no country which believes that it has sufficient well-trained mental health professionals (Kakuma et al., 2011). In South Africa, in comparison with wealthier countries, however, there are far fewer professionals (Lund, Kleintjes, Kakuma, Flisher, & the MHaPP Research Programme Consortium, 2010), with a maldistribution of resources towards urban centres. In addition, many mental health professionals do not speak the languages of the client populations (Swartz & Kilian, 2014). Valerie was thrust into working with us in areas in which we were trying to do things for which we did not have a formal template. For example, in trying to assist teachers to deal with children who were subject to high degrees of political violence, we were working with teachers who were, themselves, often not well qualified. They were traumatised and struggling to find a space within themselves to provide some measure of containment for the children in their care (Evans & Swartz, 2010; Swartz, Gibson, & Gelman, 2002). In dealing with questions of abuse in the context of child disability, we had to contend with the impact of structural issues on the personal experience of carers (van den Berg, 2002). Picture, for example, the situation of a person having to care for twenty abandoned children under the age of three at bath time in the late afternoon. Picture this, that you are the one adult tasked with managing all the children at this time. Any psychological service aiming to support these children and those caring for them had to build on existing strengths and to be realistic about challenges.

Valerie helped us, as a sounding board, on a range of projects on childhood disability (McDougall, Swartz, & van der Merwe, 2006), dealing with trauma in healthcare (Frenkel, 2002), public health challenges (van der Walt & Swartz, 1999; 2002), and thinking about how to change policies and practices in the context of scarce resources. She provided a sounding board to a globally innovative project, helping people with intellectual disability who had been sexually abused to navigate the court and justice system, and helping the system to accommodate and adapt to assisting complainants with intellectual disabilities (Dickman & Roux, 2005). She helped us think through the complex, ethical challenges associated with questions about the representation in texts of children with disabilities and their families (Swartz, van der Merwe, Buckland, & McDougall, 2012). Her ways of thinking and of helping us to think had impacts, not only on the projects she consulted to, but also more distally – for example, when we were struggling with questions of ethics around photographing people with disabilities in rural South Africa, we drew on Valerie's earlier work with us (Mji, Schneider, Vergunst, & Swartz, 2014). A major project exploring the use of guidelines in the rural public health system, focusing on HIV and TB care, also drew on insights from Valerie in previous consultations (Mayers, 2010), probably without Valerie even being aware of this. In short, Valerie helped us think about work far beyond what is usually considered mental health work, and her influence and its effects continue.

Valerie first visited us first in 1994, the year in which South Africa became a democracy. South Africa was emerging from being a world pariah and a country largely isolated from much of the rest of the world because of boycotts (including the academic boycott), which played an important part in hastening the transition to democracy. Many people in the mental health field, as with other professionals, had left the country. It was a source of wry pride to those of us left behind that South Africans were so prominent in the development of cognitive behaviour therapy (especially in the USA) and in developments in contemporary psycho-analytic based practice in the UK. We were isolated and subject to varying degrees of what Australians so aptly call "the colonial cringe" (Fallows, 1991) – the belief (however much we resisted this belief consciously) that we could not be as good as those in the imperial centre.

The first thing Valerie did when she arrived was to listen and to watch. Very soon, it became clear to us that this visitor from the global North was different from many other visitors. She saw what we were trying to do. She did not assume *a priori* that what we were doing, untrained as we were from the position of those who hold formal psychoanalytic training, must, by definition, be worse than what someone from the North could offer. The following is an example of an opposite response from Valerie's. The first major psychoanalytic-based conference in South Africa after the fall of apartheid was in 1998, and I gave one of the plenary addresses. The chair for that session, a psychoanalyst trained in the UK but based in South Africa, commented after my talk that it had focused on conscious issues, focused as it was on contemporary issues in mental health practice in South Africa. Psychoanalysis, by contrast, she said, was concerned with the unconscious. I experienced this, as I had experienced (and, to an extent, continue to experience) many interventions from foreign-trained experts, as a fundamental disavowal. The implication was that as I am not trained in psychoanalysis, nothing that I could say would be of use or interest to those trained in the discipline. I have no doubt that had I done psychoanalytic training, I would have learned a great deal which would have improved my work, just as my work would have been vastly improved by a better grounding in public health and disability studies. I have no objection to my work being criticised and seen as useless or worse, on grounds of evidence or argument. I do object, however, to being disavowed on the basis of certain forms of knowledge being foregrounded as better than other forms (and allowing exclusive access to anything useful), and also on the basis of where I am located.

Valerie never assumed that, by definition, we did not know what we were doing. This allowed her, in her enthusiasm and generosity, to see what she believed was good in our work, to affirm us for that, and to build our skills further. She did not see us as a kind of collective *tabula rasa* needing enlightenment and removal from our dark, colonial present – she was interested in what we were doing and in helping us build on where we were.

In this, of course, there is an important parallel with Valerie's work on disability, and intellectual disability in particular. Psychology and psychoanalysis both have rather unfortunate histories when it comes to disability – they have contributed to research and practice traditions which have equated disability with deficit and lack, and which have made disabled people, as Tom Shakespeare has put it, "dustbins for disavowal" (1994). A key foundation of Valerie's work on disability (Sinason, 2010) is that she sees all people, and assumes that regardless of impairment or difficulty, people have an emotional and intellectual life, and that we all have something to offer. Her recognition of this is the basis not only for the emancipatory, disability related work that Valerie has pioneered in the UK, but also for her work here in South Africa; she sees the good and builds on it. She has the imagination, the lack of defensiveness, the lack of an imperial attitude, to allow herself to see what is there – to look at things in their complexity. She does not fear deficit, or abuse, or violence, or difficulty. It is partly this lack of fear, I think, that enables her to help not only the most vulnerable people but also their helpers, who themselves are vulnerable through their positioning in the global and local politics of inequality of resources and patterns of exclusion.

Shakespeare (1994) is no psychoanalyst (in fact, as a leading British figure in disability scholarship, he is probably quite sceptical of psychoanalysis), but his description of disabled people as "dustbins for disavowal" is, for me, an articulate and accessible description of projective identification. He describes how non-disabled people put all their weak, ugly, shameful parts of themselves into disabled people, a theme taken up and developed psychoanalytically by Brian Watermeyer (2013), a Cape Town psychologist, deeply influenced by the contact Valerie has had with us. The projective identifications described by Shakespeare and Watermeyer, of course, parallel ways in which South African mental health workers (professional and not formally trained) can be looked at, but not really seen, by outsiders. This constitutes not only an act of misrecognition but also a way for outsiders not to take the emotional risk of making themselves vulnerable to seeing what may make them uncomfortable.

Fearless Valerie saw us and our work. She was able to consider the possibility, not only that we could do things but also that we might have learned things she could not have learned from her own training and context – by being truly open to learning from us, she became one of our best teachers. It is important to note here that this act of seeing is complex and difficult, I imagine, even for Valerie. She does not disavow but she also does not idealise. She sees that through our work we try to help, but also, crucially, that we, as privileged South Africans, are complicit every day of our lives in various forms of oppression; this is something which is true for all people of privilege, but is easier to run away from or not to see in wealthier and more equal societies. To use disability politics language again, Valerie does not "supercrip" us (Schalk, 2016). Just as I resent the assumption by outsiders that I know nothing by virtue of my being an African, I equally resent the fawning praise we sometimes receive from people from outside about how they admire our work because it is so difficult and we have so few resources, and we do things they could never do. It is nice to be admired when the admiration is congruent, but when all the talk is about how wonderful we are, as with the breathless valorisation of disabled people who triumph over the impossible ("supercrips"), I do not feel seen. I do not want outsiders to tell me I am wonderful as a way of not really engaging. I want what Valerie offers – a real engagement with what I do well but also, centrally, with where I can and should do better.

I have often thought about what makes Valerie's contribution to work in South Africa unique. There are many people from other countries who help us very generously and I am grateful for the many collaborations with outsiders I have been fortunate to have; some of these are from wealthier countries and some from other African countries. Valerie is unique in that she is ebullient, curious, interested in absolutely everything, devastatingly intelligent but without ever using her intelligence to harm, and she has the energy and enthusiasm of a child taking on the world.

There is something more, though, which I think has to do with real fearlessness. On one of her visits to South Africa, Valerie returned to our home where she was staying, full of enthusiasm for a meeting she had had with a prominent person working in the South African occult crimes unit. She almost gleefully opened a sheaf of amongst the most gruesome photographs I have ever seen, and showed them to us. These were photographs taken by South African law enforcement personnel of victims of extremely violent murders. It was not that Valerie was happy these people had been killed – far from it. What she expressed to us was her relief that because the violence is ubiquitous and obvious in South Africa, there were so many people in law enforcement, in mental health, and in society more generally, who were prepared to face the fact that terrible, terrible things, like ritual abuse and acts of unspeakable cruelty, exist. Readers of this volume will be familiar with the range of accusations made against Valerie, many of them related to "false memories". The reasons for these allegations are complex, and I am certainly not the best person to comment on them. But part of what has made Valerie so special to people working in mental health in South Africa, has been her willingness not only to see us but also to see and live with the very difficult issues we have to deal with. I think that part of what brings Valerie back to us (although Valerie would be in a better position than I to speak on this) is not just her willingness and need to help but that our violent context can tolerate the fact that she is able to see what, to many, many people in wealthy countries like the UK, should never been seen nor even be admitted to exist. Valerie, because of who she is, is a brave person. We are able, I hope, to support her in her bravery, not because of who we are but because we, by circumstance, are forced to see things and be brave about them. "Don't look," said the taxi driver to *Valerie*, of all people. I hope that in some way we have helped to sustain her looking.

One of the most recent collaborations Valerie has had with a South African has been in the publication of an edited volume on dissociative identity disorder (DID) with Amelia van der Merwe (van der Merwe & Sinason, 2016). This book is especially close to my heart as Amelia is doing postdoctoral work with me, and is one of the most gifted students I have worked with. This book is a major international effort, drawing on the best international scholarship on DID, and not shying away from debate and controversy. Through this collaboration, Valerie and Amelia contribute not only to knowledge, but also to righting the knowledge imbalance between North and South. By working with Amelia, Valerie has chosen to speak back to regimes which assume that knowledge resides only with privileged people in privileged countries. Valerie opens the doors to seeing more, hearing more, learning more, and helping more. This is how she has been able to help us in South Africa. I hope that her interaction with us has gone some way to helping her, too, as one (enormously good, wonderfully generous, life-changing) turn deserves another.

References

Bates, K., Goodley, D., & Runswick-Cole, K. (2017). Precarious lives and resistant possibilities: the labour of people with learning disabilities in times of austerity. *Disability & Society, 32*: 160–175.

Dickman, B. J., & Roux, A. J. (2005). Complainants with learning disabilities in sexual abuse cases: a 10-year review of a psycho-legal project in Cape Town, South Africa. *British Journal of Learning Disabilities, 33*: 138–144.

Evans, J., & Swartz, L. (2010). Training service providers working with traumatized children in South Africa: the navigations of a trainer. *Psychodynamic Counselling, 6*(1): 49–64.

Fallows, J. (1991). The economics of the colonial cringe: pseudonomics and the sneer on the face of *The Economist. The Washington Post*, 6 October. Available at: www.theatlantic.com/technology/archive/1991/10/-quot-the-economics-of-the-colonial-cringe-quot-about-the-economist-magazine-washington-post-1991/7415/ [last accessed 17.8.2017].

Frenkel, L. (2002). 'You get used to it': Working with trauma in a burns unit of a South African children's hospital. *Psychodynamic Practice, 8*: 483–503.

Gibson, K., & Swartz, L. (2008). Putting the 'heart' back into community psychology: Some South African examples. *Psychodynamic Practice, 14*: 59–75.

Groce, N. E., Rohleder, P., Eide, A. H., MacLachlan, M., Mall, S., & Swartz, L. (2013). HIV issues and people with disabilities: a review and agenda for research. *Social Science & Medicine, 77*: 31–40.

Joyner, K. (2016). The epidemic of sexual violence in South Africa. *SAMJ: The South African Medical Journal, 106*: 1067–1067.

Kakuma, R., Minas, H., van Ginneken, N., Dal Poz, M. R., Desiraju, K., Morris, J. E., Saxena, S., & Scheffler, R. M. (2011). Human resources for mental health care: current situation and strategies for action. *The Lancet, 378*: 1654–1663.

Lund, C., Kleintjes, S., Kakuma, R., Flisher, A. J., & the MHaPP Research Programme Consortium. (2010). Public sector mental health systems in South Africa: interprovincial comparisons and policy implications. *Social Psychiatry and Psychiatric Epidemiology, 45*: 393–404.

Makusha, T., Mabaso, M., Richter, L., Desmond, C., Jooste, S., & Simbayi, L. (2017). Trends in HIV testing and associated factors among men in South Africa: evidence from 2005, 2008 and 2012 national population-based household surveys. *Public Health, 143*: 1–7.

Mayers, P. M. (2010). Nurses' experiences of guideline implementation in primary health care settings. Unpublished PhD thesis. Stellenbosch University, South Africa, March 2010. Available at: https://scholar.sun.ac.za/handle/10019.1/1437 [last accessed 30.12.2017].

McDonald, D. A. (2009). *World City Syndrome: Neoliberalism and Inequality in Cape Town.* New York: Routledge.

McDougall, K., Swartz, L., & van der Merwe, A. (2006). *Zip Zip My Brain Harts.* Cape Town: HSRC.

Mji, G., Schneider, M., Vergunst, R., & Swartz, L. (2014). On the ethics of being photographed in research in rural South Africa: views of people with disabilities. *Disability and Society, 29*: 714–723.

Prinsloo, M., Matzopoulos, R., Laubscher, R., Myers, J., & Bradshaw, D. (2016). Validating homicide rates in the Western Cape Province, South Africa: findings from the 2009 injury mortality survey. *SAMJ: The South African Medical Journal, 106*: 193–195.

Schalk, S. (2016). Reevaluating the supercrip. *Journal of Literary & Cultural Disability Studies, 10*(1): 71–86.

Shakespeare, T. (1994). Cultural representation of disabled people: dustbins for disavowal? *Disability & Society, 9*: 283–299.

Sinason, V. (2010). *Mental Handicap and the Human Condition: An Analytical Approach to Intellectual Disability* (2nd edn). London: Free Association Books.

Swartz, L., Gibson, K., & Gelman, T. (Eds.) (2002). *Reflective Practice: Psychodynamic Ideas in the Community.* Cape Town: HSRC.

Swartz, L., & Kilian, S. (2014). The invisibility of informal interpreting in mental health care in South Africa: notes towards a contextual understanding. *Culture, Medicine and Psychiatry, 38*: 700–711.

Swartz, L., van der Merwe, A., Buckland, A., & McDougall, K. L. (2012). Producing boundary-breaking texts on disability issues: the personal politics of collaboration. *Disability and Rehabilitation, 34*: 951–958.

van den Berg, R. (2002). Providing a containing space for unbearable feelings. In: L. Swartz, K. Gibson, & T. Gelman, (Eds.), *Reflective Practice: Psychodynamic Ideas in the Community* (pp. 45–55). Cape Town: HSRC.

van der Heijden, I., Abrahams, N., & Harries, J. (2016). Additional layers of violence: the intersections of gender and disability in the violence experiences of women with physical disabilities in South Africa. Journal of Interpersonal Violence, 27 April. Available at: http://journals.sagepub.com/doi/abs/10.1177/0886260516645818 [last accessed 30.06.2018].

van der Merwe, A., & Sinason, V. (Eds.). (2016). *Shattered but Unbroken: Voices of Triumph and Testimony*. London: Karnac.

van der Walt, H., & Swartz, L. (1999). Isabel Menzies Lyth revisited institutional defences in public health nursing in South Africa during the 1990s. *Psychodynamic Counselling*, 5: 483–495.

van der Walt, H. M., & Swartz, L. (2002). Task orientated nursing in a tuberculosis control programme in South Africa: where does it come from and what keeps it going? *Social Science and Medicine, 54*: 1001–1009.

Watermeyer, B. (2013). *Towards a Contextual Psychology of Disablism*. Abingdon: Routledge.

Chapter 13

Like an owl in the tree

Learning from Valerie Sinason in treating patients with intellectual disabilities in Sweden

Anders Svensson

I had been working as a psychologist for ten years. For most of those years I worked with people with intellectual disabilities. I had discourses with them about their lives, their happinesses, and their problems. I liked my work. I worked at different places and gathered experience. My three kids had already been born by the time the "heavy" case began. Twenty-five years have passed since then. That heavy case is still lying under a thin membrane inside me and now it is starting to move.

I had been working at a hospital for adults with intellectual disabilities. I had been there for a while when something very unexpected happened. A suspicion emerged, and grew, that a female patient had been raped. Two years earlier, a child had been assaulted in the same area. The suspicions led to a police investigation. It was decided that my therapeutic treatment with the patient should start when the investigation had finished.

During the intervening time, I found out from a newspaper article that there was a psychotherapist called Valerie Sinason working in the UK, who had great knowledge about people with intellectual disabilities who had been sexually abused. I asked Valerie for her help with my case and, in the autumn of 1991, we had three long telephone conversations. In the course of these conversations it became very clear to me that Valerie understood my case and my situation. After twenty-five years, I still remember that feeling of being understood. As there were no experts in intellectual disability and sexual abuse in Sweden at that time, Valerie suggested that she be my supervisor when the sessions started. I explained that there would probably not be any money for supervision from my employer and Valerie answered that it did not matter. In my notes from the first session, the patient shows me how she had been clutched by someone's hands. She shows she is relieved that the sessions have begun and she shows gratitude towards me. This, I think, was a reflection – a kind of parallel process – of how I, too, felt at Valerie so kindly offering her support to me.

Here the relief ends. Here the fear appears in me. Here the terror emerges again. The feeling is precisely the same as it was twenty-five years ago: the same heavy force through my stomach and the same thoughts that repeat and repeat. It is not possible to write about those eighty-five sessions or about those incidents outside of the sessions. I would rather not speak about the insights that arose during our work. It was obvious for all of us that the case was one of ritual abuse and, in writing this now, I find that the terror that I felt twenty-five years ago returns easily, along with the feelings and the questions: "What might happen if I write about this? What could happen? Think carefully." I decide it is not possible to keep on speaking. I live a calm and peaceful life. I do not want to run the risk that somebody will stand on the sidewalk outside our house and look through our windows, or to be exposed to that terror that is connected with the silent telephone calls in the middle of the night. I also worry about what the Swedish tabloid newspapers could still write about this case. I have decided, together with Valerie, that in writing this chapter to describe and celebrate her influence on me, I will not revisit that painful case which has been described before (Sinason, 2010, pp. 263–264); Sinason & Svensson, 1994). I will write, instead, about some of the things I learned from Valerie during those years.

An open mind

I learned from Valerie to have an open, living mind during the sessions with my patient. I learned to be open to the unexpected and to the awful, and to have my ears tuned to the words that may never have been spoken before. This capacity of Valerie's for being open to hearing the hitherto unthinkable is what shines through her writing in *Mental Handicap and the Human Condition* (1992).

Patients could tell me something. I listened and followed, and at the same time, I was prepared for the new opening. It was as if I had discovered a new facility inside myself and the feeling was of catching flying balls with both of my hands. I had been accustomed to catching balls with one of my hands as a matter of routine. Now, however, I found my other hand was also open; it was prepared and very much alert. This hand captured probably the most important balls. Something could happen from one word to the next.

An altered language

From Valerie I also learned a lot about language itself. Above all, I learned to adjust my language to my intellectually disabled patient's own language. I did this by learning to use only the words that my patient understood and, also, by generally using her own words and expressions. I connected my language to her so that all the words in my therapeutic language become completely comprehensible for her and we could understand each other. This "joint" language, and the potential for enhanced communication that it opened up, gave my patient an experience of competence. It has been my experience that communication and language which is attuned to that of the patient, gives the patient a new experience of understanding and of being understood.

I came to understand how important this phenomenon is when I heard Valerie present imagined dialogues with patients through role-play in our supervision sessions. Bit by bit, I learned how it worked and what great significance this adjustment of language has. The stress of the patient is greatly reduced through the experience of being understood. I learned to pay particular attention to the way in which a session opened – the first words spoken by the patient in the session. This would give me my "lead" and then I would adapt my language in response to it.

The importance of comfort and kindness

The third lesson I learned from Valerie was the ability to give comfort. Comfort is directed to painful experiences that remain in some way in the memory of the patient. I learned to respond with kindness and empathy to the pain of the disability itself, and to understand that the impact of the disability was often a profound assault on the self-confidence of the patient. Valerie was very skilful in teaching me about where my offerings of comfort and kindness should best be directed, how to offer these, and the importance of using kind and natural words in response. I came to understand that this comfort may be one of the most important aspects of the therapeutic dialogue with a patient who has intellectual disabilities.

Working with the preconscious

I learned from Valerie that the preconscious is a critical part of my practice, and a vital tool in helping me attune to the patient's communication, language, and narration of self. In my transcripts in English of the sessions with my patient, I was faced with separate words or sentences that were incomprehensible to me. We used particular signs, such as, "##", for these. These words were incomprehensible during the session itself and incomprehensible when I listened to them on the recording of the session. Sometimes, some words became clear and comprehensible after listening to the recording several times, but some of the words persisted in their incomprehensibility. We called the incomprehensible words and sentences "black". The "white" words were those that we had no difficulty in understanding. These were words that connected with the content in the former sessions. The partially understandable words used within the setting where both patient and I were connected, were described as "grey". The "grey" was the preconscious. In our supervision sessions Valerie directed my gaze towards these "grey" parts. She explained that the "grey" parts of the sessions were the doors to our being able to help the narrative move forwards. They were also often the way to a greater depth of understanding.

In this therapy which Valerie supervised, my patient was a woman with moderate intellectual disabilities. She was also severely traumatised due to many years of abuse. After a while during the session, when she had talked for a moment understandably and coherently within the "white", she could, after a short break, say something less easy for me to understand or compute, such as, "The shoes were wet" or, "a lot of food". These statements did not connect with anything else from the earlier sessions and so did not mean anything to me. I even thought that she may have said them by mistake. Valerie, however, had a completely different approach to these statements from the preconscious. With her help, this "grey" became comprehensible to me, and a little bit of knowledge in this subject started to grow inside me. In the next session, the utterance, "The shoes are wet" may lead, for example, to the beginning of a story in which the incidents of her abuse took place in a forest where the ground was wet. Or the three words, "shoes were wet" might lead to a different memory in another context. The three words could, in fact, be the key to a locked gate.

The patient's whole story over eighty-five sessions could be compared to a lot of things. When I have described this case I have mostly used the metaphor of meadows. Every meadow is connected to two or three other meadows. There are gates between meadows and these gates may function as the creative possibilities of the preconscious. In the early sessions, perhaps until Session 5, I see us as having been in the first meadow. Then we encountered a gate and it was opened. Once we had passed from one meadow to another during the patient's story, it was as if the earlier meadow was gone from the narrative and from her memory. She never returned to a meadow, and thus to themes or incidents that we had talked about earlier. She could only talk about the meadow in which we were at the time. She told me about terrible incidents that had happened to her but these memories only existed for a short period, perhaps for a month. The therapy lasted for over thirty months. Valerie helped me understand this process and I learned as much I could from her.

In my work with the patient, although each meadow was full of meaning in itself, I was struck by the way in which, in our psychotherapeutic discourse, she never returned to the first meadow, or indeed, any earlier one. I was working without a linear narrative, or any appearance of one. The capacity to work without linear narrative is an important aspect of work with many people who may have cognitive limitations of one kind or another, whether through intellectual disability, trauma, brain injury, or because they are young children. Valerie has done so much to help me and other professionals working with people with intellectual disabilities to embrace this experience, thereby co-creating meaning and affective experience between therapist and patient.

Despite the absence of a linear narrative, there were images and words that recurred. My patient said repeatedly that the people who committed the abuse used ugly words like, "hell" and "Satan". These are the most common swear words in the Swedish language. Her complaints about their use of language was one of the few details that followed her across all of the meadows.

A moral framework

During the years of collaboration and supervision with Valerie, I learned about the great value of working with morals. I learned to put the patient's narrative into a moral context. I think that it is a matter of making the incomprehensible incidents understandable and coherent and to recognise the moral world in the narrative. The therapist's moral work is often connected with the thing I used to call comfort. In the moral context, the patient is often the victim and objectively seen as nothing else. The therapist emphasises the innocence of the patient whom they see as a kind person exposed to evil others. It is necessary to simplify the intervention and separate the good and the evil. The simplification facilitates for the patient and is somewhat, or very much, coherent with the patient's view of life. This moral work establishes clarity.

The patient's own ability to condemn or despise an abuser can be impaired and weakened and the patient can find him or herself in a constantly weak position existentially. The patient's own self is in a state of disempowerment and weakness in all aspects of life. This is a consequence of how the patient perceives him or herself and his or her handicap. This weak position is, of course, influenced by his or her experiences of people generally, and how he or she is treated by them. The devalued position of people with intellectual disabilities in society can lead, cumulatively, to a weakening of self, and certainly to a weakening of a sense of the value of the self. Such a weakening, familiar to the dynamics in abusive relationships, can serve to blur boundaries of right and wrong. Abusers commonly work to shift responsibility for their actions onto their victims. For many people with intellectual disabilities, this happens at a political or societal level. Valerie's supervision helped me address this issue in a clear and concrete way, so that I could state overtly where good and bad lay.

Below, I will give some examples to illustrate this issue of power dynamics. To give some background to this, I wish to say that I have worked with about eighty cases of sexually abused patients with intellectual disabilities. In some of these cases, the patient has been the perpetrator. In other cases, a patient has been both perpetrator and victim. In most of my cases, the patient has been the victim of sexual abuse. In most cases, the perpetrator has been a man. In five cases, it has been a woman. Three of these women were perpetrators together with a man or many men. Two women were single perpetrators. A perpetrator misleads, terrifies, and threatens the victim or maybe the victim's family. The perpetrator's position, in relation to the victim, is entirely superior in power and initiative. The perpetrator uses his or her intelligence and power against the victim and the victim's helplessness.

Example 1

A twenty-five-year-old woman with mild disabilities told me that she had been raped by a physically disabled man in a wheelchair. They both lived in a residential college. The alleged rapist had told my patient to take her clothes off and come to his bed. I asked her why she did it and she answered that she was not able to do anything else. She felt she was forced to do what he told her to do. I asked her why she did not leave. She answered that it was not possible for her. This fact of the impossibility speaks to me of her sense of utter powerlessness.

Example 2

Another example is of a man with mild intellectual disabilities who was sexually abused by his uncle for the whole of his adolescence. Even though the abuse continued for five years, the boy never told anyone. However, one time he tried to escape. When his uncle came to pick him up and rang the doorbell at the boy's home, the boy did not open the door. The uncle then pushed open the letterbox in the door and said, "I can see your legs. You are inside." This made the boy open the door and let the man in. The boy said to me, "He had seen me so I had to let him in." This was the only occasion when the boy had tried to escape or hide. He had tried, but had surrendered immediately.

Example 3

The last example involves a teenage girl with moderate intellectual disabilities who was sexually abused by a taxi driver on several occasions over several years. The taxi driver drove her to school every morning. One morning, after her parents had left the house, the girl tried to escape from the taxi driver. She did not go out, as usual, to wait for him in the street. Instead, she hid under her parents' bed. The taxi driver searched for her, looking through the windows. When he saw her, she crawled out from under the bed, and went to sit in the taxi.

A calm and peaceful sensibility

Twenty-five years have passed since my supervision with Valerie began. Reflecting now, it seems to me that it was Valerie who taught me the importance of finding a sense of calm and peace in each session. I learned from her that, irrespective of the direction of the discourse, or the quality and intensity of the feelings, or the violence of the content, there is still a space for this calm and peace, and that it is part of the therapist's work to find this and to experience it alongside their patient.

Since those years, 1991–1994, I have become used to working with, and am less disturbed by, abuse cases. At one time during those eighty-five sessions in which Valerie and I collaborated, Valerie said, "Now you have heard the worst. There will never be anything worse." Her words, of course, gave me a sense of calm which has remained in me for all of these years.

During more recent years, I have been using quotes and short narratives in lectures about the adults with intellectual disabilities with whom I have worked, to help create a "picture with words". Amongst these nearly one hundred texts that I use, there are some that depict sexual abuse or the consequences of it. I conclude my chapter with ten of these. The first three describe the case in which Valerie helped me. The last text is the oldest one and describes a case I worked with before I met Valerie. In the other texts, Valerie's spirit is present as an attitude, a respectful witness – like an owl in the tree.

Texts
1
May not
One may not do like that.
One may not.
May not do so.
May not say so
Hell, hell, hell to do so.
One may not.
When she said that, I didn't understand anything.
2
Heavy lights
Later that same summer
she whispered to me about the old men and the old women
about the disgusting songs,
the heavy lights and black things in the strange house.
In the damned house.
3
In my lap
She rises and sits down in my lap
and she says: "It's not nice for you to hear
what I am telling you.
Not nice for you, Anders. Not at all.
It's not nice for you to hear it.
I pity you.

4
The cat
I don't remember anything of my boyhood.
Except that both Mummy and Daddy did it with me.
but mummy did it just a few times.
Yes, I remember the cat.
I fell in love with the cat
who suddenly just appeared.
5
Now
Now I am spared,
spared, spared, spared.
Do you hear me?
Spared.
I don't even have to go up the stairs.
Can stay down here.
He said I am spared and I don't have to.
6
In prison
I want them to go to prison
So I can get calm
meet a boyfriend and settle down.
7
Rape
We have sessions every week.
She says the same things.
She has it written down and in copies.
And she gives me a copy every time.
The man in the brown Nissan raped me in the little forest.
Then I came to the nurse and to the doctor.
But he did it again the same summer.
It's nine years ago by now.
She tells it carefully and in the same way, for a year.
Then we begin to fantasise that there should have been
fifty women and fifty men.
The women helped her, comforted her and carried her.
The men yelled at him, frightened him, hit him
and put him in prison.
She changed, became calmer, could listen to others.
But she kept wondering:
Why didn't the hundreds of persons
come when it happened?
8
Ashamed

He is so awfully ashamed.
I thought everybody did it.
In all families.
9
I am a human
I can't fucking swallow it.
I puke at once.
I am human for heaven's sake, right?
10
Amber
Beaches of amber and a family of fishermen.
My fiancé followed me home for Christmas.
We ate downstairs in the room next to the kitchen
eggs, herring, snaps and porridge.
But upstairs, in my old girl's room
A relative came, from my sister's side
And he told my fiancé to sit under the table
while he was doing it with me.
The young psychologist could hardly imagine
that such things could happen.
He was still missing an open mind.

References

Sinason, V. (1992). *Mental Handicap and the Human Condition: New Approaches from the Tavistock*. London: Free Association Books.

Sinason, V. (2010). *Mental Handicap and the Human Condition: An Analytical Approach to Intellectual Disability* (2nd edn). London: Free Association Books.

Sinason, V., & Svensson, A. (1994). Going through the fifth window: "Other cases rest on Sundays. This one didn't". In: V. Sinason (Ed.), *Treating Survivors of Satanist Abuse* (pp. 13–21). London: Routledge.

Chapter 14

Valerie Sinason and the psychodynamics of bravery

Brett Kahr

I first encountered Valerie Sinason on Saturday 28th March, 1987, just over thirty years ago. It seems striking to me that I should remember the date. But I do ... because Valerie Sinason made such a huge impression, and I shall never forget that very first meeting.

On that occasion, the Association of Child Psychotherapists had organised a special eightieth birthday celebration for Dr John Bowlby, the legendary psychoanalyst, held, appropriately, at the Zoological Society, right across the road from the London Zoo, in recognition of Bowlby's interest in Darwinism and in ethology. I had the great privilege of having known Dr Bowlby for several years; hence, I decided that I would attend these celebrations, and as a young psychologist, I did so eagerly, keen to participate in this landmark tribute. Valerie Sinason did not actually deliver a paper herself at that memorable conference – in 1987 she had only just embarked upon her own publishing career and had not yet achieved the level of international academic and clinical distinction that would soon follow – but, as Convenor of the Association of Child Psychotherapists' External Programme Planning Committee, she did serve as both the pro-genitor and as the principal organiser of the day's proceedings and, also, as chairperson for one of the sessions.

In my estimation, most chairpersons at conferences rarely perform their function well. Members of the mental health profession often host their panels in a particularly unimpressive manner. The vast majority will mumble their way through an inadequate introduction, and, quite frequently, chairpersons will offer only meagre words of praise for the speaker, often as a result of envy. I cannot even begin to list the number of conferences that I have attended over the years at which chairpersons have simply muttered: "Well, you all know Dr So-and-So, therefore I will dispense with the usual pleasantries and just invite him (or her) to deliver the paper."

I must confess that I cannot recall precisely which of the invitees Valerie introduced but I do remember that she undertook her task brilliantly. Not only did she project her mellifluous, animated, audible, musical voice to the very back of the auditorium, and awaken all the sleepy attendees from their post-prandial slumber, but also she provided the most generous of introductions to the speaker in question.

Valerie not only chaired in this exemplary and welcome fashion but also took the time and the trouble to express particular thanks to Miss Dorothy Southern, Dr Bowlby's long-serving private secretary. Sinason told us that Dorothy Southern had worked for Bowlby for more than thirty-five years – in fact, I later discovered that she had begun to look after Bowlby as early as 1951! – and Sinason underscored that such a lengthy association between these two people certainly provided us with an important insight into John Bowlby's capacity to forge and maintain long-term attachment relationships. By offering this piece of biographical detail about Dorothy Southern, Sinason not only paid homage to a wonderful woman who had never received any public recognition for her work, but in addition she convinced us all that Bowlby actually practised what he preached, and that he possessed the capacity to maintain secure, long-term bonds in his own private life. If we had discovered that Bowlby could not keep a secretary and that he kept replacing each of his assistants year after year, this knowledge would hardly have inspired our confidence in his ability to understand the importance of reliable, ongoing attachments!

Little did I know, back in 1987, that this sort of seeming "throwaway" comment, welcoming Dorothy Southern to the conference, actually epitomised the very essence of Sinasonianism: namely the capacity and, indeed, the necessity to treat everyone with equal dignity and value, whether a world-famous octogenarian grandee or his humble secretary, known to so few.

I remember that Bowlby's niece, the child psychotherapist Juliet Hopkins (later Dr Hopkins), delivered a paper on this occasion, which I rather enjoyed, and I also recall quite vividly that Bowlby himself presented some material from his forthcoming work on the childhood of Charles Darwin, which would eventually be published in book form in the year of his death (Bowlby, 1990). But in spite of the extraordinary honour of hearing Bowlby speak for the last time, and in spite of the high quality of the other presentations, the voice of Valerie Sinason left a far greater impression on me.

Not long thereafter, I had the pleasure of bumping into Valerie Sinason at a psychoanalytical conference held at the University of East London, and I plucked up the courage to introduce myself. Having published virtually nothing at all at that point, apart from a few *pièces d'occasion*, Sinason had no reason to know me; nonetheless, she greeted me in her characteristically warm fashion, and a collegiality soon ensued. When she discovered that I had only just begun to work psychotherapeutically with an intellectually disabled person as part of my forensic psychotherapy training at the Portman Clinic in London, she very graciously invited me to present a paper about this particular patient to the Mental Handicap Workshop at the Tavistock Clinic next door (Stokes & Sinason, 1992).

I accepted Valerie's kind and generous offer in spite of my tremendous trepidation. After all, the Tavistock Clinic, at that time, represented the very pinnacle of psychodynamic institutions in Great Britain, and I feared that I might not be up to the challenge. But Valerie welcomed me in a most kind and enthusiastic manner and she introduced me to a large group of colleagues in the Mental Handicap Workshop, and then offered me the opportunity to discuss my forensic case, namely, that of a man who had suffered from peri-natal anoxia at birth and who sustained brain damage a result, and who, in later years, became violent and attacked elderly women.

As a mere psychotherapeutic stripling, with but a modicum of experience in facilitating long-term dynamic psychotherapy, I described my case with some hesitation, convinced that all the geniuses at the Tavistock Clinic, including Valerie, would lacerate me for having failed to make the right in-depth inter-pretation or for having neglected to comment on the negative transference or, indeed, for any number of other psychological infelicities.

When I finished speaking about my work with this very troubled and disadvantaged man, I looked to Valerie, expecting that she would launch into a lengthy, articulate, and wise re-analysis of my material. In fact, she paused for several seconds, and then a look of great sadness descended upon her face, and she exclaimed, "Well done! What a painful case! That poor man! Well done on managing as you have done."

Although I had expected criticism, Valerie Sinason showered me with encouragement. After breathing a sigh of relief – probably a very audible one – we then opened up the discussion to the entire membership of the Mental Handicap Workshop, and everyone shared their thoughts in a frank and helpful manner, and I succeeded in learning a great deal more about my patient than ever before. But such an honest exchange could have unfolded only after Valerie's initial blessing as chairwoman. With her simple and decent remark, she made me feel like a young colleague rather than a mere trainee in need of a reprimand.

Not long thereafter, Valerie invited me to attend the meetings of the Mental Handicap Workshop on a regular basis, which I did with enthusiasm, and then, after a time, she invited me to become a member of the Mental Handicap Team in which we discussed new referrals and ongoing cases. As my clinical experience in the field of "mental handicap" (subsequently known as "learning disability" and, eventually, as "intellectual disability") grew and grew, I had the privilege of taking on new patients and benefiting from Valerie's benign and wise supervisory lens. After several years more, I began to work for Valerie formally as Course Tutor for the mental handicap trainings in the Child and Family Department at the Tavistock Clinic, and our associ-ation developed from there.

Over these last thirty years, I have met few colleagues who have displayed greater warmth and affection and generosity. Valerie Sinason has become one of my most esteemed teachers, mentors, guides, and friends. We have taught together, lectured together, collaborated on projects together, discussed clinical and organisational matters together, and much more. Above all, I have never failed to learn from her seemingly endless fountain of wisdom. My gratitude remains both immense and lifelong.

But in spite of Valerie's unique kindness and decency as a human being and as a professional colleague, it would be quite inadequate to characterise her simply as being nice. She possesses another crucial characterological component: a component far more rare, namely, her *bravery*. While many people might be friendly, loving, decent, facilitative, creative, and ethical – all qualities which Sinason enjoys aplenty – very few have the capacity to be brave as well. And in offering this testimonial of respect and appreciation for Valerie Sinason, I wish to focus on her unique and admirable ability to be brave and strong in the face of pain and hatred and resistance and danger.

Strikingly, in spite of the many topics investigated so carefully by countless numbers of psychoanalytical clinicians and writers over the last century, no one has, to the very best of my knowledge, explored the subject of bravery. Even Professor Sigmund Freud, who wrote about *everything*, offered very few insights into the psychodynamics of bravery or courage, and he certainly never crafted a well-developed discussion of the concept. Freud made only occasional comments about brave and courageous people throughout his corpus of works, and he often did so merely *en passant*. For instance, in his monograph on the great artist and scientist Leonardo da Vinci, published in 1910, Freud (1910b, p. 122) praised the Italian maestro:

> Thus he became the first modern natural scientist, and an abundance of discoveries and suggestive ideas rewarded his courage for being the first man since the time of the Greeks to probe the secrets of nature while relying solely on observation and his own judgement.[1]

Perhaps one might regard Freud as the very first brave person in the history of psychoanalysis. After all, he displayed the courage and the temerity to challenge traditional nineteenth-century approaches to the treatment of mental illness (Kahr, 2013, 2017). At a time when quite a large number of physicians either neglected their hysterical neurotic patients – especially females – or performed horrific surgical procedures upon them (e.g., hysterectomies, ovariectomies, even clitoridectomies (e.g., Brown, 1866)), Freud (1895) promoted the much more simple, much more humane talking cure. By developing an overtly psychological approach as a means of alleviating mental illness, Freud risked the disapprobation of innumerable colleagues (cf. Jones, 1955; Kahr, 2009), and yet, in spite of the hatred that he had to endure, he maintained his conviction in the utility of psychoanalysis and he remained bravely and unswervingly committed to his clinical discoveries.

At a period in medical history when physicians would often lacerate the bodies of both female and male psychiatric patients, Freud invited his analysands to recline comfortably on a couch and to relate their stories of misery and woe in the comfortable and confidential privacy of his consulting room (Kahr, 2013, 2017). In this respect, he anticipated the anti-psychiatric revolution which would emerge during the 1960s and beyond (e.g., Laing, 1960; cf. Double, 2002, 2006; Heaton, 2006) and brought tremendous tenderness and compassion to the care and cure of the psychologically unwell.

In similar vein, I would also regard Donald Winnicott as a brave man. During the 1920s and 1930s, Winnicott, then a young physician practising in the field of children's medicine, began to investigate the ways in which psychoanalysis might help colleagues to understand some of the more troubling symptoms of infancy and childhood. At a time when medical practitioners often dismissed children's nausea or bedwetting or tremors as irritating bids for attention, Winnicott endeavoured to demonstrate that such psychosomatic symptoms result from difficulties within the home environment (e.g., Winnicott, 1930a, 1930b, 1931a, 1931b, 1933a, 1933b, 1936, 1939) and embraced psychoanalytical models of understanding when such models were highly contentious and under attack from physicians of the time.

In later years, Winnicott demonstrated his bravery in many other ways, not least in his pioneering work as a media psychologist, delivering unique broadcasts on the radio, helping mothers to understand the meaning of their babies' lives and minds: a task which no other mental health profession had undertaken previously in such a public way (e.g., Winnicott, 1945a, 1945c, 1945d, 1945e, 1945f, 1945g, 1949a, 1957a, 1957b, 1987, 1993; cf. Kahr, 1996, 2015b, 2017b). Through this work, Winnicott became the very first psychoanalyst in Great Britain to reach an audience of literally millions of people.

As if Winnicott had not already demonstrated enough bravery by championing psychological paediatrics and media psychology, he also proved his courage by daring to speak out forcefully against what he regarded as the cruel, indeed sadistic, somatic psychiatric treatments so prevalent during the 1940s, namely, leucotomy and electroconvulsive shock (e.g., Winnicott, 1943a, 1943b, 1943c, 1944a, 1944b, 1944c, 1945b, 1947a, 1947b, 1949b, 1949c, 1951a, 1951b, 1951c, 1954a, 1954b, 1956; cf. Kahr, 2011, 2015a, 2019). In doing so, Winnicott had to endure much snide commentary from psychiatric colleagues (e.g., Millar, 1947; Young, 1947; cf. Kahr, 2019).

Although Sigmund Freud and Donald Winnicott remain beacons of inspiration for their bravery and for their fortitude, very few mental health professionals have followed in their footsteps. In my experience, most clinicians simply aspire to become merely "good enough": decent people who apply Freudian, Jungian, Kleinian, Winnicottian, and Bowlbian ideas in their daily work, but who rarely make a paradigm-shifting impact in our field. Fortunately, men such as Freud and Winnicott have provided a template in which mental health professionals might engage in acts of bravery, and no doubt their work inspired Sinason.

Across the course of her clinical lifetime, Valerie Sinason has demonstrated immense bravery in many different ways. First, she championed the use of psychodynamic methods of treatment in work with disabled and handicapped patients. During the 1970s, virtually no one had ever worked psychoanalytically with nonverbal or brain-damaged patients; and yet Sinason, fortified by her successful experiences, pioneered the field of disability psychotherapy, exploring how classical psychoanalytical notions and methods could help to strengthen the shattered minds of her disabled patients. Through these clinical investigations, she discovered that many of these learning disabled men, women, and children had suffered tremendous physical, sexual, and emotional abuse, which exacerbated their symptoms tremendously. At that time, few colleagues could bring themselves to hear about Sinason's clinical findings, and many of her senior mentors at the Tavistock Clinic thought that she must have imagined these stories of abuse, doubtful that human beings could actually treat their children in such a grotesque way. Undeterred by the resistance, Sinason turned to her patients for guidance. As they kept revealing similar tales of trauma, Sinason persisted in her efforts to understand the traumatological origins of psychopathology, and in doing so, she discovered instances in which abuse will unfold on an almost unspeakable scale, namely, in multi-perpetrator paedophile gangs and in religious cults. Indeed, victims of such unparalleled abuse would, subsequently, often develop dissociative identity disorders or psychotic disorders as a desperate means to rid their minds of these atrocious experiences.

Valerie demonstrated her bravery and her courage in many other ways: first, by believing the narratives of her patients, rather than dismissing them as delusional; second, by confirming the data again and again over time, mindful of the possibility that patients might exaggerate or lie; third, by lecturing publicly and by teaching about her work and thus subjecting her findings to intense collegial scrutiny; fourth, by publishing her clinical findings internationally; and fifth, by amalgamating her discoveries with those of other colleagues, thus ensuring that her data corresponded with that of pioneers in other countries. In this way, Sinason has proved herself a most brave personality and a most courageous mental health practitioner by embracing the subjects that most of her colleagues have avoided.

As a result of her labours, Dr Valerie Sinason has become the honorary mother of the field of disability psychotherapy. Furthermore, she has created an organisation, the Clinic for Dissociative Studies in London, in which those abused in multi-perpetrator groups receive compassionate psychotherapeutic treatment after having failed to obtain proper help from their local psychiatric teams. Through her teaching, through her supervision work, through her public lectures, and through her books, chapters, papers, and media broadcasts, Sinason has changed the landscape of mental health care in Great Britain and beyond as a result of her tireless research into the nature of traumatology. Such an undertaking requires immense bravery and unyielding fortitude.

Her many books offer outstanding proof of what she has accomplished. Indeed, Sinason has bequeathed to us a veritable library of standards, such as *Mental Handicap and the Human Condition: New Approaches from the Tavistock* (Sinason, 1992); *Understanding Your Handicapped Child* (Sinason, 1993); *Treating Survivors of Satanist Abuse* (Sinason, 1994); *Memory in Dispute* (Sinason, 1998); and *Attachment, Trauma and Multiplicity: Working with Dissociative Identity Disorder* (Sinason, 2002), to name but a few of her classic titles, many of which have now appeared in revised, updated editions (e.g., Sinason, 2010, 2011). But, additionally, as described in this volume, she has written books about abuse and trauma, in collaboration with Professor Sheila Hollins specifically for men and women with intellectual disabilities who have often suffered dreadful forms of cruelty, such as *Jenny Speaks Out* (Hollins and Sinason, 1992); *Bob Tells All* (Hollins and Sinason, 1993); and *Mugged* (Hollins, Horrocks, and Sinason, 2002).

Bravery stems from many roots, and it would be foolhardy for me to attempt to understand the origins of Sinason's special qualities in this regard. As a modest woman, she would, no doubt, attribute her bravery to all that she had learned from her teachers, her clinical supervisors, her psychoanalysts, her mentors, her colleagues, her students, and her patients. In view of the fact that Valerie Sinason has the capacity to listen very carefully and open-mindedly, I have little doubt that these many people fortified Sinason in her researches. But I do not believe that her teachers allowed her to become brave. I strongly suspect that her courage and fortitude long predated her training in the mental health profession.

Perhaps one day Sinason will write a memoir which explores these roots more personally and more authentically; and, indeed, in her interview with Dr Alan Corbett, printed in this Festschrift, she has spoken about the way in which her parents have influenced her life and work. Happily, I had the privilege of meeting both her late mother, Mrs Tamar Segal, and her late father, Professor Stanley Segal, and I know that she derived much inspiration from these toweringly brave people. Tamar Segal distinguished herself as a poet who wrote many moving public tributes, and Stanley Segal excelled as a pioneering educator who demonstrated that children with severe or profound disabilities could indeed learn to read and could be educated, at a point in history when everyone regarded them as beyond hope. Both Tamar and Stanley had extremely powerful voices and they used their verbal intelligence and their compassion to defy convention.

With such bravery deeply ensconced within her very fibre, Valerie has developed a remarkable capacity to be bold and to engage clinically with patients whom others would prefer not to know. In order to provide but a brief snippet of Sinason as a clinician – and one would really need a whole book in order to do justice to this subject – I wish to offer a vignette of one of my favourite examples from her bold clinical practice.

Many years ago, during her long tenure as Consultant Child and Adolescent Psychotherapist at the Tavistock Clinic in London, Valerie Sinason worked tirelessly with patients burdened by severe and profound mental and physical handicaps (e.g., Sinason, 1992, 2010). At one point, Sinason had the opportunity to treat an adolescent called "Eve", who suffered from Goldenhar Syndrome: a rare congenital condition of unknown aetiology. As Sinason (1991, p. 17) explained:

> This means she has no outer ear, a curved deformed spine and thin wasted paralysed legs. She has no speech but a few Makaton signs and a few grunts and cries. She was referred for eye-poking, wailing, bottom-poking and smearing.

Indeed, Sinason (1991, p. 17) described Eve as "the most handicapped patient" that she had ever seen at that point in her career.

On the day of Eve's first appointment at the Tavistock Clinic, Sinason stood by the entrance to the lift, awaiting Eve's arrival in a wheelchair, escorted by a care worker. As the doors of the lift opened, Sinason (1991, pp. 17–18) experienced a horrific shock and explained that, "She was looking at me through one curled hand. I knew she had seen my shock. My first thought was cowardice and corruption. How could I cover up my initial response? Then intelligence returned". After catching her breath, Sinason (1991, p. 18) then spoke her first words to Eve:

> I said, "Hello, I am Mrs Sinason and you are Miss E, and perhaps you have got one arm covering your eyes because you know that when people first see you they get a shock at how handicapped you are." She put her hand down and looked at me with great intelligence and we were in business.

With quick-witted brilliance, Sinason had scrutinised her counter-transference, noted her own sense of embarrassment and shame at having demonstrated shock in front of her patient, and then came to realise that this might represent Eve's lifelong experience of humiliation at looking so very tragically deformed. Sinason had found a style of language which allowed Eve to feel immediately recognised and understood; and thereafter, Eve benefited from the tremendous compassion and experience for which Valerie Sinason has become known worldwide within the mental health profession, and consequently the patient enjoyed a most successful course of psychotherapy.

This brief vignette provides, I trust, a glimpse of Sinason as the brave clinician, able to work with those whom others would prefer to avoid.

Knowing Valerie Sinason as I do, I strongly doubt that she would ever describe herself as brave. I suspect that she would simply explain that she did little more than listen to her patients, study their narratives, work with them psychotherapeutically, and do her best to be of some help. But, I can boast on her behalf, because, having worked alongside her clinically, I can report that many of the men, women, and children who consulted her had already received diagnoses of being untreatable by numerous other professionals. Thus, to succeed where many others had already failed requires great courage and bravery.

Happily, Valerie has created a new canvas for mental health workers. As a mother, indeed, grandmother, in the profession, she has encouraged the work of at least two or three new generations of practitioners who have grown up in a post-traumatology world, and who no longer have to fight the brave battle to be believed when they report that a patient might have suffered from gross abuse in an intrafamilial or extrafamilial context. Few have epitomised the Sinasonian legacy as deftly as the late and much missed progenitor of this volume of essays, Dr Alan Corbett, whose remarkable books on psychotherapy for people with intellectual disabilities (Corbett, 2014) and on the treatment of male survivors of sexual abuse (Corbett, 2016) have earned a landmark place in all our professional libraries. During his lifetime, Dr Corbett frequently expressed his gratitude, both publicly and privately, to Dr Sinason, whose support and inspiration fortified him professionally and, at times, personally as well.

Young people entering the psychological profession will find it difficult to believe that, not so very long ago, many psychiatrists and psychologists, even psychotherapists and psychoanalysts, doubted the realities of child abuse. Indeed, having trained at so-called gold standard Oxbridge and Ivy League institutions on both sides of the Atlantic Ocean during the 1970s and 1980s, I can report, with deep horror and regret, that none of my teachers ever mentioned child sexual abuse at all. Even as a young clinician working in a psychiatric hospital during the early 1980s, no one ever dared to speculate as to whether the patient who claimed to have a throbbing lump in his throat had ever had to endure enforced fellatio as a child; likewise, no one ever risked wondering whether the patient who used to hump the legs of a chair, inserting wooden spokes into his rectum, might have suffered from anal abuse during his early years. In both cases, the Consultant Psychiatrist dismissed these patients, quite simply, as psychotic. Fortunately, new recruits to our profession can reap the fruits of the battle fought by Sinason and others to place abuse and disability squarely on the map as proper areas of study.

I predict that, in a short while, the work of Valerie Sinason will become so deeply internalised by the mental health profession that newcomers may not even know of the battles that she had to fight in order to allow her abused and traumatised patients to be heard, to be believed, and to be offered psychological treatment. As Dr Henry Dicks, one of the pioneers of dynamic psychology in Great Britain, and sometime psychiatrist at the Tavistock Clinic during the 1930s and 1940s, once wrote, "my generation have had the experience of all pioneers – of our position being first ignored, next decried and then quietly imitated without acknowledgement of sources" (1970, p. 324). It should hardly surprise us if, as time unfolds, the work of Sinason becomes so mainstream, that few will even recognise its historical origins. Should that become the case, then Sinason will truly have succeeded, because her fight for the rights of the mentally tormented will soon become as straightforward as the battle for female suffrage, for gay rights, for social justice, and for racial equality.

On a recent trip to the Library of Congress in Washington, D.C., as part of my research into the life and work of Sigmund Freud, I stumbled upon a little note that Freud (1897a) penned to his German colleague Dr Wilhelm Fliess, in English, on 1st January, 1897, and which he then incorporated into a much longer letter, some two days later (Freud, 1897b). I shall quote, herewith, the less well known English version in its entirety, signed by Freud (1897a) with his characteristically abbreviated valediction of "Sigm.":

> New Years Day 1897
> We shall not be shipwrecked. Instead of the passage we are seeking, we may find oceans, to be fully explored by those who come after us; but, if we are not prematurely capsized, if our constitution can stand it, we shall succeed. Nous y arriverons. No previous New Year has been so rich with promise [.] I am not afraid to take on all the devils in hell.
> Sigm.

Upon reading this remarkably bold and brave salvo from Sigmund Freud, an image of my great *inspiratrice* Valerie Sinason popped instantly into my mind. Like Freud before her, she has failed to be shipwrecked, in spite of the calumnies that she, like so many great pioneers of traumatology, has often had to endure. She has taken on all the devils in hell in the course of pursuing this extremely taxing body of work. But, as Freud exclaimed in French, "*nous y arriverons*": "we shall arrive there" or, rendered more colloquially and more aptly, "we shall get there". Like Freud before her, Sinason has reached her destination and, thankfully, she has brought us all along with her.

Note

1 The original German sentence reads: "So wurde er der erste moderne Naturforscher, und eine Fülle von Erkenntnissen und Ahnungen belohnte seinen Mut, seit den Zeiten der Griechen als der erste, nur auf Beobachtung und eigenes Urteil gestützt, an die Geheimnisse der Natur zu rühren" (Freud, 1910a, pp. 55–56).

References

Bowlby, J. (1990). *Charles Darwin: A Biography*. London: Hutchinson.

Brown, I. B. (1866). *On the Curability of Certain Forms of Insanity, Epilepsy, Catalepsy, and Hysteria in Females*. London: Robert Hardwicke.

Corbett, A. (2014). *Disabling Perversions: Forensic Psychotherapy with People with Intellectual Disabilities*. London: Karnac Books.

Corbett, A. (2016). *Psychotherapy with Male Survivors of Sexual Abuse: The Invisible Men*. London: Karnac Books.

Dicks, H. V. (1970). *Fifty Years of the Tavistock Clinic*. London: Routledge & Kegan Paul.

Double, D. B. (2002). The history of anti-psychiatry: an essay review. *History of Psychiatry*, *13*: 231–236.

Double, D. B. (2006). Historical perspectives on anti-psychiatry. In Duncan B. Double (Ed.). *Critical Psychiatry: The Limits of Madness*, pp. 19–39. Houndmills, Basingstoke, Hampshire: Palgrave Macmillan.

Freud, S. (1895). Zur Psychotherapie der Hysterie. In Josef Breuer and Sigmund Freud, *Studien über Hysterie*, pp. 222–269. Vienna: Franz Deuticke.

Freud, S. (1897a). Untitled Note. 1st January. Box 49. Folder 28. Sigmund Freud Papers. Sigmund Freud Collection. Manuscript Reading Room, Room 101, Manuscript Division, James Madison Memorial Building, Library of Congress, Washington, D.C., U.S.A.

Freud, S. (1897b). Letter to Wilhelm Fliess. 3rd January. In Sigmund Freud (1986). *Briefe an Wilhelm Fliess 1887–1904: Ungekürzte Ausgabe*. Jeffrey Moussaieff Masson and Michael Schröter (Eds.), pp. 230–233. Frankfurt am Main: S. Fischer / S. Fischer Verlag.

Freud, S. (1910a). *Eine Kindheitserinnerung des Leonardo da Vinci*. Vienna: Franz Deuticke.

Freud, S. (1910b). *Leonardo da Vinci and a Memory of His Childhood*. Alan Tyson (Transl.). In Sigmund Freud (1957). *The Standard Edition of the Complete Psychological Works of Sigmund Freud: Volume XI. (1910). Five Lectures on Psycho-Analysis, Leonardo da Vinci and Other Works*. James Strachey, Anna Freud, Alix Strachey, and Alan Tyson (Eds. and Transls.), pp. 63–137. London: Hogarth Press and the Institute of Psycho-Analysis.

Heaton, J. M. (2006). From anti-psychiatry to critical psychiatry. In Duncan B. Double (Ed.), *Critical Psychiatry: The Limits of Madness*, pp. 41–59. Houndmills, Basingstoke, Hampshire: Palgrave Macmillan.

Hollins, S., Horrocks, C., and Sinason, V. (2002). *Mugged*. London: Gaskell / St. George's Hospital Medical School.

Hollins, S. & Sinason, V. (1992). *Jenny Speaks Out*. London: St George's Mental Health Library.

Hollins, S. & Sinason, V. (1993). *Bob Tells All*. London: St George's Mental Health Library.

Jones, E. (1955). *The Life and Work of Sigmund Freud: Volume 2. Years of Maturity. 1901–1919*. New York: Basic Books.

Kahr, B. (1996). *D. W. Winnicott: A Biographical Portrait*. London: H. Karnac (Books).

Kahr, B. (2009). Psychoanalysis and sexpertise. In Christopher Clulow (Ed.). *Sex, Attachment, and Couple Psychotherapy: Psychoanalytic Perspectives*, pp. 1–23. London: Karnac Books.

Kahr, B. (2011). Winnicott's *"anni horribiles"*: the biographical roots of "Hate in the Counter-Transference". *American Imago, 68*: 173–211.

Kahr, B. (2013). *Life Lessons from Freud*. London: Macmillan / Pan Macmillan, Macmillan Publishers.

Kahr, B. (2015a). Winnicott's *anni horribiles*: the biographical roots of "Hate in the Counter-Transference". In Margaret Boyle Spelman and Frances Thomson-Salo (Eds.), *The Winnicott Tradition: Lines of Development – Evolution of Theory and Practice Over the Decades*, pp. 69–84. London: Karnac Books.

Kahr, B. (2015b). Lecture on "The Roots of Mental Health Broadcasting". Afternoon Workshop on "Donald Winnicott, the Public Psychoanalyst: Broadcasting Beyond the Consulting Room". International Conference on "Donald Winnicott and the History of the Present: A Celebration of the Collected Works of D.W. Winnicott". The Winnicott Trust, London, in association with the British Psychoanalytical Society, Byron House, Maida Vale, London, and the British Psychoanalytic Association, British Psychotherapy Foundation, London, and the Association of Independent Psychoanalysts, London, at the Board Room, Mary Ward House Conference and Exhibition Centre, Holborn, London. 21st November.

Kahr, B. (2017). *Coffee with Freud*. London: Karnac Books.

Kahr, B. (2018). The public psychoanalyst: Donald Winnicott as broadcaster. In Angela Joyce (Ed.), *Donald W. Winnicott and the History of the Present: Understanding the Man and His Work*, pp. 111–121. London: Karnac Books.

Kahr, B. (2019). *Winnicott's* Anni Horribiles*: The Creation of 'Hate in the Counter-Transference'*. London: Routledge/Taylor & Francis Group.

Laing, R. D. (1960). *The Divided Self: A Study of Sanity and Madness*. London: Tavistock Publications.

Millar, W. M. (1947). Physical therapy of mental disorder. *British Medical Journal*, 14 June, p. 861.

Sinason, V. (1991). Interpretations that feel horrible to make and a theoretical unicorn. *Journal of Child Psychotherapy, 17*: 11–24.

Sinason, V. (1992). *Mental Handicap and the Human Condition: New Approaches from the Tavistock*. London: Free Association Books.

Sinason, V. (1993). *Understanding Your Handicapped Child*. London: Rosendale Press.

Sinason, V. (Ed.). (1994). *Treating Survivors of Satanist Abuse*. London: Routledge.

Sinason, V. (Ed.). (1998). *Memory in Dispute*. London: H. Karnac (Books).

Sinason, V. (Ed.). (2002). *Attachment, Trauma and Multiplicity: Working with Dissociative Identity Disorder*. Hove, East Sussex: Brunner-Routledge / Taylor and Francis Group.

Sinason, V. (2010). *Mental Handicap and the Human Condition: An Analytic Approach to Intellectual Disability*. Revised Edition. London: Free Association Books.

Sinason, V. (Ed.). (2011). *Attachment, Trauma and Multiplicity: Second Edition. Working with Dissociative Identity Disorder*. London: Routledge / Taylor and Francis Group.

Stokes, J., & Sinason, V. (1992). Secondary mental handicap as a defence. In: A. Waitman & S. Conboy-Hill (Eds.), *Psychotherapy and Mental Handicap* (pp. 46–58). London: Sage Publications.

Winnicott, D. W. (1930a). Enuresis. *Proceedings of the Royal Society of Medicine, 23*: 255.

Winnicott, D. W. (1930b). Short communication on enuresis. *St. Bartholomew's Hospital Journal, 37*: 125–127.

Winnicott, D. W. (1931a). *Clinical Notes on Disorders of Childhood*. London: William Heinemann (Medical Books).

Winnicott, D. W. (1931b). A clinical note on convulsions, p. 257. In Anonymous. British Paediatric Association: Proceedings of the Fourth Annual General Meeting. *Archives of Disease in Childhood, 6*: 255–258.

Winnicott, D. W. (1933a). Short communication on enuresis. *British Journal of Children's Diseases, 30*: 41–42.

Winnicott, D. W. (1933b). Pathological sleeping. *British Journal of Children's Diseases, 30*: 205–206.

Winnicott, D. W. (1936). Appetite and emotional disorder. In Donald W. Winnicott (1958), *Collected Papers: Through Paediatrics to Psycho-Analysis*, pp. 33–51. London: Tavistock Publications.

Winnicott, D. W. (1939). The psychology of juvenile rheumatism. In Ronald G. Gordon (Ed.), *A Survey of Child Psychiatry*, pp. 28–44. London: Humphrey Milford / Oxford University Press.

Winnicott, D. W. (1943a). Prefrontal leucotomy. *The Lancet*, 10 April: p. 475.

Winnicott, D. W. (1943b). Shock treatment of mental disorder. *British Medical Journal,* 25 December, pp. 829–830.

Winnicott, D. W. (1943c). Treatment of mental disease by induction of fits. In Donald W. Winnicott (1989), *Psycho-Analytic Explorations*. Clare Winnicott, Ray Shepherd, and Madeleine Davis (Eds.), pp. 516–521. London: H. Karnac (Books).

Winnicott, D. W. (1944a). Shock therapy. *British Medical Journal*, 12 February, pp. 234–235.

Winnicott, D. W. (1944b). Introduction to a symposium on the psycho-analytic contribution to the theory of shock therapy. In Donald W. Winnicott (1989), *Psycho-Analytic Explorations*. Clare Winnicott, Ray Shepherd, and Madeleine Davis (Eds.), pp. 525–528. London: H. Karnac (Books).

Winnicott, D. W. (1944c). Kinds of psychological effect of shock therapy. In Donald W. Winnicott (1989), *Psycho-Analytic Explorations*. Clare Winnicott, Ray Shepherd, and Madeleine Davis (Eds.), pp. 529–533. London: H. Karnac (Books).

Winnicott, D. W. (1945a). *Getting to Know Your Baby*. London: William Heinemann (Medical Books).

Winnicott, D. W. (1945b). Physical therapy in mental disorder. *British Medical Journal*, 22 December, pp. 901–902.

Winnicott, D. W. (1945c). Getting to know your baby. *New Era in Home and School, 26*: 1–3.

Winnicott, D. W. (1945d). Why do babies cry? *New Era in Home and School, 26*: 3, 5–7.

Winnicott, D. W. (1945e). Infant feeding. *New Era in Home and School, 26*: 9–10.

Winnicott, D.W. (1945f). What about father? *New Era in Home and School, 26*: 11–13.

Winnicott, D. W. (1945g). Their standards and yours. *New Era in Home and School, 26*: 13–15.

Winnicott, D. W. (1947a). Physical therapy of mental disorder. *British Medical Journal*, 17 May, pp. 688–689.

Winnicott, D. W. (1947b). Battle neurosis treated with leucotomy. *British Medical Journal*, 13 December, p. 974.

Winnicott, D. W. (1949a). *The Ordinary Devoted Mother and Her Baby: Nine Broadcast Talks. (Autumn 1949)*. London: C.A. Brock and Company.

Winnicott, D. W. (1949b). Hate in the counter-transference. *International Journal of Psycho-Analysis, 30*: 69–74.

Winnicott, D. W. (1949c). Leucotomy. *British Medical Students' Journal, 3(2)*: 35–38.

Winnicott, D. W. (1951a). Leucotomy in psychosomatic disorders. *The Lancet*, 18 August, pp. 314–315.

Winnicott, D. W. (1951b). Ethics of prefrontal leucotomy. *British Medical Journal*, 25th August, pp. 496–497.

Winnicott, D. W. (1951c). Notes on the general implications of leucotomy. In Donald W. Winnicott (1989), *Psycho-Analytic Explorations*. Clare Winnicott, Ray Shepherd, and Madeleine Davis (Eds.), pp. 548–552. London: H. Karnac (Books).

Winnicott, D. W. (1954a). A psychiatrist's choice. *The Spectator*, 12 February, p. 175.

Winnicott, D. W. (1954b). Letters to the Editor of the *Spectator*. In *Physical Treatments of the Mind and Spiritual Healing: Articles and Correspondence Reprinted from the Spectator*, p. 12. London: The Spectator.

Winnicott, D. W. (1956). Prefrontal leucotomy. *British Medical Journal*, 28 January, pp. 229–230.

Winnicott, D. W. (1957a). *The Child and the Family: First Relationships*. Janet Hardenberg (Ed.). London: Tavistock Publications.

Winnicott, D. W. (1957b). *The Child and the Outside World: Studies in Developing Relationships*. Janet Hardenberg (Ed.). London: Tavistock Publications.

Winnicott, D. W. (1987). *Babies and Their Mothers*. Clare Winnicott, Ray Shepherd, and Madeleine Davis (Eds.). Reading, Massachusetts: Addison-Wesley Publishing Company.

Winnicott, D. W. (1993). *Talking to Parents*. Clare Winnicott, Christopher Bollas, Madeleine Davis, and Ray Shepherd (Eds.). Reading, Massachusetts: Addison-Wesley Publishing Company.

Young, M. L. (1947). Physical therapy of mental disorder. *British Medical Journal*, 5 July, pp. 32–33.

Chapter 15

An interview with Valerie Sinason reflecting on her life and the evolution of disability psychotherapy

Alan Corbett

AC: I want to start by asking what brought you into working with disability. What was the path?

VS: For a long time I thought the real reason was that my father was a disability pioneer. He was a teacher first of all, for what was then known as the "E stream" in a comprehensive school. He was disgusted by the very idea of streaming, and also appalled by the stigma experienced by the children *because* they were in the E stream. He produced the first textbooks for children with a disability – I see them now as a kind of forerunner to the *Books Beyond Words* (2017) – about space travel. This meant they knew about sputniks before the rest of the school did. They put on an assembly showing their knowledge of the new Russian space travel and the kudos this conferred on the children removed some of that stigma.

When he first became a headmaster of a school for children with an intellectual disability, my father was the first teacher to force his staff to stop beating children and using canes. He actually got them to break up canes to make a three-dimensional map of the world, which was, again, an amazing, transformational activity. It showed how pain could affect knowledge. When he first became a head teacher, he brought in school uniform to make the children feel smarter. He had bingo nights for parents to teach them numbers and spelling. He had animals in the playground long before there were city farms, and he had the local mayor come in to address a school assembly. As his daughter, I was acutely aware of and following these changes, and I was deeply committed and identified with what he was doing. My brother and I went with him on every school trip. In a way, my dad's work was experienced by us as an invisible, handicapped sibling. When Dad came back from school, he talked to us in what we called his "assembly voice", and we would say, "Dad, we are not that slow!" But we also realised that, in his positive efforts to reduce stigma and shame, he was cushioning children from being expected to know anything. In this way, I think he was *not* seeing where there could be a greater psychological capacity in his pupils. In the middle of deeply admiring him, my brother and I had that feeling we were onto something he'd missed.

Years later, when Neville Symington started his Subnormality Workshop at the Tavistock Clinic (Stokes & Sinason, 1992) I found I was at home because what I'd grown up with gave me an understanding of the lived experience of people with learning disabilities. So, this was what I had always understood to be the start of my path but, years later, while working on the revised edition of *Mental Handicap and the Human Condition* (2010), I realised that my mother's mother, who lived with us all her life, not only was illiterate, but also had a mild learning disability through trauma. This had remained somehow a secret within our family – the knowing of it not allowed. It had stayed secret to me over all those years, even though I was a disability specialist.

My mother was so defended against anything other than the knowledge that her mother was a brave woman with a cruel life. My grandmother lived at a time when women were not encouraged to go to school, and she apparently had a wicked stepmother who didn't want her to go to school. She was kept at home and so she never learned to read. But I realised this wasn't the whole story: my other grandmother, who was also illiterate, was absolutely brilliant. She was sharp and shrewd. So I knew that there was a difference between my grandmothers but I didn't have permission to see the difference as learning disability until after my mother was dead. My brother doesn't agree, nor do my lovely uncle and aunt.

My grandmother had a kind of benevolence, but couldn't see clearly, and was frightened and incapable of safe, adult capacity. My mum could. And my dad could sometimes see a political vista more clearly than an individual one. On the council estates we lived on until I was sixteen, they created the first children's community centres and were asked to stand as local Labour MPs. This made running groups easy for me.

I have also only recently realised that the fact that neither of my parents had parents that brought them up and that they had benevolent siblings, meant that they passed onto me the concept of a collaborative authority. Also, growing up as children, we were incredibly respected: we were equal voters in the family. There were boundaries and restrictions, but always with thought and reason. Because of that, school was actually quite shocking for me. My parents challenged the obliteration of children's voices. This meant that when I went to South Africa, it was straightforward for me to be part of efforts to transform a township. Dad had given every Member of Parliament a copy of *No Child is Ineducable* (Segal, 1966) and that led, over time, to *The Plowden Report* (1967) and *The Warnock Report* (1978), which led to legislation to guarantee disabled children's rights to an education. He did this calmly and with an eye to the greater vision. I got this from him, without having to work on it! I think I'm still putting together all the reasons of how this upbringing affected me and has affected my work.

AC: It's interesting, isn't it? Intellectual disability is on both sides of your family. And your father was an educationalist. Your path to being, eventually, a psychoanalyst was through education and teaching. I wondered: how conscious was it at the beginning of your therapy career that you would gravitate towards disability?

VS: It wasn't at all conscious. Before starting my training as a child therapist at the Tavistock Clinic, I had qualified as a secondary school English literature teacher. I had my children and was at home for five years. I hadn't thought of being a child psychotherapist because nowhere in my family did anything psychoanalytic play a part. Had I not trained as a therapist, I do think I would have been a teacher who wrote books and who cared about children that were traumatised. But no, disability was not there. I worked with immigrant children, mainly from poor backgrounds, and I was riveted with everything that I saw. I guess that would link with my having grandparents that were immigrants, and being very aware of the experience of the pain of newness and loss of identity that can come with arriving in a strange country.

AC: It's interesting because in the book we've got contributions from a number of disability therapists who were originally child therapists. How much do you think your original training as a child therapist impacted on your eventual work with adults?

VS: I think child therapy provides a brilliant training because of the infant and toddler observation. In the observation over one year or two, you're not there to intervene, you're there to observe. Because of that, you really feel the power of a baby's emotional experience. There is no equal experience, in terms of dealing with profound multiple disability. A person with profound disability may, for example, have only a few Makaton signs, or no signs, or no speech that's intelligible. Having a child therapy training gives you an understanding of body language. It means you are not perturbed by there being no speech, or by uncoordinated physical movements. As a child therapist you are used to the face-to-face encounter rather than the couch, and my experience is that most trauma adult patients don't like not seeing – they need to check your expression is still empathic.

Also, a child therapist can't have the same dignity. For example, when a trainee, I used to be amazed at seeing calm people sitting on the stairs at the Tavistock with a child refusing to go in the room. You just don't get embarrassed in the same way with the mainstream adult population.

I never felt that I had some sort of secret authority through a key to the unconscious. A child therapist, in a way, has learnt to be transparent in a way that isn't necessarily a part of training. As well, I think there's a kindness, a general, compassionate feeling towards whatever child you see. I didn't find this to be an automatic prerequisite for an adult therapist, which really shocked me.

AC: There is something about that, isn't there? I remember the first IPD [Institute of Psychotherapy and Disability, 2017] gathering, "Treating with Respect", in the early 2000s, and you reinforcing that idea to all of us: respect and kindness is central to this whole notion of working with disability.

Thinking about child therapy, too, it's interesting what you said about being riveted. Lots of people *aren't* riveted. They are bored or disengaged or ambivalent. I wonder if there's a way, thinking back to your parents and this incredible mission that your father was on, that you see something and react to it and seek to change it. Has there been a kind of political edge, in the broader sense of the word, to your work, just as there was with your father's?

VS: Realising that how someone is treated in the outside world is a part of their soul and their identity – which, by the way, John Bowlby had always said, and is there with the Bowlby Centre training – and is also there with relational psychoanalysis. But it wasn't there as a strong thought in child therapy at the time I trained. Nor was it, at the time I trained, in adult psychoanalysis. Of course, Winnicott spoke of the outside world (1949 [1964]) and so did Martha Harris, the founder of the Tavistock training, but I think that the psychoanalytic privileging of the inner world, which was a precious territory, and in the early days had met with such attack from the outside, had led to an almost defensive response. There was a wish to make the inner world the sovereign territory and not see that there was an important mixture of internal *and* external. I think, on a psychological level, that my childhood was a mixture of both being seen clearly and *not* being seen.

AC: I see a link in what you've just said: in disability therapy, there's a political element and there's also, as there is in child therapy, a systemic element. As a child therapist, you don't just think about the child, but you're also having to think about Mum, Dad, or the absence of Mum or Dad.

VS: I hadn't made that connection. Absolutely right.

AC: I wondered if part of what your particular background has given to the new discipline of disability therapy is the understanding that it's actually a *systemic* project. It's about the external as well as the internal. Perhaps your early experiences bequeathed you that.

VS: Yes, absolutely.

AC: I think there remains an ongoing debate about the "purity" of therapeutic approach. I remember early on in Respond, you described your approach as "Esperanto", explaining that it needs to be conducted in an amalgam of languages. Do you still feel that now, all these years later, or have you gravitated more towards one approach over another?

VS: I now think disability therapy is the best form of therapy for everybody. In the beginning, I and others were all talking about the things we do *differently* in this (disability) work, and we were fascinated that we were encouraging curiosity. We were wanting to make sure people with learning disabilities, in therapy and outside, weren't shamed for showing their aggression. We were also looking at dependency issues and shame over that. Whilst we kept to the "kosher" interpretation, we had spirit and warmth in our voices, and in our clothes. This was in contrast to a pseudo-depressive position uniform that a certain wave of therapists seemed to go into in that period. It could lead to them looking dull and depressing. It was Anna Scher, the actress and drama teacher, who we both know, Alan, who, with a rough group of sixty, depressed secondary school kids, holding classes on her own, immaculately made-up and glamorous, said, "The more depressed the client group, the more you should show you value them, by coming out to see them." And Isca Wittenberg, my supervisor and Deputy Chair of the Tavistock, said, "Neutrality doesn't have to mean ugliness." So I think disability therapy can have a warm, curious, empathic response that's not shaming and this is actually how *all* our patients should be treated.

AC: You've mentioned one of your supervisors there, and I'm really curious about who has supervised you. I think you've got a very particularly detailed way of supervising people. Several contributors to the book share their experiences of it. In fact, you were my first real supervisor. You work as a kind of jeweller, as if crafting a piece of jewellery. You take transcripts apart – it is a process of deconstructing and reconstructing. It's an amazing experience.

VS: Oh, thank you!

AC: I'd never had that before, and I then thought: this is what supervision is always going to be like. With people like Anne Alvarez it is, but with others, it isn't. What were your supervisors like and what did you take from them that you still use?

VS: Well, after I qualified, the first supervisor I chose to have was Anne Alvarez, and she always provided some nibbles and a drink. I took that as model of how it should be done: she always cared both about the patient *and* me. I did have experience of some of the non-chosen supervision, on both my trainings, where it could feel that the supervisor was on the side of the patient against me, which wasn't helpful; or of the supervisor being in quite a cold, theoretical state, querying the exact words and interpretation, without me feeling there was any real empathy for the patient. Sometimes, especially in seminars where trainees presented work to the group, there was actual antipathy when the patient was an abuse victim or also had abusing wishes. It was to a level that shocked me.

In supervision, Isca would say, "Now, isn't that an interesting dream he's brought!" She was awake, interested, and riveted! I like people who are not jobbing therapists, but have got a passion for what they're doing: people who don't see the job as an ordinary nine to five, but as a privileged entrance to somebody else. The patient has allowed you in, and therefore the work with them deserves the greatest amount of thinking on your part. I also got a lot of supervision of the best kind, from my last analyst, Mervin Glasser. I had deliberately chosen a forensic analyst, and he was just so warm, and this was especially helpful with particular patients.

Of course, the way I supervise that you describe, Alan, I do it that way partly because I'd done an English degree and I loved English literature. Language has always been central for me. I think we are all the therapists we are, partly from the jobs we've had before. For example, you, Alan, have such wonderful management capacities. I hadn't see that kind of luminous management before I saw you working at Respond. The structures that would aid the process had been really thought out, but you did it without shaming, without heavy authority. I could just enjoy it. It wasn't something to feel rivalrous over because the capacity to put in structures just didn't even exist in me and it was a pleasure to see it. Those structural issues wouldn't be the things that I would note first in a session, but rather the linguistic issues. And the trauma issues. Also, of course, Pearl King supervised me for two decades and cared about the reality of cult victims with DID [dissociative identity disorder].

AC: Am I right in thinking that Murray Cox supervised you, and also you *and* Sheila [Hollins], in your forensic group?

VS: This was years later, with Sheila Hollins and I having our sixteen-year group [the St George's Group] for learning disabled victim/perpetrators. We went to Murray for Shakespeare supervision, and he was just wonderful. He would hear the whole session and he would give us a lovely way of tabulating it: circles for each person; a line for halfway through group time; arrows, so we could do a very speedy write-up after (which we haven't put together yet). But he'd then give us Shakespeare quotes that came to mind.

AC: Incredible.

VS: But what I remember best and being moved by most was not actually about one of our patients. He told us about when he first went to Broadmoor to put on Shakespeare, a woman came up to him and said, "Mr. Shakespeare, Mr. Shakespeare, tell me a quote about me!" And he said, "Well, what's happened to you?" She told him how in a psychotic, post-natal depression she'd killed her baby and she had never recovered from it. He paused for a moment and said, "That it should come to this". It's one of those comments that's stayed with me for twenty years. Those are the sort of things I learn by – a quote or a sentence that somebody has said in a session.

AC: And that's it really, isn't it? Going back to this kind of jeweller's concept of supervision, and that sense of detail, it strikes me that you're always looking at it from a linguistic point of view as well. You're trying to map out the unconscious through this process, including even with non-verbal patients. That always astonished me, that we could spend a whole session thinking in a linguistic way about someone who didn't have words!

VS: Yes, absolutely.

AC: Going back to the group with Sheila [Hollins] – she writes about it in this volume, too, and I hope it's written up at length at some point because I don't know of any other group quite with the background of patients and the length of the therapy itself. I'd like to ask what you think the men got from the group that they wouldn't have got from individual therapy?

VS: They got shared meaning. They were in a society, the society of the group. That gave them value and a group of peers – because they were living with professionals, workers, support workers, nurses, but not with peers. This allowed a culture to build up in which helped developed a sense that there was meaning to them, to their experiences and feelings. They were "Invisible Men", as your book title describes (Corbett, 2016). Rude things were said about putting learning disabled, forensic patients together in a group, things like: "Well, if they're together, they'll just be wanking off together." But in sixteen years, there was none of that. We all know how much depends on the attitude of the therapists and Sheila [Hollins] and I were treating them with respect.

AC: How incredible to sustain a group for sixteen years.

VS: Yes. Eventually it ended, very much against my wishes. The patients all complained, wrote their own letter to management, we went to the MP; but even with Sheila [Hollins] as a Professor, it made no difference, the group was closed. They had a real lesson in politics.

AC: A painful lesson, I presume, for you as well.

VS: Yes.

AC: A piece of work being killed off.

VS: Yes.

AC: I think in the disability world we have to face that a lot, perhaps much more than in the non-disability therapy world: funding gets pulled; people are moved; people are scheduled to be anywhere else but their therapy. How active do you find yourself having to be with individual patients and their teams, about sustaining the work when it's under attack?

VS: I did have to be active. At the time, Deborah Marks called the work that Sheila [Hollins] and I were doing, "psychoanalytic advocacy" (Marks, 1999, p. 111–112). I think she was drawing attention to the things that seemed to worry mainstream therapists, things like: Were we wild?; Were we doing the right thing?; Why were we getting involved in things that weren't therapy? And we were saying: "Apart from a small number, the client group can't do these things we do on their own behalf. We are being their voice over what's happening in the rest of the world. If other people in their support teams take that on instead, then we will be very grateful to go back into the normal boundaries of therapy."

Now, when someone refers someone with a disability to me, I can refer them to Respond, I can refer them to the Bowlby Centre. Before, there was nowhere. I'd say we're in the same position with dissociation [DID]. I know we're not focusing on that in this conversation, but in that work you simply cannot, as a therapist, avoid the political position of someone's diagnosis being ignored; or the trauma they've gone through being treated as a lie. So that's a complicated one in Britain. In South America and other places, therapists would be *expected* to be making comments on what's politically happening.

AC: Yes, I wanted to ask about that because the book also has got thoughts from some of the people you've worked with across the world – in Sweden and South Africa. What have you noticed about different attitudes, both towards disability but also therapy?

VS: Yes. They make a wonderful contrast, Sweden and South Africa. In Sweden, the human rights of people with learning disabilities were better than in Britain, and the provision was better too. For example, there was a rule that someone should be offered a job of their choice! Well, think of all the unemployed people in England without a disability that don't get that. Also, there was a law saying that people should have some choice over the home they lived in. In restaurants in Sweden you saw families out with their disabled children in way that you don't in Britain, with nobody staring. But against that, they didn't have any therapy provision. So I was connected to the two groups in Sweden that formed therapy provision, but they got the politics right first, and that was fascinating.

In South Africa, there was nothing. But the country was, and is, in a spirit of openness that makes up for so much that's missing. When I'm there and colleagues are depressed, you know, about the horror, say, of 300 women being raped every second, I think, "You've got it in the newspapers as a fact!" In Britain, conversely, we now have the idea that a survivor should be *prosecuted* because the way he or she was treated has meant it appears there was some distortion in his or her evidence. We have the current backlash against the inquiry (Independent Inquiry into Child Sexual Abuse, 2017) and the scapegoating of some police officers who took an approach which said that not everything anybody says is true, but that there is a reason why they're speaking and we think there is something there.

In South Africa there's hardly any provision but there is a belief in what people are saying. One year, I had a Zulu group of 200 people and an interpreter. You could really feel, genuinely, that something had shifted in that group, about the treatment for disabled people. There was a communal acceptance in the same moment of a new insight. This happened when the learning disabled grandson of a chief had died in hospital. I was asked to address this meeting because the group were worried politically at speaking out and I didn't know why. The Chief, with a translator, had said, "Do handicapped people go up in smoke when they die?" And I was puzzled, wondering what belief in the group I was not aware of. I said, "That's an interesting question. Has anybody here ever watched somebody handicapped die?" The Chief said, "Well, it's like this. My son, he had a son, and that son was ill. And my son, he carried my grandson to hospital because we don't have ambulances here in this township. And my son, he couldn't get food for me for three days while he was in the hospital with his son. And then my son, he comes back and he gets me food and then we hear from the hospital that my grandson has died, and it costs five grand for a death certificate, and we don't have five grand, so did he go up in smoke? And then the ancestors would not be shamed."

I said, "Ah, well, how generous of you to think he went up in smoke, because if he went up in smoke then we don't have to be shamed that this government haven't given you an ambulance, and we wouldn't have to be shamed that there was no one getting you food while your son was away, and we wouldn't have to be shamed there was no telephone here, and we wouldn't be shamed that you weren't given the money for a death certificate, and the ancestors would not be shamed. But we *are* all shamed, and no, as you know, he didn't go up in smoke, but that's you being generous." That was a highly mutative moment in my life in this work. South Africa hasn't reached the lower middle-class, ugly shame level. In South Africa you could see, as the brick buildings went up instead of the shacks, that there was a shame over disability that got bigger. Before that, someone with a disability could be useful just standing all day stirring illegal drinks, or they could be your useful "rape container" and not be killed because they felt they had a place as the local sex worker. But moving up a level, that's when the stigma and the shame came in. I had a strong personal and political wish to do something about that transition.

AC: Which, I imagine, some welcomed and some didn't. It makes me think about now about resistance to change in this work and the things you have done. How you do react personally when you're under attack?

VS: It has changed over the years. In the beginning, I could take my father's words as comfort. He would quote Galileo: "Every moving force creates its own backlash", and say to me, "What do you expect? You cause a movement or a change, there *has* to be a reaction. And be kind to it, because the change will be making people feel guilty." So, in the beginning when I understood the handicapped smile and I realised I was making people feel guilty when I spoke about it, I spoke about *my* guilt that I always used to smile back. I changed my approach and I got fewer attacks. Then the attacks came when I spoke about abuse and, again, I could see people couldn't bear it. But, as I've got older, I have found it more tiring. I think, "Oh, not this again!" I still have a naivety, even after twenty-five years. I failed to realise that it's a fact that each year more people are born and they haven't been educated in this way of thinking, so we are all starting from scratch every year. It's an illusion to think we've built up a body of knowledge, except in certain liberal places. That's why the way of dealing with it remains the same for me: the basic way is writing. This is why, Alan, I think your book, *Invisible Men* (Corbett, 2016), is so important. People can take a book, they can argue with it, it stays with them. It can't but help inform them. So I consider written words the best way.

AC: It's important to acknowledge, even in a disability focused book, that you've moved on to work with patients with DID, which is an even more contentious, controversial area, and which evokes enormous attack. Do you ever regret moving into such controversial specialist areas? We could be talking now, looking back on your career as a "worried well" psychoanalyst. What would that have been like?

VS: I do have some narcissistic pangs. We dealt with all those first attacks on disability therapy and then had a wonderful acceptance at government level. That came from us! It's changed thousands of lives and if that learning disabled woman in Sweden (Sinason & Svensson, 1994) had not been referred to me, I could have enjoyed those changes so much more. I would have had lots more time to give to the IPD, and all sorts of other disability related work, so it did constrict my disability time (although many of my patients with learning disabilities also had DID). The DID work has meant I've had a repeat of those attacks, but even bigger ones. However, I've also met the finest people I could meet, clinically and theoretically, and it is disability colleagues that can cope with this best. So, just as we've said, child therapists have got an extra place in disability therapy and disability therapists have been crucial to working with DID. Such therapists understand stigma, and patients who have separate pockets of life and experience that can't sit comfortably together. Those therapists know that people have gone through the worst that people can go through. When Anders [Svensson] rang me, I answered. If I'd had a kind of career trajectory in mind, I might have bypassed all sorts of amazing things I've been involved with.

AC: You are talking as well here, about resilience. I think this is one of the qualities you need in this work. What qualities do you think are essential for a therapist working with people with disabilities?

VS: When we are thinking of therapy to groups that have not been given legitimacy, there needs to be a commitment to a moral principle that's over and beyond a professional approach. So, this work calls for people that have a sense of justice, for whatever reason. Also, I think therapists need to be able to deal with the fact that the newness of work will create a backlash, as my father said.

My supervisor for the last decade now is Philip Stokoe. He has a social work background and has worked in that capacity with children and adults who have experienced extreme early trauma. As well as his clarity and humour, he has something quite Winnicottian in his work. He also has a Kleinian psychoanalytic approach. I find that combination just perfect. But, in terms of theory, I think the crucial issue is projective identification. If you're not aware how someone's pain can be forcibly projected and transmitted, you can't do this work, or deal with the rage of groups like false memory societies, abuser networks – the denying, disavowing networks. You need to understand how the pain of the dynamic of the patient gets into society.

AC: David O'Driscoll has written in this book about the history of disability therapy. I just wonder what you feel the future of disability therapy is? Is there a risk of it being so specialist? Are we in danger of creating a new ghetto for ourselves by being disability therapists, and should we be striving to be therapists who work with all sorts of patients?

VS: I think we need both. We need to offer "top-ups" to therapists – that's what we've tried to do in the IPD and through the UKCP. I think we need to be operating at the specialist level and at the barefoot level at the same time. And I think the principles we have, and are there in the IPD, too, are a good fit for untrained workers, semi-skilled workers, and parents. Unsurprisingly though, we are not being aided to disseminate it.

AC: It seems that the ideas that you have been sharing in this conversation, Valerie, they have a kind of simplicity and "obviousness" about them that will make sense to anyone who's working in relationship with people with intellectual disabilities in whatever capacity – as a family member or a member of staff. But on the other hand, you've been saying it's also complicated and difficult and has important theory behind it. We don't need to be afraid of saying that and documenting it.

VS: Yes, absolutely. When you explain containment to a tribal African group, who are sitting in a large circle that includes you, and you talk about how everybody feels when a baby cries, and then how they feel when the baby is calmed, everybody in the circle understands. As we all know, an untrained group can respond far quicker than a trained group. We mustn't forget that, just as DID is an affront to the concept of identity, especially Western identity, an intellectual disability is an affront to thinking about what defines a human, about what makes us different from other animals. It touches our fears of what our family might produce. That's why people may not want to go near it.

AC: I think you're so right that those really challenging questions can be communicated. But I also think it depends on who's communicating. You have the ability to communicate something in a very clear way, but also in a way which is highly poetic. And I just wanted to say thank you, both for the interview but also for what you've given disability therapy over the years. Without you, it wouldn't exist, and that's what this book catalogues: that you've created a discipline, and few people can say that.

References

Books Beyond Words. (2017). https://booksbeyondwords.co.uk [last accessed 27.11.17].
Corbett, A. (2016). *Psychotherapy with Male Survivors of Sexual Abuse: The Invisible Men*. London: Karnac.

IICSA Independent Inquiry into Child Sexual Abuse. (2017). www.iicsa.org.uk/ [last accessed 4.12.17].

The Institute of Psychotherapy and Disability. (2017). www.instpd.org.uk [last accessed 30.12.2017].

Marks, D. (1999). *Disability: Controversial Debates and Psychosocial Perspectives.* London: Routledge.

The Plowden Report. (1967). *Children and their Primary Schools: A Report of the Central Advisory Council for Education (England), Volume 1: The Report.* London: HMSO.

Segal, S. (1966). *No Child is Ineducable: Provision and Trends.* Oxford: Pergamon Press.

Sinason, V. (2010). *Mental Handicap and the Human Condition: An Analytical Approach to Intellectual Disability* (2nd edn). London: Free Association Books.

Sinason, V., & Svensson, A. (1994). Going through the fifth window: "Other cases rest on Sundays. This one didn't". In: V. Sinason (Ed.), *Treating Survivors of Satanist Abuse* (pp. 13–21). London: Routledge.

Stokes, J., & Sinason, V. (1992). Secondary mental handicap as a defence. In: A. Waitman & S. Conboy-Hill (Eds.), *Psychotherapy and Mental Handicap* (pp. 46–58). London: Sage.

The Warnock Report. (1978). *Special Educational Needs: Report of the Committee of Enquiry into the Education of Handicapped Children and Young People.* London: HMSO.

Winnicott, D. W. (1964). *The Child, the Family and the Outside World.* London: Pelican Books. [reprinted London: Penguin, 1991].

Index

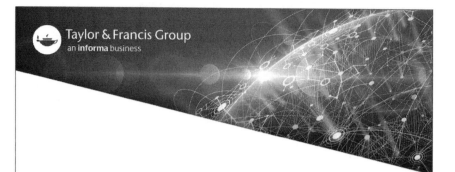